INFRINGING NEUTRALITY

THE RAF IN SWITZERLAND

1940–45

ROGER ANTHOINE

INFRINGING NEUTRALITY

THE RAF IN SWITZERLAND

1940–45

TEMPUS

Front cover: In June 1954, Swiss entrepreneur Martin 'Bomber' Schaffner raised the sunken Steckborn *Lancaster* out of Lake Constance. The picture shows the intact fuselage emerging from its fifty-year stay underwater. ('*Weltwoche*' via J.P. Wilhelm)

Back cover: The crew of the Birmenstorf *Wellington* with their debonair guards, probably the day before their repatriation. Observer/navigator William Shields is third from left, back row, and pilot James Avery, second from right. Seated in the middle row are rear gunner Ronald McEwan and wireless operator Joseph Cash. Air bomber Wilfred Boddy is sitting on the ground on the right. (Coll. Ernst Killer via Max Rudolf)

First published 2006

Tempus Publishing Limited
The Mill, Brimscombe Port,
Stroud, Gloucestershire, GL5 2QG
www.tempus-publishing.com

© Roger Anthoine, 2006

The right of Roger Anthoine to be identified as the Author
of this work has been asserted in accordance with the
Copyrights, Designs and Patents Act 1988.

British Library Cataloguing in Publication Data.
A catalogue record for this book is available from the British Library.

ISBN 0 7524 3420 9

Typesetting and origination by Tempus Publishing Limited
Printed in Great Britain

Contents

Foreword

My grandfather was a coal miner before the war. He was also fascinated by flying machines. This was perhaps a reaction to his spending most of his active life in the dark entrails of Earth. In any case, he never failed to attend the rare aviation events that took place on the green meadows of our generally bleak community. Also, he always took along his toddler grandson who thus began to crave for things in the air and for the white-clad idols who took them up.

Years later, with his native Belgium suffering under German oppression, the grandson took a modest part in subversive operations. In that capacity he was often out in the countryside at night. Those were the times of peering at the dark void of the night sky, of listening to the drone of invisible RAF bombers on their way to Germany, of reflecting on the brave men who were putting their lives at stake for freedom.

Those were the times when many of those heroes would be found amongst hills and forests, killed violently in the wreckage of their once powerful mounts, for under full moon or in thick cloud, danger was always lurking, be it in the form of prowling nightfighters, of treacherous flak or of hostile weather.

Those were also the times when the urge never to forget the deeds of the winged freedom fighters originated, developing into an impulse to put their sagas on record lest they be forgotten. Hence books, articles and lectures on Second World War Allied aviation. Hence also, after the grandson had moved near Switzerland, this review of how the RAF fared in and over a country which was luckily spared the shocking experience of war.

Roger Anthoine
Peron (France) near Geneva
January 2006

Abbreviations/ Glossary

(see also Table 1: Ranks)

0.30   Standard machine-gun in RAF bombers during most of the war: .3in (7.69mm)

0.50   Standard heavy American machine-gun: .5 in (12.7mm)

AOC   Air Officer Commanding

App.   *Appointé*, a Swiss Army rank (see Table 1: Ranks)

Ar. Ter   *Arrondissement Territorial*, a Swiss geographical area

B-17   Boeing's four-engined heavy bomber, the so-called '*Flying Fortress*'. With the B-24, it was the mainstay of the USAAF in Europe. Some examples served with the RAF

B-24   Consolidated Vultee's other four-engined American heavy bomber, the '*Liberator*'. With the *B-17*, it performed heavy strategic boming daylight missions over Europe. One Group flew clandestine night missions dropping supplies to underground fighters in Western Europe and Scandinavia

Bat.   Battalion

BBC   British Broadcasting Corporation in London

Bbdier   bombardier, a crew member in the USAAF, equivalent to the Air Bomber in RAF parlance

Bf.109	German fighter aircraft, a single-seater built by Messerschmitt. Became the mainstay of the Luftwaffe's fighter arm. Like the FW.190, it was sometimes used to intercept RAF night raids
Bf.110	the most successful Messerschmitt twin-engined nightfighter responsible for the demise of thousands of RAF bombers
BGp	USAAF Bomb Group, roughly equivalent to the RAF Squadron
C.	Centigrade (temperature)
Chap	Chapter
Cie	Company, a military unit in Switzerland as well as in most armed forces
CO	Commanding Officer
CoA	Certificate of Airworthiness
DFC	Distinguished Flying Cross: a coveted RAF decoration given to commissioned officers only
DFM	Distinguished Flying Medal: the equivalent to the DFC for non commissioned officers! DFM is also the acronym for the Swiss Département Militaire Fédéral, i.e. War Department
Div.	Division. Can indicate either large ground force units or USAAF aerial armadas made up of Groups and Wings
Do.217	Dornier twin-engined German bomber also developed as heavy nightfighter
DSO	Distinguished Service Order. A British decoration.
EMG	Etat-Major Général, the Swiss general staff.
FAFL	Forces aériennes françaises libres, the Free French Air Force fighting with the Allies
FFI	Resisters from the Forces Françaises de l'Interieur

FGp   Fighter Group: the USAAF fighter unit roughly equivalent to the RAF Squadron

flab   Acronym for Flieger Abwehr, the Swiss anti-aircraft artillery comparable to the German flak or British ack-ack

F'Hafen   Friedrichshafen, a town on Lake Constance, Germany

Flak   Acronym for Flug (or Flieger) Abwehr Kanonen. The dreaded anti-aircraft artillery defending the Reich against Allied aerial incursions

FO   Foreign Office

F/Sgt   Flight Sergeant

ft   Foot or feet. The unit measuring height or altitude in aviation (0,305m)

FuG   Funkgeräte – the broadcasting and receiving radios used by the German armed forces. For instance, the FuG-16Z radio was designed for *Bf.109*-G3 fighters of the Luftwaffe

FuMG   Funkmessgeräte. Radio detection apparatus (radar) for the German Luftwaffe. For instance, the FuMG-62C was the Wurzburg radar built by Telefunken

Fus.   Fusilier, a rank within the Swiss Army

FW.190   As the Bf.109, but designed by Focke-Wulf. The best German propeler-driven fighter

Gib   Gibraltar

Gp   Group – the US equivalent of the Squadron in the RAF where the word qualified the large unit comparable to the US Wing

Hali   The Handley-Page *Halifax* four-engined RAF bomber. It was the second 'heavy' to enter service after the *Stirling*; .6,176 *Halifaxes* were built, against 2,382 Short *Stirlings* and 7,374 Avro *Lancasters*, which were undoubtedly the best Allied bombers of the Second World War

HE   High Explosive

HCU   In Heavy Conversion Units, crews who had trained on other types were acquainted with the flying of four-engined bombers

HM   His Majesty

HQ   Headquarters

IFF   Identification (of) Friend or Foe. Radio transmitter identifying aircraft as friendly. Similar to present-day transponder

in   inch

Inf.   Infantry

Jafü   Jagdführer. German fighter controller

JG   Jagdgeschwader. German fighter Wing

Ju.52   Junkers 52. Three-engined transport of the Luftwaffe

Ju.88   Junkers 88. Twin-engined German bomber also developed as a nightfighter

Kc/s   Obsolete Kilocycle per second. Now KHz

Kdo   Kommando

KG   Kampfgeschwader: German bomb Wing

KHz   Kilohertz. Quantifies radio frequencies. Has replaced the Kc/s

KU   Kampf Unfall. German report of downed aircraft

KIA   Killed in Action

Lanc   Avro *Lancaster*. The mainstay of RAF Bomber Command operations from 1942 onwards

LMF   Lack of Moral Fibre. Describes RAF individuals unwilling or unable to carry on fighting the enemy

LN   *Luftnachrichten*. German radio transmission and intercepts network

MAAF   Mediterranean Allied Air Force

MI   Military Intelligence (British). Comprised several sections such as MI.9

MiD   Mentioned in Despatches. A form of British recognition for valour. Gazetted in the official *London Gazette*

m   mètre, metre

mi.   statute mile

mntn   mountain

NCO   non-commissioned officer

NJG   *Nachtjagdgeschwader*. German nightfighter Wing.

ObFw   *OberFeldwebel* = German equivalent to RAF F/Sgt.

ORS   Operational Research Section. An RAF organisation analysing raid results

OSS   Office of Strategic Services. American organisation for subversives operations

OTU   Operational Training Unit. Preceded crew arrivals into RAF operational Squadrons

P-47   Republic *Thunderbolt*. Single-seat, single-engined American fighter

P-51   *Mustang*. As P-47 but built by North American

PFF   Pathfinder Force. RAF elite aerial units preceding Main Force bombers for precision marking of targets.

PoW   Prisoner of War

PRG   Photo Reconnaissance Group. (USAAF)

PRU   RAF Photo Reconnaissance Unit flying unarmed Spitfires or *Mosquitoes.*

QG   General Headquarters.

QGA   Army Headquarters, Switzerland.

RAAF   Royal Australian Air Force.

RAF   British Royal Air Force in which airmen of many nationalities flew in the Second World War from the Commonwealth, the occupied countries and others. Its Bomber Command aircraft flew mostly at night

RCAF   Royal Canadian Air Force

RCM   Radio Counter Measures

Ret.   retired

Rgt.   Regiment

RNZAF   Royal New Zealand Air Force

rpm   revolutions per minute

SAAF   South African Air Force

SHAEF   Supreme Headquarters Allied Expeditionary Forces

SN-2   German radar aboard Luftwaffe nightfighters. A development of the Lichtenstein radar

SOE   Special Operations Executive. The British subversive organisation dealing with underground operations

Spit   *Spitfire*

SQ.   Squadron

Ter.   Territorial. Swiss geographical area

US   United States. Often used for 'American'

USAAF   United States Army Air Force(s). Their heavy bombers generally operated in daylight. Until 1947, US aircraft belonged to the ground forces

(Army). The 8th and 9th Air Forces flew out of the British Isles; the 12th and 15th from North Africa and Italy. Worldwide, there were up to twenty American Air Forces during the Second World War

V-1   Vergeltungswaffe-1, the Luftwaffe's flying bomb

V-2   Vergeltungswaffe-2, the Wehrmacht' A-4 rocket

VE   Victory in Europe

WAAF   Women's Auxiliary Air Force in the RAF

WAC   Women's Army Corps in the US Army

* * * * * * * * *

TWO PRACTICAL NOTES ABOUT...
the times...
In view of the various time rosters in use in wartime Britain (Standard, Summer or Double Summer times) and on the Continent, no attempt has been made at conversion of the hours quoted. The times quoted are those in force in the countries where the events occurred with perhaps a mention of either (CH) or (GB) indicating Swiss or British time.

and credits for illustrations
Most of the photographs, maps or sketches appearing here are credited in their captions. However, some sources could not be identified and we extend our apologies to their authors: should they surface in time for possible reprinting runs, they would of course be properly recognised. For photographs, special thanks must go to two sources: the Swiss FliegerMuseum in Dübendorf and particularly to its keeper Andrea Lareida, who patiently dealt with the writer's repeated requests for relevant photographs; and Jim Wright in Corby, England, whose tireless energy located and produced a host of pictures of crewmembers from several continents, killed in operations in Switzerland.

Acknowledgements

Between August 1990 and July 1993, *Aeroplane Monthly* (now *Aeroplane*) published my series of short articles on the RAF and Switzerland. The response was so positive that the idea germinated to enlarge the series in book form. I was thus most grateful to the magazine's editors, Richard Riding and Michael Oakey, for permission to elaborate on my original material in order to start the 'RAF and Neutral Switzerland' project.

The design, however, proved to be so rich in untouched material that a companion volume was deemed necessary to cover downed evader aircrew reaching Switzerland to avoid captivity prior to returning to operational status in England. Thus was born *Aviateurs-Piétons vers la Suisse*, the first volume of a trilogy expected also to encompass the USAAF.

Putting together the RAF segment was initially thought to be a couple of years' involvement. The project actually took much longer to mature. Several years were spent reading some 300 books, writing as many extra letters, delving with dozens of supplemental archival files, screening a couple of films and many rolls of (sometimes barely readable) microfilms, and interviewing almost 100 people on three continents. It also proved useful to retrace, on the ground and in the air, the tracks followed by actors of this saga.

Many persons or organisations contributed useful information and helped to make this book as complete and accurate as possible. The names of those whose contributions were deemed essential appear in the main text or in the following paragraphs. It is recognized that the bits of information or the clarifications they provided contributed to weave historically and technically credible backgrounds to the dramas that occurred in Swiss skies half a century ago.

Others who should not be forgotten helped with their funds of documents or from official records depositories in Berne, Kew and London. My gratitude is owed to all, a special mention being deserved by: in Australia, David Wilson at the RAAF Headquarters, Canberra; in Canada, Janet Lacroix of the Canadian Forces Joint Imagery Centre; in Dübendorf, at the Swiss Air Force museum where most

Swiss 'Einvernahmen' (Interrogation reports) are stored – Toni Bernhard, Hans-Jürg Klossner and Andrea Lareida; in London, Eric Munday at the Historical Branch of the Ministry of Defence.

Among individuals there were: in Belgium, Maurice Goessens in Gerpinnes and Félix Thiry in Braine-Alleud; in Britain, Oliver Clutton-Brock in Newbury; in Oxted, Norman Mackie for his comprehensive skill in flying operational *Lancaster*s and *Mosquito*es and for letting me use his unpublished memoirs, and in Aldwick, T. 'Hamish' Mahaddie for his encouragement and his experience as a Pathfinder commander; in Switzerland, Peter Kamber in Burgdorf, Peter Schneider in Oberdorf, Hans-Heiri Stapfer in Horgen, Albert Violand in Sierre, Theo Wilhelm in Regensdorf, and in Geneva, Robert Pettersson. For others' unselfish co-operation, it is a pleasant duty to mention them hereafter with principal sources in relation with the chapters involved. There, 'CH' obviously abbreviates 'Switzerland', and 'GB', the United Kingdom. Official sources are also shortened, with 'Berne' meaning the Bundesarchiv in Berne, 'Düb' relating to the Dübendorf Air Museum, and 'PRO', the Public Records in Kew/London (now National Archives). Finally, if helpers have been overlooked, they are humbly asked to forgive the author's unwilling oversights.

• For Chapter 2, references about airspace violations rest into the PRO files such as FO.371/34881-2 and -/39846 and in Berne's E27/14354 (vol.2-3) and 14355(3-4-6).

• For Chapter 3, my thanks go to David Annani in Gwynedd (GB), who clarified the Nigel Smallpage episode; Mme Rosa in Thonex-Geneva, with her collection of wartime 'Schweizer Illustrierte Zeitung', and Herr Trüssel, curator, city archives Stans (CH). The main sources are files E27/ 14355 (vol.4) and 14356 (6-7-8) and 14362 in Berne, and file 53/14/6 in Düb.

• Chapter 4 owes much to Paddy Hope in Leeds (GB), Aridio Pellanda in Morat (CH), and to the crew's official evasion reports in my file EV4/1006 +1007 and Berne's E27/14355(4).

• For Chapter 5, credit is owed to Max Rudolf in Birmenstorf (CH); Kpl Schifferle, Stadtpolizei Baden (CH) and Fw. Heierle at the Polizeikommando, Aargau. In Berne, files EMD/AA6 5791-1-vols 4 and 9 were basic archival documents. The Swiss Air Accident report, 1303, issued in 1988, also helped, as did the evader report EV7/135, and Bomber Command's files, AIR 14/3473 and AIR 24/262B at PRO.

• Le Bouveret's early *Lancaster* catastrophe in Chapter 6 has been well documented, thanks to, in the UK, the pilot's brother, Walter Badge, R. Le Claire and Jim Wright, the air bomber's son. Without him my description would have lapsed much more than it does. Jim's unrelenting search of his father's RAF career, particularly his last day, proved not only an example of filial devotion but an unending source of information. Likewise, in Switzerland, Pascal Blanchard's continuing research proved most valuable, and Leo Clerc's eyewitness account solved part of the mystery that resulted in the head-on crash against a cliff. Pascal Barman also contributed significantly to the research. Other witnesses were also interviewed in Bouveret: Ms Ely Borgeaud, Auguste Cachat, René Curdy and Bernard Denis. The Berne file E27/14355 (vol.5) and PRO's AIR27/1234 also proved important, as did R. Buley, Headmaster at Shebbear College in Devon, and Swiss witnesses such as Mme Claude Durussel, Emile Monnet, Alfred Richon, Georges Richoz and M. Loutan.

• Chapter 7 owes much to the following Swiss witnesses or researchers: Ms Barlatey; Annie Bickel; François Brunelli; Elisabeth and Jacques Dubas; Sœur Fr.Duval; Charles Hemoz; Pierre Gianada; Ernest Lagger; Christine Lescaut; J-B Moix; Marcel Oggier; Marc Pfefferlé; Abbé Auguste Pont; Jacques Reichenbach; Michel Ranguelov; René Rosset; Hans Schaub; P. Schneider and Gerald Theodoloz, all in or near Sion (CH). Last but not least there were, again, Pascal Blanchard in Villeneuve (CH), and R. Le Claire and Jim Wright in England. In New Zealand, Derek Morgan gave valuable information on his brother, the pilot of this ill-fated aircraft; Jim Quinn of the 467 Squadron Association in Australia also helped. Finally, for many of the photographs featuring the sorry remains of *Lancaster* ED.531, I am indebted to Germaine de Preux, Jeanne Ometz, Charles Reichenberger and Bernard Schmid – all in Sion (CH). Swiss Air Accident report 1603 (1995) helped, but most relevant data rest in Berne's files, E27/14354(2) and 14567(1) and 14572(7) and AA8(25); in Düb's file 53/14/2 and box 6; and in PRO's AIR27/539 and 815 and 1930 and 1234 and 2677.

• Chapter 8, 'Sihlsee's Spin', was spun thanks to several participants, primarily 'Bish' Alistair Crowley-Smith, the pilot involved, and his charming wife Miriam, sadly both deceased. His fellow crewmember, Arthur Truscott, and Eric Hiley, also contributed significantly. Hedi Kälin's account of her meeting with the bootless Smith, minutes after his arrival in Switzerland, was also essential. Similarly, M. Lienert-Reichmuth in Euthal (CH) provided background information with his collection of wartime local newspapers. In England, A.C. Wedderburn of the 100 Squadron Association had recollections of another survivor of Lanc ND.595, Ron Carr. Amongst official sources there are: evader reports 4A/1932-3 and 1936; in Berne, files E27/14354(3) and 14355(6) and 14356(7) + 14567(1)and 14571; in Düb:Vol.2 of the Einvernahmen files; at PRO, Report K.206 in file AIR 14/3473 and 3731 and 27/797.

• The tragedy of the 'Saignelégier *Lancaster*' in Chapter 9 has been reconstructed with the help of Isobel Atcheson in Australia. In Britain, Ken Reece provided his survivor's recollections, later complemented by his brother George. Also in the UK, help was provided by S/Ldr Mervyn Davies, RAF (Ret.) and Jack Farmer, whilst in Switzerland, Edi Gyger's generous help was essential. There, J-P

Gigandet, Thierry Hadorn and Michel Lando also deserve this mention. Official sources include: PRO's files FO371/39846 + AIR14/2073 +2677 + AIR27/539 +1089; Düb's Vol.2 of the Einvernahmen files and box E6; Berne's files E27/14354 (2) and 14355 (6 + 7) and 14/356 (7) and EMD/5791-1-8.

• Chapter 10 was substantiated by historian John–Paul Basset and Fred Coney, Hon.Chairman of the 'Mildenhall Register' (15 Squadron). Apart from the customary Swiss Einvernahme (interrogation report) by J.R. Lécher & Co., it was, however, from such Swiss witnesses as Ernst Beletti, Robert Forster and Alice Remund that this Chapter benefited most. Archival sources rest in Berne files E27/14354(2) + 14355(6) + 14356(7) + 14567-8 and 14593. At PRO they were AIR14/3473 and 27/204, as well as Blott's Evasion Report 4A/1930, and in Düb, Vol.2 of the Einvernahmen files and Box E7.

• For the mysterious and barely documented loss of the 'Uttwil *Mosquito*' in Chapter 11, the crew's personal records, the Berne files E27/14355 (6) and 14593 and 13843-1 and 1A, plus PRO's AIR16/962, were the basic sources. Hans-Heiri Stapfer (CH), and the Swiss accident reports (1989)/1412 and 1494, also helped, as did PRO researcher W/Cdr (Ret.) F.F. Lambert, himself a distinguished wartime *Mosquito* pilot.

• The 'Grappelen Alpine disaster' in Chapter 12 could be described thanks to several Britons: Ms Lesley Bridges, Donald Brinkhurst, Don Bruce, Al Greethurst and P.D. Kayes (both of 101 Squadron Association), and the ubiquitous Jim Wright. Emil Brunner and Jean-Pierre Wilhelm (CH) also contributed to my background. A particular recognition must, however, go to S/Ldr (Ret.) Bernard Noble and his excellent and privately published book-cum-family history, *Noble Endeavour*, which gives in-depth information on the RAF career of his uncle, W/O Bertram Noble, pilot of the Grappelen *Lancaster*. Berne's files E27/14355 (6-8) and 14356 (6-7-8) and 14391 and 14567(1) + 14657 and 5791-1-1A and AA (8) (25), and PRO's AIR14/1246 and 3781 and AIR27/803 were also used, while in Düb it was Vol.5 of the Einvernahmen files.

• The saga of the 'Hamikon *Lancaster*' in Chapter 13 could not have been correctly described without Otto Hochstrasser, who saw its final moments. In nearby Hitkirch, the Elmiger family had recollections of survivor Piggott's arrival. I also owe much to the mid-upper gunner's cousin, Michael Clark (GB), who was ctive in having a memorial erected to commemorate 27/28 April 1944, and to Rolf Zaugg (CH) whose time, effort and expense saved from oblivion the top turret of either ME.720 or ND.759 *Lancasters*. Useful archive files comprise: Berne's E27/14355(6) and /14356(7) and /14391 and /14658; PRO's = AIR14/1246 and /2791 and AIR27/1089 and /1090 and WO208/3324 (Evader Reports 2642 and 2671) and FO371/39846 and Düb's Vol.5 of Einvernahmen. From Canada, via, again, Jim Wright, came the personal records of RCAF personnel killed here.

• For Chapter 14, thanks are due to: pilot Bob Peter in Australia; to Murray Bartle and Vin Graham for their most informative recollections, and particularly to Noel Davis for allowing the use of his memoirs written in May 2000. Formal documents can be found in PRO's AIR27/381, in Berne's file E27/14355 (3 and 6) and 14356(7), and at Düb in Vol.5 of the Einvernahmen files.

• The quasi-simultaneous arrival of 'two *Mosquitoes'* at or near Dübendorf in Chapter 15 was described thanks to their crews, namely the late Henry Morley, and thanks to Gordon Harper and Reginald Fidler who let me use their personal accounts. Wartime *Mosquito* navigator, Paddy Hope, also let me draw upon his precise skills. Bill Bridgman of the 515 Squadron Association and many officers of the *Mosquito* Aircrew Assn also contributed to this research. Likewise, I drew upon Berne's file E27/14355(8) and 14356(7), and on Düb's Vol.7 of the Einvernahmen files.

• The late Charles Bratschi was instrumental in providing much hitherto unpublished data on the arrival of the French aircraft described in Chapter 16. The handling of the sleek Bell *P-39 Airacobra* is well documented by Richard Kent in *Flying Combat Aircraft of the USAAF* (Iowa State University, 1975) and Jacques Mutin searched his unique pictorial archives to provide the photograph showing the very *Airacobra* in which François Laurens was killed. Of course, the Dübendorf files contain their usual amount of relevant information, mainly E27/14354(5+6) and E27/14742 to 793.

• Chapter 17 is documented by many newspaper and periodical sources, and of course by Bonjour's history of Swiss neutrality. However, the mainstay of information were the Berne files E27/14354 (2 and 3) + 14355 (4 and 7) and 14356 (5 and 6 and 7 and 8) and 14425 (for the Kembs dam), as well as PRO's FO371/34881 and AIR27/1930. Several witnesses such as Antoine Berntsen also shared their recollections with the author, as did the late Richard Williams, regretted President of RAFA-Switzerland.

• Chapter 18 is the product of various sources already quoted above, and last but not least, of the 1958 Imperial War Graves Commission's register of the names of those who fell in the 1939-1945 war, and are buried in Vevey's cemetery in Switzerland. Düb's file E27/14792 provided data on the Swiss radio beacons at the time, and EMD-5791/1, information on the IBM involvements. Evader reports such as 4A/1930 and 6/2465 proved useful not only to reconstruct the Blott & Co.'s repatriation trip across German-Europe, but other sagas as well. My thanks also to Carol Wicht in Choëx (CH) for providing accurate details on her late husband's career.

• For Chapter 19, PRO's FO Index 1940-1943 plus FO371/34880 were used, and 'Marking Time', the periodical for Swiss internees, also provided inside information. Berne's file EMD/5791-1-9 contributed, whilst the search for the fate of the 'Swiss *Mosquitoes'* was helped by Albert Violand and Düb's keeper Andrea Lareida. Various figures on compensations appear in Berne file E27/14567-8.

Many books and periodicals also helped to consolidate my knowledge of events in the air war involving Switzerland, including:

A Lancaster Pilot's Impression on Germany, Richard Starkey, 1999
Always Prepared, 207 Squadron RAF, John Hamlin, 1999
Australian Air Power, Europe, John Herrington, 1962,1963
Bericht zur Heimatkunde (...) 1939-45, Max Rudolf
Bericht der Kommandant, (Swiss) Fliegertruppen, 1946
'Bomber Command Association's 'Newsletter''
Bomber Command War Diary, Martin Middlebrook and Chris Everitt, 1985;
Bomber – Fighter and Coastal Squadrons, 3 vols, Philip Moyes, 1964,1969,1982
Bomber Intelligence, William E. Jones, 1983
Fremde Flugzeug in der Schweiz, Theo Wilhelm, 2000
Geschichte der Deutschen Nachtjagd, Gebhard Aders, 1977
Histoire de la Neutralité Suisse (Vol.4-5-6), Edouard Bonjour, 1970
Lancaster Bomber, Bruce Robertson, 1974
Luftnachrichtentruppe, Karl Hoffmann, 1968
New-Zealanders in the RAF, 3 vols, H.L. Thompson, 1953,1956,1959
On Wings of War, (166 Squadron), James Wright, 1996
Pathfinder Force, Gordon Musgrove, 1976
Pilot Notes (various aircraft), wartime, HMSO
Portrait of a Bomber Pilot, Chris Jary, 1995
RAF Bomber Command Losses, (7 vols), William Chorley, 1992 to 2002
Right-Hand Man, Geoff Copeman, 1996
SOE in France, M.R.D. Foot, 1966
Strategic Air Offensive against Germany, (4 vols), C. Webster and N. Frankland, 1961
The Time of my Life, Jack Dickinson, 1999
Uncommon Valour, A.G. Goulding, 1985

A final note of regret is due here, that has to do with the ever encroaching bureaucracy pervading most fields of human activities, including historical research. Examples abound, not only within public archival depositories, but also in industry and benevolent circles. A particularly unpropitious example rests, of all places, with an humanitarian organisation in Geneva. Whereas in the 1970s, when researching *Forteresses sur l'Europe-17 August 1943* (Rossel, Brussels, 1980), I easily had access to their sources identifying casualties and PoWs, but by the 1990s those archives had been closed, resting under the regal protectorate of a proliferating staff. It therefore became more complicated, nay impossible, to identify some of the airmen involved, resulting in obscure heroes being deprived of the credit their deeds and sacrifice warranted.

R.A.
January 2006

1

Love and Hate

The young aviator stood bemused near the wreck of the brand new Mosquito *laying broken near Dübendorf airport, Switzerland. Minutes earlier, Flight Sergeant Reginald Fidler had survived the crash-landing of his* Mossie. *Now, helping his pilot out of the heap of wood and smouldering electric bundles that had been their cramped cockpit, Fidler was looking up in awe at another* Mosquito *apparently bound to touch neutral Swiss soil in the same crippled condition that had been theirs!*

The date was 30 September 1944 and the two Mosquitoes *were to be the last Royal Air Force aircraft to arrive and be impounded in Switzerland. Meanwhile, however, and since the Second World War had started in Europe, the RAF had been involved in numerous dramatic events over this central European country which strove to adhere to a self-imposed policy of neutrality.*

The saga of Switzerland and the Allied air forces in the Second World War is one of love and hate. Starting in June 1940 and almost until the end of the conflict, the first was bombed, strafed and showered with incendiaries by the second, her airspace sovereignty was repeatedly violated, her nationals killed and maimed, albeit in comparatively small numbers, and her complaints virtually ignored by aircrew and officialdom alike. Fiercely neutral since 1815, Switzerland proved extremely touchy on the subject of Grenzverletzungen, i.e. infringements of her borders. The Second World War started on 3 September 1939 and during the remainder of that year, there were 143 border violations by French and German aircraft.[1] The number rose to 708 in 1940, when the two neighbouring belligerents battled near the western Swiss borders. That year, 1940, was also when the British Royal Air Force began overflying neutral Switzerland in the course of raids against northern Italy that were to last until 1943. Thereafter, RAF bomber violations only happened when the attacking streams flew close to the Rhine border on their way to targets in Southern Germany. In 1941 belligerent over-flights numbered 413, with roughly the same number (419) in 1942. The figure was to double in 1943 (874), and to skyrocket to 2,212 in 1944, when the waves of the air war came breaking near the borders. As for 1945 when the war came to an end, after the first four months, the figure reached the stunning total of 1,732. Out of the 6,501 aerial violations recorded within Swiss airspace, 881 could be attributed to Axis aircraft and 604 to their Allied opponents, but there is little doubt that the latter could also be blamed for most of the balance. Indeed, aerial violations started early in the war to strain Anglo-Swiss relations, and later were to threaten ties with the US government.

DISASTER AVERTED

As early in the war as just after noon, Wednesday 13 February 1940, Swiss defences were ready to react to the intrusion near Geneva of a large three-engined mono-plane, when the machine veered to stay just outside the border over Ferney.[2] No shot was fired and fortunately so, since it transpired the aircraft was *A.702*, a Swiss Junkers *Ju.52* turning base for Geneva airport! Just as lucky was another Junkers straying over Birsfelden aerodrome on 17 March 1941. The airfield, lay-ing very close to the German border near Basle, was defended by Oblt.Liebrich's *Grenzkompanie I/257*, whose standing procedure was to refrain from shooting unless ordered by an officer. Notwithstanding this, gunner Hug let go a volley of forty-seven rounds towards the erring machine, fortunately without scoring any hit.

Indeed, the defences could react violently when not in doubt: in the spring of 1940, Swiss fighters and anti-aircraft artillery shot down several German aircraft. In the summer, the situation came to a head with Germany, to such an extent that the Swiss had to relent: their fighters were barred from operating too near the borders. In January 1941 the Swiss flab defences[3] were instructed not to shoot anymore at anything less than a three-plane formation. Accordingly, no foreign aircraft arrived in Switzerland in 1941 or 1942, except on its own volition. But in April 1943, orders were rescinded. The defending forces were then to attack without warning any formation of two or more aircraft, Swiss fighters having to challenge intruding machines to a landing, and to shoot if a second challenge remained without effect. Meanwhile, surrounded as she was by the Axis nations and depending on their 'goodwill' for maintaining her lifelines of supplies from the outside world, Switzerland was faced with preventing the Royal Air Force, and later on the US Army Air Forces to use her as a safe convenience in their aims to attack targets in northern Italy and Southern Germany.

SWISS COMPLACENCY

After losing a number of aircraft cutting corners over Switzerland, a chastened Luftwaffe only rarely infringed upon Helvetic borders. The Third Reich, however, resented the apparent abandon with which the RAF started to overfly a neutral country where flak and fighters could not oppose its deeds. For instance, the RAF raid on Munich on 19/20 September 1942 was routed south, i.e. near or on the Swiss border, in order to avoid German defences laid on the direct route from England. Heinrich Gremminger, the Swiss Consul in Münich, was quick to point out how badly local officials resented the apparent Swiss *laisser faire* in the matter. The event did undoubtedly contribute to German threats of 'do something or otherwise we shall ...' The Swiss reacted along two avenues. Lacking radar and nightfighters, they were at a loss to oppose the RAF night-flying raiders in their own element. But their flab could and did fire at them, sometimes with dramatic results. Indeed, the RAF did provide the Swiss with good reasons to act violently – on 16/17 December 1940, for instance, when British bombs intended for Mannheim had been scattered on Basle.[4] Swiss countermeasures of a more conventional venue laid at diplomatic level. Depending on the events, protests were lodged by their legations in Berlin, Rome or London. In the British capital, Swiss Minister (i.e. Ambassador) Walter Turnheer was to become an *habitué* of the Foreign Office as violations by British night bombers became more and more frequent. His protests usually prompted RAF and Air Ministry to issue soothing statements for diplomatic consumption. This had not always been the case, however. An early answer from Bomber Command to the FO, issued in October 1940, bluntly stated: '[against] objectives in Italy, the primary aim is to reach [them]. If it is necessary to fly over Switzerland in order to do this, action should be taken accordingly'. Exactly a year later, the phraseology was somewhat toned down after Switzerland had experienced more accidental bombings. 'Crews', wrote AVM Norman Bottomley, the Deputy Chief of Air Staff, in yet another note to Bomber Command, 'were instructed to avoid flying over Swiss territory whenever it is at all possible within tactical limitations'. After still another year, in the December of 1942, things became unhinged following a massive infringement of Swiss airspace during a raid on Turin on 29/30 November, repeated on 8/9 December.[5] In Berne (the Swiss 'federal city', i.e. capital) Foreign Affairs Minister, Marcel Pilet-Golaz[6] complained so bitterly to British Ambassador Clifford Norton, that the matter went up to Anthony Eden, London's Foreign Office Minister. Soon after this, the chief of the RAF Bomber Command, Air Chief Marshal Arthur Harris,[7] was reminded in no uncertain terms of, 'the importance of reducing to a minimum the occasions on which RAF aircraft fly over Switzerland en route to Italy'. Generally sympathetic to the difficulties faced by Bomber Command, the Foreign Office stated its awareness of, 'the risk of violations resulting from stress or weather or other genuine operational necessity', but at the same time felt that a) no aircraft should be routed over Switzerland and b) crews should realise the gravity of violating Swiss neutrality. The note also stated that repeated violations imposed a serious strain on British relations with the Swiss government, jeopardising the important facilities obtained from Swiss neutrality. What the FO had in mind were tangible benefits in special industrial supplies, covert operations, intelligence and propaganda, to which was later added the status making neutral Switzerland the protective power of belligerent Britain.

RAF ROUTES TO ITALY

At that time, in theory, RAF navigators laid their routes to Italian targets in Genoa, Turin or Milan, well clear of Swiss territory. A turning point was for some months over the city of St-Julien, in French Haute-Savoie, a few miles south of the border and close to the tip of an easily recognisable check point: Lake Geneva. Navigation errors, with or without quotation marks, were easy to make. Two examples were obvious in the Autumn of 1941. One occurred during the night of 10/11 September 1941, when seventy-six aircraft were detailed to bomb Turin. Seven of them reported overflying Geneva and the fifteen despatched by 4 Group had their maps clearly marked for a penetration of Swiss airspace leading to the eastern end of Lake Geneva, well into Switzerland. Three weeks later, in a raid to Genoa on 28/29 September, the briefed route gave a turning point 30 miles (50km) west of Geneva, i.e. roughly over Bourg-en-Bresse. Most aircraft adhered to the order, but at debriefing some villains confessed to having cut corners. One navigator took advantage of the extraordinary clear night and headed straight from St-Dizier in France to Montreux, and thence to Genoa across the Swiss Alps. On the way back he returned by way of Geneva and Jersey. The crew was one of the fifty-odd who reported 'moderate, fairly accurate flak over [Switzerland at] Lausanne and three searchlights at Sion in the Rhône valley'. Such mishaps resulted in Swiss diplomatic complaints that were answered after a lengthy process involving Foreign Office, Air Ministry, RAF Bomber Command and sometimes reaching down the line to operational units, i.e. Groups and Squadrons. Ironically, both of the above incidents happened days after a formal note from London had replied to Swiss complaints aired on 19 August. All efforts would be made, it said, to avoid Swiss airspace. However, HM Government could not:

> modify their plans for the bombing of military objectives in northern Italy and it
> is unfortunately impossible to guarantee that in flying on so long a range there will
> be no errors of navigation... if they occur [Switzerland is] fully entitled to take all
> proper action for the defence of [her] neutrality.

THE GENEVA LANDMARK

The diplomatic joust over airspace infringement would last until the end of the war, but meanwhile, on November 1942 for instance, Sir Archibald Sinclair, the Secretary of State for Air, wrote to Anthony Eden, who, from the FO, was in charge of softening Swiss feelings, stating the routeing 'enables pilots in reasonable visibility to use the lake of Geneva as a landmark to check their course and.... avoid Swiss territory'.

Sinclair then relayed a remark by Arthur Harris, himself a distinguished pilot and one never afraid of words, stating that, 'anybody who hears an aeroplane is inclined to think that he personally or his house, is used as a landmark. [So] there is no doubt that the noise of 200 aircraft flying round St-Julien, reverberates for

50 miles or more inside Switzerland and thus gives rise to complaints'. After a long dissertation explaining why the RAF could not have overflown Switzerland on the night of 22/23 November, Harris confirmed that: 'Groups have been informed of the necessity of keeping clear of Switzerland whenever possible.'

The end of the sentence left the air open to personal decisions by those directly concerned, the combat airmen, provided of course that the directive filtered down to them in a not too diluted form. They, the crews, indeed had the last word, and for good reasons since they were the ones who struggled to survive in an environment of fear and death quite remote from the niceties of diplomacy. The crews did not always know it but Harris, their Commander-in-Chief, was extremely sympathetic to their plight when, at New Year 1943 and apparently exasperated by the Swiss overflights obsession, he minuted to his Groups: 'Brief the crews accordingly. They will still transgress. Who cares'.

Anyway, in the case at hand, Harris kept for himself that on the said November night, 222 of his bombers had been dispatched to Stuttgart in Southern Germany. In view of the then still crude navigational aids available to aircrew, some of the machines could very well have strayed too far south, impinging on the Swiss border.

Finally, as if to enhance the ridiculousness of the situation, the Swiss perception that their country had just been somewhat of a convenience, was to be vindicated soon after the war, in February 1946, and by, of all people, a top-ranking RAF official. Attending a memorial ceremony at Vevey's RAF cemetery, an outspoken New Zealander, Air Marshal Sir Arthur 'Maori' Coningham, stated he knew Switzerland well, having overflown it many times in the course of large RAF raids.[8]

TURNING POINT, LAKE BOURGET

Just as straightforward were statements from aircrew. F/O Thomas Wiley was a rear gunner on a 78 Squadron *Halifax* that came down in France on 11/12 December 1942. He evaded capture and, when debriefed in London, said: 'We were returning over Switzerland when one of the motors cut.' As it was, and as seen in the second September 1941 incident, another turn spot more remote from Geneva and the Swiss border had eventually been selected by Bomber Command to placate the Swiss. Lake Bourget near Aix-les-Bains/Chambéry thus became check point to the Alps and northern Italy. In practice, however, night-flying RAF crews still took shortcuts over Lake Geneva and even further east, nearer a line running from Basle to Lugano. An extreme example, which could hardly be blamed on aircrew alone, occurred on the occasion of the first large raid on Friedrichshafen on 20/21 June 1943. After bombing, the raiders – *Lancasters* of 5 Group, RAF – did not turn back but flew on to bases in North Africa, in what was to be the first 'shuttle' raid of the war. The route after target had deliberately cut across eastern Switzerland, to northern Italy and the Mediterranean. More violations occurred in August, such incidents being recurrent until the end of the war. Also, starting in 1943, there were infringements by daylight-flying USAAF formations.

These, however, were usually slight and accidental shallow penetrations even if the Americans did 'very well' on their own when it came to bombing Swiss towns by mistake.[9] Even so, on the whole Switzerland proved most sympathetic towards Britain and the United States. An apocryphal radio exchange between Swiss flab and an RAF bomber pilot ran as follows:

Swiss: 'You are overflying neutral territory; we are shooting at you...'
RAF: 'Yes, we know. Please note your aim is too low'
Swiss: 'Yes, we know. Please do not descend...'

Made up as it was, the story reflects well the mood of the times. The Swiss, behind all their aims of neutrality and impartiality, could barely hide their positive feelings for the cause of democracy and freedom. But as for every love story, this did not go without hitches. There were cases when the RAF and the USAAF became victims of the Swiss endeavour to adhere to a strict neutrality in order to soothe a particularly watchful and fierce entourage. Over the sixty-eight months, during which warring countries surrounded Switzerland, a total of thirty-two belligerent aircraft would crash within her borders: twenty-eight Allied and four Axis machines. Out of those accidents, sixteen were claimed shot down by fighters and ten by flab, the others coming to grief because of weather or battle damage sustained elsewhere. Six further Luftwaffe machines were also downed by the Swiss, going on to crash outside their borders.

HELVETIC ASYLUM

Helvetic sensitivity was much more relaxed when it came to giving asylum to damaged aeroplanes. During the war, Switzerland became a safe haven for surviving crewmembers from 59 German aircraft, 167 American, one French, one Hungarian and 13 RAF machines, counting one *Lancaster* that 'landed' in Lake Constance, just inside or near her home waters. Surprisingly, however, the first British flying machine to arrive was, as will be seen, an incendiary balloon not listed as a manned aircraft.

What was the fate of airmen stranded in Switzerland? Swiss policy was quite simple: aviators obviously lost during a training sortie were sent back with their mounts to the Reich or Italy as it happened. They usually spent one night as guests of the Confederation, pending clarification of their status, and while their aeroplane was examined and refuelled. On the other hand, combat crews were interned, which meant they were in uniform,[10] more or less confined to quarters in Swiss army barracks and later on in the war, in requisitioned hotels in isolated areas such as Berne, Davos or Wengen. Some of the inmates arrived in rather bad shape and Switzerland did care for them, as, for instance, in a special 'camp' for those suffering from deep burns, in Tolochenaz, east of Geneva. During the course of Second World War, Switzerland gathered a sizeable number of 'winged refugees'. Among them were 101 German and Italian airmen, but it was the Allied contingent that reached staggering figures: 1,673 men (including 76 casualties) out of which, from the year 1943 onwards, Americans were overwhelmingly prominent (1,563 and 41 killed),[11] there being only 34 RAF aircrew interned after landing or parachuting in the country, besides 35 casualties (see Chapter 18 whose figures include four FAF pilots).

Then there were at least 319 'walking aviators': escapees from Axis compounds for Prisoners of War and the evaders downed in hostile lands or seas who had had enough luck and stamina to journey to the safe haven of central Europe. Indeed most airmen were well aware of the tiny country's position as a oasis of peace in a world aflame. Some had a chance to taste of her hospitality when all else failed; others, the unlucky ones, rest forever in the shade of her renowned mountains. This volume is essentially the story of the Royal Air Force 'Winged' (Flying) Refugees,[12] gathered from interviews with survivors and witnesses on the ground, and from official records in Switzerland, Britain and Germany. It will, however, be one of the contradictions unearthed by researching the matter, that the first RAF crew member to lose his life in Switzerland did not die as the result of an operational accident: he drowned entering the country!

THE FIRST RAF CASUALTY

Royal Air Force casualties in Switzerland were comparatively light: thirty-six of its wartime airmen being buried or reported missing in the country.[13] Acquiring the dubious distinction of being the first RAF casualty in the country was a young sergeant air gunner. His name was Sidney Bradley. He had spent a month of hardship travelling over 200 miles (320km) fraught with danger, only to drown in the border river Doubs on Tuesday 16 June 1942.

The river's tumultuous waters squeeze between abrupt Jurassic limestone cliffs, offering a formidable barrier coinciding over some 28 miles (45km) with the border separating north-western Switzerland from the then German-occupied France. The region, sparsely populated, mountainous and spreading over both countries, attracted those wanting to evade and escape, and others willing to flee German control and rejoin the free world. Even without considering the presence of German patrols intent, with their dogs, at preventing escapes into neutral territory, crossing the Doubs in these parts was a hard endeavour. A measure of the difficulty can be derived from the names given to several spots such as the aptly named 'Echelles de la Mort' (The Ladders of Death) overlooking the deep canyon north of La-Chaux-de-Fonds.

Sid Bradley hailed from Aigburth near Liverpool; he was nearing his twenty-second birthday when he was shot down on 19/20 May 1942. After training at No.4 Air Gunnery School he had flown on his initial operation on 10 April and had been on ten sorties. He had been first Wireless Operator/Air Gunner aboard a *Wellington III* serialed X.3472 and coded SR-D by 101 Squadron.[14] His aircraft, captained by Sgt Jack Beecroft, had been one of the eleven RAF machines lost during an ineffective raid on Mannheim. The *Wellington* had developed engine trouble over France and, according to the crew, had belly-landed 'some 9 miles (15km) south-west of Mézières'.[15] Subsequent research indicates the spot was actually 27km (17mi.) further south, at Leffincourt.

In any case, having succeeded in the arduous task of belly-landing the heavy machine at night in unknown enemy territory, pilot Beecroft elected not to set the aircraft alight, in order not to draw attention to his crew. Only the Gee navigation equipment and the IFF identifier were detonated before the five men made for the south. All eventually reached the Swiss border, where the pilot and a gunner, Henry Harwell, swam across the Doubs while, chastened by Bradley's fate, the two other survivors sought a safer passage, only to be captured by a German patrol.

Poor Bradley was only discovered on 27 June. He was to be the only Allied casualty among the 350-odd evaders who swam or walked into wartime Switzerland.[16] He is said to have been cremated in nearby La-Chaux-de-Fonds, although some sources report his burial in the town's cemetery on the 27th. His remains now rest at Vevey's British cemetery on the shore of Lake Geneva with thirty-three other fellow crewmen who died in Switzerland. To them the poignant words seen on many of their headstones are a relevant tribute:

> They shall grow not old, as we that are left to grow old
> Age shall not worry them, nor the year condemn.
> At the going down of the sun and in the morning
> We will remember them.

2

Why the RAF?

One may wonder why the Royal Air Force could be involved with Switzerland in the Second World War. After all, that peaceful and tiny country had been neutral since well before the turn of the century and was situated far inside the continent, at least 400mi.(650km) away from Britain. The answer becomes obvious when considering the strategic implications of the British air arm during the war.

Actually, the RAF was not, by far, the first to perpetrate violations of Swiss neutrality. Such German and French deeds occurred months earlier, between September 1939 and May 1940, when France and Germany came to grips close to the northern Swiss border.

FIRST MISHAPS

The earliest instance seems to have been a Luftwaffe action – on the ground. It occurred on 27 November 1939 when three uniformed Luftwaffe airmen walked into Switzerland. They had been shot down four days earlier at Cotebrunne near Besançon, and evaded capture by the French to become the first of some 350 flyers, including 155 RAF evaders, to walk across the borders and seek refuge within the Swiss haven of peace.[1] On 10 May 1940, matters became more critical: German bombs fell on Courrendlin, near Délémont and close to the French border. Six days later, a Heinkel *He.111* was shot down by Swiss fighters near Winterthur. The same defenders downed two more Heinkels on 1 June and one more on the morrow. On the fourth, a pair of Messerschmitt *Bf.110*s were claimed by Swiss fighters, who lost one of theirs. On 8 June, two more *Bf.110*s were downed by the Swiss after one of their antiquated *C.35* reconnaissance aircraft had been brought down. French airmen also made mistakes. On 4/5 June 1940, they launched sorties against Southern Germany with the BMW factory in Munich, the Badische Anilin Werke in Ludwigshafen and several airfields as targets. Not intended as an objective was Tagerwilen, a Swiss village close to

Konstanz, and its airfield on the lake of the same name. Although the crew has not been identified, it is known that the raider was the solitary Farman 221 No.8 of Groupe de Bombardement II/15. Flying out of St-Yan, its crew claimed to have attacked Friedrichshafen airfield with its 2,200kg (4,845lb) bomb load. The intended target is just 28km (17mi.) east of Tagerwilen, on the opposite shore of Lake Constance, and this makes the Farman a serious contender for the first and probably only bombing of Switzerland by French aircraft. In any case, the Vichy French government paid the princely sum of 7,042.75 Sw.Frcs in 1941 for the damage.

PRECARIOUS NEUTRALITY

Belligerent forces and neutrality did indeed not always get along as well as the cosy diplomatic circles would have liked. An example occurred much further south when the Italian Regia Aeronautica raiding Bahrein in the summer of 1940 overflew and bombed Saudi Arabia. In Switzerland proper and much later in the war, an avalanche of American aircraft – there were 167 of them, mostly four-engined bombers with their ten-men crews – practically swamped the country's internment facilities.[2]

To return to the Royal Air Force, its aircraft were also involved with neutral countries other than Switzerland. Such was the case after the fall of France for that part of the country governed by the Vichy regime, i.e. south of the Demarcation Line which between June 1940 and November 1942 separated the occupied and non-occupied parts of the country. RAF machines transiting at night between England and Gibraltar or the Mediterranean front, often cut corners across 'Vichy'. The same applied to the south west, over Spain and Portugal and across the Continent, over Sweden and Turkey.

The earliest involvement of the British air arm with Switzerland occurred early in the war with accidental bombings of towns and land, and fortuitous arrivals of drifting balloons intended to play havoc with German facilities. The latter are dealt with in Chapter 3, and this chapter will thus endeavour to analyse the reasons why manned RAF aircraft interfered with Swiss neutrality between 1939 and 1945.

To proceed with such an analysis of the RAF *v.* Switzerland, one can examine several periods or reasons:

- the early raids on Italy commencing in June of 1940;
- the more methodical attacks on Italy leading to the collapse of the country in September 1943;
- the more or less unintentional overflying of Swiss neutral territory in the course of reconnaissance sorties or of attacks on Southern Germany;
- the need for distressed aircraft to seek refuge in the safe haven of Switzerland.

ITALIAN TARGETS

In the summer of 1940, the debacle of France and the Italian entry into the fray on 10 June presented the RAF with a new set of requirements as Italian targets became politically desirable.

As for the raids that were to take place later against Italy, the policy meant long-range sorties towards an area south of Switzerland,[3] across enemy-occupied France with the barrier of the Alps thrown in as additional difficulty. Furthermore, the period closely followed the revelation that daylight raids proved too costly for bombers which, contrary to pre-war expectations, did not, by far, always get through unscathed. Since mid-April, Bomber Command strategic attacks were staged at night only.[4]

Those two ingredients laid the seed of infringements of Swiss neutrality, usually translating into rather mild border violations but occasionally resulting in serious mishaps. Harmless towns and villages could thus be subjected to accidental bombings. The earliest of such incidents took place in the course of the very first RAF raid on Italy on the night of 11/12 June 1940. This was twenty-four hours after Italy had declared war on France and Great Britain, when thirty-six big twin-engined Armstrong-Whitworth *Whitleys* were detailed to attack the RAF's industrial target, SDL.606. Five bomber units took part in the raid: Nos 10, 51, 58, 77 and 102 RAF Squadrons[5] which despatched up to nine *Whitleys* each. Listed in their 'Order 103' were the Fiat aviation factories in Turin, with several alternate objectives such as the Ansaldo plants in Genoa, as well as Milan and Savona.

The raid did not prove a great success, with only nine aircraft bombing Turin, and two others attacking Genoa. Of the remainder, twenty-three turned back due to poor weather over the Alps, fifteen of which brought their bombs back. Of the others, some sowed their loads on 'alternate targets', including some Swiss real estate (see below and Chapter 17).

ALPS AND THUNDERSTORMS

In view of the distance involved, the raid was staged with a refuelling stop in the Channel Islands, in Jersey and at Cliffield-Guernsey, the sorties thus lasting over eighteen hours. At dusk on 10 June, the heavily loaded machines took off at some ten minutes intervals from those short airfields. Weather at base was good and mild, but soon turned extremely bad over the Continent. Heavy electrical storms were encountered, with icing in cloud. All this resulted in several aircraft turning back. One of them was P.4957, flown by S/Ldr Hanafin, which was struck by lightning, the rear gunner being shocked and the wireless operator suffering from burns when his R.1082 set blew up.

One machine met with a still less enviable fate, crashing in France with the loss of all five aboard: this was Sgt Norman Songest's crew in N.1362 of 77 Squadron, who came down at Lignières-la-Doucelle, NW of Alençon[6] where the bomb load obliterated aircraft and men.

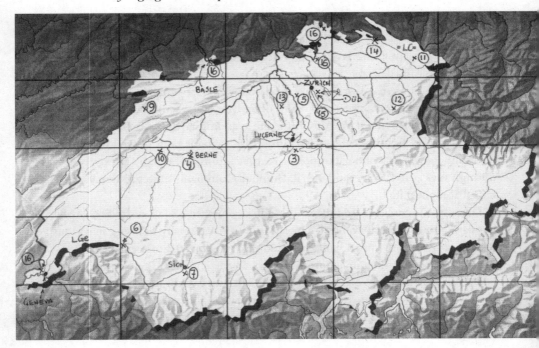

Map of Switzerland showing the locations of landings and crashes of RAF and associated aircraft in the Second World War, numbered after the relevant chapters. LC is for Lake Constance, LGe for Lake Geneva, and Düb stands for Dübendorf. (Off. Fédl. Topographie)

Others laboured to gain altitude over the Continent in order to cross the alpine barrier. Here, the *Whitleys* were confronted with the difficulty of overflying the mountains, heavily overloaded with ice accretion, a meteorological occurrence which resulted in many aircraft having to turn back or jettison their loads.

SWITZERLAND HIT

On this night of 11/12 June 1940 it was 0115hr, Swiss time, when a first stick of six bombs exploded in Switzerland. It was a typical *Whitley* reduced bomb load on this raid. Aimed with the help of a large parachute flare, the explosives harmlessly churned empty fields near Daillens, 10km (6.5mi.) north of Lausanne on the Swiss shore of Lake Geneva and 100km (62mi.) north of Turin.

Ten minutes later, seven more bombs hit Renens near Lausanne, killing a Mrs Dante on the fair grounds and maiming her husband; eight others were also wounded nearby. Here, another *Whitley* had been striving for almost half an hour to locate a worthwhile Italian target; the crew eventually aimed at rail sidings adjacent to a waterfront, topography much similar to one existing in Genoa.

Later on, some 50km (31mi.) south-west of Lausanne, the weather had turned out mild, hazy and cloudy in Geneva's outskirts. There, Pierre Meyer was quite unaware of the weather when he was harshly thrown out of bed to find himself gasping and bewildered under heaps of plaster rubble. Swiss clocks showed exactly 0145hr, and more British bombs had hit Switzerland. They wrecked Meyer's cottage, 'Les Clématites', in the then green suburb of Carouges-Roseraie, but at least its owner was alive. For others, the event proved much more tragic. The culprit missile was just one of a stick of six bombs which left a wake of destruction, wounding fourteen people and killing two more. Julia Escher had been lured onto her balcony by the hum of an aircraft dodging thunderheads above: splinters cut short her life. Nearby, a soldier – Fernand Chollet – was mortally wounded on his straw berth in his Beau-Séjour billet.[7] The lone aircraft had circled for forty-five minutes, evidently trying to ascertain its position and releasing 'a yellowish flare' in the process. The crew most probably ended up spotting the Arve River and the western tip of Lake Geneva between clouds, again mistaking the landmarks for comparable ones in Genoa, both targets nestling indeed more or less at the foot of overhanging hills. Having turned to the south east over Cologny, the *Whitley* came back 'downwind' over the Arve River, apparently aiming at rail facilities in La Praille. Its bombs missed, falling short by one mile (1.6km).

Three aircraft were thus involved in this initial bombing of Switzerland. The accident was fully recognised as such by the British Foreign Office as early as 18 June, diplomatic apologies being followed by complete compensation.[8]

WHO DID IT?

Trying to identify the crews involved remains a difficult exercise and no definite answer can be provided. However, from a contemporary Bomber Command report one can proffer tentative considerations, since:

> eleven crews bombed: nine at Turin and two at Genoa
> fifteen brought their bombs back to England;
> two attacked unidentified targets;
> eight did not submit reports, including the one lost.

One can thus focus on the ten last-listed aircraft and subtract the one lost, since it crashed in France with its bomb load. There then remains a short list of nine machines the most likely to have bombed the suburbs of Geneva and Lausanne on the night of 11/12 June 1940. Then, going further down in the analysis by checking the reported times of bombing, it can be noticed that F/O Bissett in P.4981, a 51 Squadron machine, 'became heavily iced up and forced, whilst still in cloud, to release the bombs twenty minutes after the estimated time of arrival over target'. The time of bombs away was 0100hr, said the crew, which means they had reached the supposed target area some forty minutes after midnight. Knowing that the average bombing time of the machines reaching the Italian targets was around 0120hr, one cannot help wondering if Bissett's crew could not be one of the best candidates for having presented wartime Switzerland with the first British bombs.[9]

At least two other bidders can also compete. One is S/Ldr P.Beare who, icing up in 102 Squadron's N.1471 coded DY°R, jettisoned his load 'over the Alps' at around 2200hr on the 11th, which seems to be far too early to have attained the mountains. The other contending crew could be F/Lt Tony O'Neill's, from 58 Squadron, who also jettisoned his load 'in the icy stygian murk' of the Alps before turning back.

On behalf of those pioneer crews flying *Whitleys* and *Wellingtons* on long flights from UK bases, endowed with none of the navigation aids[10] that later became available, one should remember the difficulty of finding distant targets at night in all sorts of weather. Indeed, at the time, Bomber Command reckoned that only one out of every five aircraft despatched found its target.[11] No wonder then that in 1940 the tally of Swiss border violations amounted to 556 by Allied and unknown aircraft, most of which must have been straying RAF machines.[12]

A final note as a measure of how effective opposition was, be it enemy or weather: by the end of 1940 no less than eight of the thirty-six aircraft participants in the 11/12 June raid were to be lost in operations, a casualty rate of 22 per cent!

THE HEAT ON ITALY

Later, from the Autumn of 1942, the offensive intended to throw German forces out of Africa began, and Churchill indicated that 'the heat should be turned on Italy'. RAF Bomber Command then resumed its attacks against targets in Northern Italy. Altogether, between June 1940 and August 1943, it conducted fifty-seven raids on Italy from its East Anglian bases, spread amongst industrial cities or ports such as Genoa (twelve),[13] La Spezia (five), Milan (twelve), Turin (twenty) and tactical targets at or near Bologna (four), plus one each at Cislago, Leghorn (Livorno), Savona and San Giovanni.[14]

In the course of those sorties, border violations were invariably recorded by Switzerland, the most flagrant being during the Milan operation on 24 October 1942. This was the only one to take place in daylight and the Swiss were thus able to clearly identify *Halifax* intruders, even though most aircraft were *Lancasters*.

At this stage one can wonder, as did the Germans, why Swiss defences were not more actively engaged against the British night raiders. The answer is two-fold and quite unrelated to the fable of a biased sympathy towards the Allied flyers. During all of Second World War and more so in the early months of the war, Swiss fighters were quite unprepared for night operations. There was no night-fighter nor radar guidance in the Swiss inventory, and only its flab artillery could react to airspace violations. Even so, particularly in the first years of the conflict, the flab was not particularly efficient above 5,000m (15,000ft) and less so at night, lacking as it was in searchlights and heavy guns. This situation was, of course, not fully appreciated by foreign diplomatic circles nor even by Swiss politicians as shall be seen in Chapter 19.

Later in the war, raids on German targets in Southern Germany also added to the risk of RAF bombers drifting too far south into Swiss airspace. There was also the calculated gamble taken by the planners of such raids in routeing streams of bombers close to the Swiss border in order to ease navigation and/or to avoid German defences. One, among many such occasions, occurred on the night of 15/16 March 1944, when residents of north-eastern Switzerland were startled by the rain of thin, black, paper strips, silvered on one side and dumped by the thousands from 'foreign birds humming their ignominious death march'. They were actually 'windows' intended to put German radar off their mark. On a less light side, that same night witnessed the arrival of a couple of ailing bombers. They had willingly infringed Swiss airspace to reach the Swiss safe haven (see Chapters 9 and 10). They were but two by-products of the raids on the Third Reich and on eastern France becoming more numerous while the German defences grew in efficiency. RAF casualties mounted accordingly, with crippled aircraft limping into the safety of Switzerland.

AIR SERVICE THWARTED

Finally, there is a chapter of wartime British/Swiss air relations that ought to be covered here. In October 1940 and until 1943, Britain put out diplomatic feelers in view of establishing a (regular or irregular) courier service by air with Switzerland. The request was instigated by MEW, the Ministry of Economic Warfare, intent on smuggling strategic goods out of Switzerland. Their idea of an air link was no different from the one made to Sweden which led to an 'airline' run by fast unarmed *Mosquitoes* plying the dangerous Kattegat route between Leuchars in Scotland and Broma airport near Stockholm. Had the Swiss agreed, a direct liaison operating over occupied France would have been even more risky for the crews involved. As it was, the Swiss government turned down the proposal on 31 January 1941, even after the British had suggested adopting an indirect route via Lisbon.[15] Britain came back on the subject until 1943, but the Swiss kept turning down the scheme of an air service.

TABLE 1

COMPARISON OF RANKS

RANKS AND THEIR ABBREVIATIONS (Air Forces)

RAF	USAAF	LUFTWAFFE
Marshal of the RAF	General (5 stars)	Generalfeldmarschall
Air Chief Marshal (ACM)	General (4 stars) (Gl)	Generaloberst (Gl.O)
Air Marshal (AM)	Lieutenant General (Lt.Gl)	General der Flieger (Gl.Fl)
Air Vice Marshal (AVM)	Major General (Maj.Gl)	Generalleutnant (Gl.Lt)
Air Commodore (A.Com)	Brigadier General (Br.Gl)	Generalmajor (Gl.Maj)
Group Captain (Gp/C)	Colonel (Col)	Oberst (Ob)
Wing Commander (W/Cdr)	Lieutenant Colonel (Lt.Col)	Oberstleutnant Ob.Lt)
Squadron Leader (S/Ldr)	Major (Maj)	Major (Maj)
Flight Lieutenant (F/Lt)	Captain (Capt)	Hauptmann (Hptm)
Flying Officer (F/O)	First Lieutenant (l.Lt)	Oberleutnant (OLt)
Pilot Officer (P/O)	Second Lieutenant (2.Lt)	Leutnant (Lt)
Warrant Officer (W/O)	Warrant Officer or Flying Officer (W/O ou F/O)	Stabsfeldwebel (Stbsfw)
Flight Sergeant (F/Sgt)	Master Sergeant (M/Sgt)	Oberfeldwebel (ObFw)
Sergeant (Sgt)	Technical Sergeant (T/Sgt)	Feldwebel (Fw)
Corporal (Cpl)	Corporal (Cpl)	Unteroffizier (Uffz)
Leading Aircraftsman (LAC)	--	Obergefreiter (OGfr)
Aircraftsman 1st Class (A1C)	Private First Class (Pfc)	Gefreiter (Gfr)
Aircraftsman 2d Class (A2C)	Private (Pvt)	Flieger (Flg)

Some Swiss abbreviations:

App	appointé
Cap	capitaine
Four	fourrier
Gend	gendarme
Plt	premier lieutenant

3

Baffling Balloons

Apart from stray bombs (see Chapter 17), the first encounters between Switzerland and the wartime RAF Commands occurred when British balloons drifted over, or landed in, the country. Those, indeed, were the first RAF aircraft to touch Swiss ground… sometimes with unpleasant results.

By the end of 1942[1] the Swiss would have gathered dozens of the wind-borne contraptions which they classified into several categories: nuisance, weather-reporting and propaganda. There was also the occasional barrage balloon accidentally cut loose from its moorings somewhere in England.[2] A fifth category was more lethal: incendiary balloons carrying bottles of phosphor or plain sacks of inflammable material such as wood-wool.

FIRST FIND

The first such 'weapon' was found early on Friday 13 March 1942, at Hemmiken near Basle, only a few kilometres south of the German border. It was a leaf-let-carrying device already devoid of its load, by then probably duly scattered over Germany or, in view of the prevailing winds, over France. The balloon was extensively studied by the Swiss, as witnessed by *Fig. 8* in the picture section. Leaflets, physically harmless as they were, sometimes came down with surprising outcomes as witnessed in Montignez, in the Jura mountains, on 19 October 1944, when a farm roof suffered from the wholesale fall of bundles of propaganda liter-ature. Ironically, the unhappy owner could not even decipher what the wretched objects said, their being written in German!

Innocuous as they might seem, scattering over and on Swiss territory, the leaf-lets were themselves very much resented by the country's highest authorities, as they allegedly indicated a violation of the neutral airspace by a belligerent aircraft. Such a protest from the Swiss Minister in London to the Foreign Office, concerned an incident on the night of 21/22 December 1942. In that instance it took only a few days for the Air Ministry to forward a satisfying answer: the RAF, it said, had indeed mounted an attack on Munich (i.e. north east of the Swiss border) during which weather conditions of 8 to 10/10ths cloud and a northerly wind were encountered. The Pathfinder Force preceding the raid had been routed to a point some miles north of the frontier, and returned on a reciprocal course. 'It was probable', said the RAF, 'that the leaflets which fell on Romanshorn were dropped by this force and were carried into Switzerland by the northerly wind. No aircraft crossed Swiss territory.'

Two weeks after the Hemmiken balloon, on 27 March 1942, Hermann Römer, a farmer in Sennhof near Winterthur, found a weather-reporting device of uncertain origin, despite its markings 'L/196/23223'. The man was allowed a five-franc bonus for his trouble, not a negligible sum at the time, but was denied keeping the mooring cable he could well have used on the farm.

TO DISRUPT GRIDS

A few days later, on 30 March 1942, another balloon, this one of very British lineage, was found at dawn in the heart of Swiss heritage land: the Rigi range, near Lucerne. The rubber contrivance bore the inscription '5A/7277-22 Dec 1941' and was one of a batch of twenty-two found within twenty-four hours in the country. All were nuisance appliances for they carried the tell-tale metal wires intended to disrupt power lines and grids, understandably in Germany.

The year 1942 was a period when the RAF operated its so-called 'M-Balloon Unit', a small outfit of some forty men under the command of F/Lt. J. Woodcock.[3] Based at Walmer, near Deal, and ideally sited on the easternmost coast of Kent, it was also a stone's throw from Kingsdown, the British radio-intercept station that eavesdropped on the Luftwaffe and other German radio transmissions. Whenever propaganda or tactical requirements coincided with suitable wind conditions, Walmer let loose broadsides of some 200 balloons that went drifting across the North Sea or the Channel, sometimes with unpredictable effects!

Indeed, M-Balloon's endeavours were sometimes a nuisance for others than groundlings, as witnessed by P/O Nigel Smallpage. This PRU *Spitfire* pilot of 140 Squadron was returning from a sortie over Zeebrugge, Belgium on 30 July 1942, when he almost collided with a flock of gas bags.[4] The spherical 'missiles' were probably part of 'Operation Outwards' and each one trailed a wire designed to short-circuit the power lines they could foul whilst drifting low over the Continent.

Back on earth, Monday 10 August 1942 seems to have been the core of a record launching period at Walmer, and the day saw many bags added to the Swiss inventory. In the morning, for instance, soldiers of *Gebirge (Mountain) Battalion 11* spotted a balloon drifting from east to west (!) at about 4,000m (13,000ft), deep into the Alps near the Rhône glacier. An hour later, a mountain patrol near Binn, also in the high eastern Valais, saw a descending gas bag, perhaps the same. It was found the day after, half deflated. In the evening, a shredded balloon and its load of leaflets were located further north by Oblt Lütolf's *Gebirgkurs 4*, a mountain training unit sweating near the Dossenhütte, at nearly 2,600m (10,000ft) south of Meiringen.

The Swiss 'crop' was samples of the 402 balloons released from England under strong surface winds on the two previous evenings. They carried 555 bundles of propaganda literature meant for the Saar, the Rhur and cities as far apart as Emden, Rendsburg and Braunschweig.

At one stage in 1943, it was rumoured in some Swiss circles that the rash of balloons could be a retaliatory measure because of alleged sympathies towards the Third Reich. The truth was that the balloons were despatched in the scope of *Razzle* operations intended to set fire to crops and forests and generally poison the land in Germany. Bombers raiding Southern Germany were routed to overfly the Black Forest to scatter *Razzle* devices.[5]

BURNING CROPS

The idea had germinated before the war and, soon after the defeat of France, incendiary-carrying *Wellington* bombers started raiding the Black Forest in the hope of laying it waste. Such raids took place as early as 14/15 June 1940, and went on into the autumn. Results did not live up to expectations, and the waste was probably more on RAF inventory than on Axis possessions. For instance, on 5/6 September, a 149 Squadron *Wellington* on a *Razzle* sortie was lost near Berck on the French coast; the crew parachuted and were captured. The pilot later escaped to Sweden, became the first escaped aircrew to return to England (on 30 July 1941) and served on to become Air Marshal Sir Harry Burton.

In 1943, it was thought in England that the *Razzle* idea had been taken up by the Germans. This was when, in connection with the search for 'wonder weapons', British intelligence heard of an enemy 'pilotless light aircraft carrying incendiary bombs'.

The threat never materialised but on the other side of the world, Japanese '*Razzle* balloons' were launched against the US mainland. It started in September 1942 when a submarine-based light plane, a Yokosuka E14Y1 '*Glen*', flown by pilot Nobuo Fujita, dropped 76kg incendiary bombs that set fire to southern Oregon forests near Brookings. Later on, from 3 November 1944 onwards, the staggering figure of 9,300 of the so-called '*Fu-go*' bomb-carrying balloons were released in Japan. Sailing on the then little-known jet streams, some ended up as far as Michigan. Most, however, fell in the Pacific or in the western United States. For instance, on 10 March 1945, a '*Fu-go*' disrupted power lines in Washington State, near the Hanford facility manufacturing nuclear fuel for the 'atomic' bombs. Worse, on 5 May 1945, five children and a woman were killed in Oregon.

Whatever practical results the *Razzle* campaign did, or did not, achieve in their country, the Germans made use of the threat as a propaganda gimmick, as witnessed, for instance, by trilingual posters displayed in Belgium in June 1941. In

Switzerland proper, the posters could well have elicited a positive response from the population after massive arrivals of incendiary and nuisance balloons between 30 March and 2 April 1943. The 'raid' generated numerous disturbances, a few samples of which follow.

INCENDIARIES ON THE HOSPITAL

On the night of 1 April, an incident could have had more tragic consequences than a simple April Fool's-day event. Six incendiary bottles landed on a hospital roof in St-Loup near La Sarraz; fortunately the fire was put out before it grew too large but exactly one year later, American bombs on Schaffhausen were not so benign.[6] The same day, again in 1943, a trailing wire shorted a high-voltage power line near Buttisholz, Canton Lucerne, and to add insult to injury the culprit and its carrier flew off to generate more evil further on! That night again, 1/2 April 1943, police uniforms were burnt near Bulle, when their owners tried to neutralise seven phosphor-filled bottles. The bill, amounting to 239.85 Sw.Frcs, was later presented to Britain.

At least two persons were injured in Switzerland by the otherwise generally useless balloons: two schoolboys suffered phosphor burns while playing with a balloon contraption discovered in a forest on 27 June 1943. The boys' identities remain unknown but news of their ordeal made it to the highest official circles: on 4 August the commander-in-chief of Swiss military forces, General Henri Guisan, wrote to his political superior, Conseiller Fédéral (Federal Councillor) Karl Kobelt, asking for formal protests to be lodged with the British Foreign Office. Likewise, photographs were included to be passed on to London with complaints about: 'fires, disruption of power lines, poisoning of meadows… which could result in serious hindrance of [our] national economy… due to a singularly blind method of warfare.'

As it was, the 'balloon offensive against Germany' went on, its deeds continuing to harass a most unhappy Switzerland.

UNTIL THE END

Figures for 1944 and 1945 are self-explanatory: in the last seventeen months of the war, the country gathered 116 nuisance, 17 incendiary, 5 barrage (two of which of German origin), 5 leaflet-carrying and 70 weather-reporting balloons, 213 in all, out of which Germany contributed 14 weather bags. Indeed, the silent missiles kept sailing under the westerly winds almost until the end of the war! M-Balloons carried out its last release on 30 March 1945, when 100 bags, carrying 388 bundles of leaflets, ascended from the advanced base at Tirlemont-Bunsbeek in Belgium. It was intended that the material be released over Dessau, Leipzig, and it is not known how many ended up within Swiss borders on that day. However, in the last months of the war, eleven nuisance balloons and twenty-four weather balloons, half of them of German origin, still found their way into the Confederation, together with one leaflet-carrying American bag – which brings in the question of identification.

Many of the first balloons found on Helvetic territory could at first easily be identified as of British origin. However, after recriminations had been lodged through diplomatic channels following personal injuries, markings disappeared from the rubber bags. This made formal identification, and complaints, difficult, even if the bags remained identical in shape, size and manufacture.

THE JAPANESE HOAX?

Concurrently, an odd incident occurred on 28 April 1944. On that afternoon, Fritz Gyger was happily pedalling towards home in Steffisburg, near Thun. Passing the Eggen sawmill, he noticed a 'whitish' shape up in a fir tree some 15m high. Believing he had spotted a parachute, and aware of the nearby airbase, he advised the Dürennast police station. When Constable Lotar Laudi arrived, they joined forces to pull down the silken object. This proved to be a round hull, around 1.5m in diameter, supporting eight shrouds knotted together, and terminating with a thin metal wire to which an aluminium capsule, 6cm (2.36in) in diameter, was attached. This had obviously contained some incendiary substance, since there were traces of fire on the device. The oddest discovery, however was the markings inscribed on the hull. They read: 'Passed, Imperial Japanese Government. 12'! For some time, the plot laid thick within the Security Detachment of Col. Schafroth's *Gruppe Ib*; that is until its chief, Capt. Mumenthaler, decided the balloon could not have drifted all the way from Japan to Europe, and that the markings were a British or American hoax meant to clear the Allies and put the blame for any mayhem on Germany's allies.

4

Pioneer *Mosquito*

AIRMEN AND AIRCRAFT:

Pilot: F/Lt Gerald Wooll
Navigator: Sgt John Fielden
PR *Mosquito* Mk.IV, DK.310, 1.PRU code L°YG

High in the crystal-clear air above Switzerland, the Mosquito *was in a dire predicament. The blinding sun shining directly in the eyes of the crew did not prevent them from perceiving the foreboding barrier of high peaks. Adding to their predicament, a solid cloud layer blanketed the ground under them, as well as any obstacle that might be lurking beneath. And there was more: they had an engine problem and were steadily losing height. In an alpine environment!*

It had been 0925hr, British Double Summer Time, on this Monday 24 August 1942, when F/Lt Gerald Wooll, a tall, dark and moustachioed Canadian pilot, had lifted his PRU *Mosquito* off Benson airfield in Oxfordshire. Within five hours he was to become the first Allied pilot to land in neutral Swiss territory.[1] Quite appropriately, this ambassador of a new type of international relations would arrive at Belp, a non-assuming aerodrome near Berne, the Swiss federal city and, ironically, adjacent to the Rugen mountain, inside which the Swiss Air Force had its underground headquarters!

LONG-RANGE RECCE

In 1942, Benson was the hub of British aerial reconnaissance, a task performed under the aegis of Coastal Command, Royal Air Force, by No.1 PRU. From October onwards, this unit would grow into five fully-fledged squadrons, with the *Mosquitoes* gathered within 540 Squadron. In August, however, 1.PRU was still flying[2] a motley collection of light blue and pink, unarmed *Spitfires* and blue *Mosquitoes*. Depending on range requirements, machines and crews were sometimes farmed out on detachment, to the west in Cornwall, or way north, in Scotland. However, whatever they brought back from their sorties was generally analysed at the central interpretation unit at Medmenham, practically next door to British and American Bomber Commands headquarters, at High Wycombe. It is interesting to mention here that at the time, British photograph interpretation was greatly improved by the use of a Swiss-made machine, the Wild *A5* plotter, a cumbersome precision device that could determine the dimensions of small objects seen in vertical photographs.

On 24 August, 1.PRU dispatched seven sorties: one flew out of Wick in Scotland, to Norway, and three from St Eval to the Atlantic coast of France. The remaining three originated from Benson, two being *Spitfire* flights to northern France. The last take-off was of *Mosquito* LY°G. This was an Mk.IV, serialised DK.310, that had been converted into a PR.IV machine whilst retaining its original but unusual livery of dull-green/dark sea-grey with sky undersurfaces. The aircraft had only joined PRU a fortnight previously, as another addition to the small complement of *Mosquitoes* being built-up by the unit since September 1941.

It seems that DK.310 had been 'diverted' to Benson, arriving on 19 July to make up for the loss of W.4089, which had failed to return from Strasbourg and Ingolstadt a week earlier.[3] The *Mossie* had only flown a few sorties, including three from Gibraltar, where it had staged to cover the oncoming invasion of North Africa. Today, Wooll and his observer, Sgt John Fielden, shared the *Mosquito's* cramped cockpit, not really designed for two men of their stature. They were on their way to Italy, on assignment to spy upon shipyards at Venice, Trieste, Pola and Fiume (now Pula and Rijeka) at the northern tip of the Adriatic sea.[4]

Wooll, a Canadian born on 15 September 1913 in Peterborough, Ontario, had worked there in refrigeration engineering. An aviation buff, he had flown light planes before sailing to England, arriving there in June 1939. He immediately enlisted in the RAF, and in May 1940 had already been promoted to Pilot Officer, operational in Coastal Command, searching for enemy submarines in the Hebrides. In November he was one of the pilots chosen to ferry a *B-17C* from the USA to Scotland.[5]

Wooll's logbook shows that he also served on *Hudsons* and *Beaufighters* in Coastal Command. On 16 April 1942 he had had a chance to fly a couple of captured German aircraft, a Messerschmitt *Bf.110* and a Heinkel *He.111*; this was just before converting to *Mosquitoes* upon being assigned to No.1 PRU, where he was now a flight commander. One of his early sorties had been on 16 May, over Saarbrücken and Amiens.

Sgt John Fielden, his navigator-observer, was twenty-two, and known by all and sundry as 'Maxie'. Strongly built and proficient at soccer and rugby, he hailed from Wigan, Lancashire. He had been employed by British Wire & Ropes Ltd in Wakefield, Yorkshire, prior to volunteering, in May 1940, for pilot duties, and eventually training for the navigator and radio trades. He had been posted to the PRU in March 1942.

TOP TANKS

Their mission had been scheduled for a fortnight. The task would necessitate a round-trip of 1,600 statute miles (2,560km). This distance had been the reason for a stopover at Ford, near Worthing, on the English Channel, in order to top-up the fuel tanks. DK.310 was a B (Bomber) Mk.IV *Mosquito* variant. Such an aircraft normally carried a maximum fuel load of 539 British Imperial gallons (2,447 litres), allowing an operating radius of an equal number of miles: 540 actually (865km). As the trip Benson—Fiume—Trieste and back, was 1,600 miles, a standard aircraft would have been short of fuel for the last 520mi. (832km) or so, not counting the modest fuel complement taken in at the Ford intermediate landing.

The *Mosquito*'s engines, a pair of Rolls-Royce *Merlin 21*, yielded 3.4 miles per gallon (1.2km/l) at 25,000ft (7,620m),[6] which meant that the standard bomber version would need another 155 Imp. gal. (700 litres) to complete the task. However, this particular aircraft, converted as it was into a PR.Mk.IV, had received, among other modifications, four fuselage tanks. Two fitted behind the cockpit and were pressurised; the other pair nested in the bomb bay. Together, they added 287gal. (1,303 litres) of tankage, and offered sufficient reserve to reach Yugoslavia and return.

Leaving Ford at 1030hr British time, climbing south-east on 120 degrees, heading towards Italy, Wooll's *Mosquito* crossed the enemy coast in the Dieppe-Le Tréport area, having almost reached its operational altitude of 25,000ft (7,620m) some thirty minutes after lift-off. Fielden's course then brought the aircraft south of Nancy, showing a ground speed of 280mph (450 km/h). About here, ground contact was lost at about 1145hr (GB), but it could be computed that it would be a matter of half an hour to reach the Swiss border, just east of Basle. This estimate fits with a Swiss observation at 1316hr (Swiss time), reporting yet another border violation north of Baden, where the Aar River joins the Rhine. It thus seems that the south-westerly wind had blown the plane slightly to port of its intended course.

Why did the crew elect to fly across neutral Switzerland on this occasion? Certainly not for economy of range, since going around the eastern tip of the country meant a detour of a bare 30km (19mi.) if the right heading had been chosen from the start. This, however, would have meant overflying the strong anti-aircraft defences on the German shore of Lake Constance. Obviously, the crew was not too keen to run this extra risk.

CUTTING CORNERS
Overflying neutral Switzerland was 'off limits', as previously indicated. Still, many crews did cut corners knowing full well that high-altitude interception by the Swiss air arm was most unlikely. At that time, Swiss fighter units flew a total of 82 Messerschmitt *Me.109Es* and 157 Morane *D-3801s*,[7] none of which was able to reach PRU altitudes before the intruder had flown out of the country. Furthermore, Swiss radar being non-existent, the defences could only be alerted by 100-odd sound location units, a slow and inaccurate process at best. Finally, flab anti-aircraft artillery consisted of about 1,000 20mm and 34mm guns, and 170 75mm pieces guided by 44 Gamma gun-laying units, plus fourteen searchlights. All this proved to be quite impotent for high-altitude interception, particularly at

night. German ferry flights to and from Italy, as well as RAF day reconnaissance, were very often heard, if not seen, above Switzerland. No wonder then, that a high-ranking Swiss Air Force officer, Oberst Fritz Rihner,[8] was later to confess that his forces were ineffective in harming 'the fast, high-flying and unreachable Allied reconnaissance aircraft'!

By 24 August 1942, even though the Swiss had already coped with no less than 1,415 aerial border violations, they had yet to obtain a close-up view of an RAF roundel-marked aircraft. Indeed, thus far, there had only been Swastika-stamped dark Luftwaffe machines to come down in Switzerland: eighteen of them. Thirty of their crewmembers had been considered belligerent and interned; the others, having arrived in trainers, were immediately sent back across the border to Germany.

The situation would soon take a turn as Wooll's arrival marked the opening of the sluices for a flood of RAF and USAAF machines: by the end of the war, 13 RAF and 167 American aircraft would have crashed or landed in the country!

At around 1130hr (GB), Wooll's *Mosquito* was overflying a solid undercast, hiding the lakes and hills of central Switzerland. Visible in the distance, however, were alpine peaks protruding in the clear, and soon the sky spy would trigger its four cameras on oil farms, steel mills and dock at Venice-Mestre and, for good measure, on the renowned canals of the Doges' city. But more urgent worries arose suddenly. Near his left knee, Wooll noticed something amiss: the coolant temperature gauge for the starboard *Merlin* read much too high at 150°C. Looking outside, glycol fumes could be seen coming out of the engine's overflow vent!

This was a harsh reminder that, previously, other crews flying to Danzig and Perpignan had also noticed that the starboard engine ran hotter than its port brother. True to form, and to his navigator's sense of precision, Fielden noted the time: 1227hr (GB). In order to prevent it from seizing, the engine was shut down, a victim of that curse of high-powered, in-line piston engines: their cooling. The drill is automatic for experienced multi-engine pilots. Wooll closed the throttle, punched the feathering button, turned off the fuel cock and ignition, and closed the radiator shutter.[9] This last move would actually not be necessary: in the *Mosquito* the radiators are sunk into the wing-leading edge, the cooling airflow being controlled by a flap-shutter at the back. The flaps are closed to start engines, and opened for take-off. In the case of engine failure, they ought to be closed on the bad engine and opened on the remaining one to prevent its overheating.

ON ONE ENGINE

In Wooll's aircraft, the shutter had stuck in the closed position after starting engines caused the boiling away of about 10 litres (2 Imp. gal.) of water-glycol coolant and the subsequent engine mishap. This, the Swiss would find out later, when performing a thorough technical study of the unexpected gift received from the heavens.

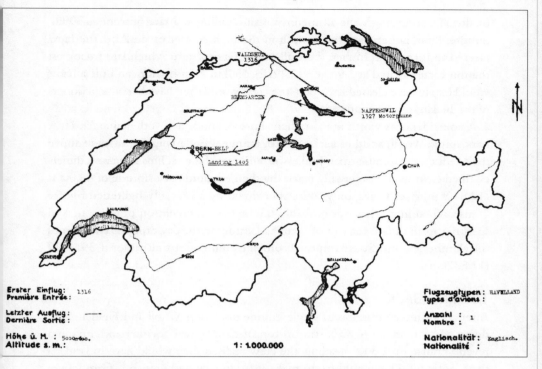

Sketch attached to the Swiss military report on the border violation by Mosquito DK.310. Note the rough track estimate and the precise timing of the infringement, starting at 1316hr (CH), near Waldshut, to terminate at Berne forty-nine minutes later.

How many *Mosquitoes* were lost during the war due to such an incident is only a matter of conjecture. What is known, however, is that exactly the same trouble plagued at least three other PRU machines. The first was DK.358 which, on 8 December 1942, developed a glycol leak on the starboard engine over Austria. The pilot Freddy McKay, and his navigator, Stanley Hope, failed to reach England on one engine: they bailed out north of Mons, Belgium, and were captured.

Similar occurrences involved two other of the few European neutral countries! On 11 November 1943, 540 Squadron's CO, W/Cdr Donald Walker, was killed in Spain after the same incident disabled, again, the starboard engine of his *Mosquito*.[10] Then, on 9 August 1944, another of the Squadron's *Mossies* had photographed Königsberg when, once more, the starboard engine began to overheat, its coolant boiling away. The much luckier pilot, F/Lt John Richards, succeeded in landing in Sweden.

When Wooll feathered the large de Havilland propeller on the right of his navigator, the position must have been over the southern tip of Lake Zürich, Fielden reckoning they must have been some twenty minutes away from target. Fuel-heavy and on one engine, the *Mosquito* could only maintain some 12,000ft of altitude; accordingly the altimeter was unwinding at a rate of some 4–500ft/ minute. Thus, rather than risk a crash in the high barrier of the Alps, the crew elected to turn back. In fact, the wall of the Gran Zebru which laid smack on the route, culminated at 3,900m (12,792ft), 150km (93mi.) away, and the aircraft would barely have cleared it. At best, the crew would then have become prisoners of the Italians on the south side.

A coincidence is worth noticing here. Further south, across the same Alps that confronted Wooll, another aerial photographer was clawing for altitude above the Mediterranean: a German Junkers *Ju-86P* out of Crete. This unarmed, diesel-engined twin would eventually reach the then extraordinary altitude of 42,000ft (12.810km) over Cairo, only to be shot down by a specially lightened *Spitfire V* dispatched into what was probably the highest interception of the war. And speaking again of *Ju-86s*, a pair of them had, earlier in the day, dropped two bombs on Camberley and Southampton from the tremendous altitude of 39,000ft (11.887km).

TURNING BACK

After about fifteen minutes of single-engine operation, Wooll and Fielden were down to 16,000ft (4,878m), still on top of clouds over Switzerland. Flying a reverse course on a 300° heading, the crew realised they would have to land on the Continent. They could try to make it to unoccupied France,[11] from where they could hope to reach Gibraltar as evaders helped by the underground. If they chose this avenue, they would have to steer a 230° course and fly against head-winds for some 300km (185m). This would entail about forty-five minutes' flying time, and a probable descent through cloud over unknown terrain. They seemed to have first adopted such a solution for they flew for six minutes or so in that general direction. In the process, they overflew the Beromunster broadcasting station on whose 556Mc/s(MHz) transmissions Fielden apparently homed, even if he failed to disclose the fact in a subsequent interrogation.

By this time, the remaining *Merlin* had also begun to overheat because of an oil leak, as the Swiss would later discover. The crew noticed oil pouring on the cowling, and the paint curling off. From time to time, the pilot switched the 'bad' engine back on but temperature rose immediately so that it had to be shut down again. All this prompted Wooll to make up his mind. They were obviously over neutral Switzerland and so he would seek a hole in the undercast, land as soon as possible and destroy the aircraft to prevent its equipment from receiving unde-sired scrutiny.

The crew had heard of the fate of one of their PRU *Spitfire* colleagues, P/O Leslie Whitaker who, three weeks earlier, on 4 August, had bailed out over Sweden, and into internment in that neutral country.[12] For any aircrew in dif-ficulty, this was indeed a much better proposition than getting acquainted with German PoW camps!

Unknown to Wooll and Fielden, it was in the vicinity of Eggiswill, in the renowned Emmental district, that the clouds parted, revealing soft green hills and pastures. The aircraft was now losing 1,000ft a minute. Gently banking, Wooll spiralled down through the break and overboard went log, codes and secret documents such as radio flimsies. They kept their maps, expecting to burn them when they set the aircraft alight. This would later prove most embarrassing. The Swiss investigators would then notice the tracks drawn across their country and holler at deliberate border violation. Fielden and his pilot did, however, succeed in soothing the interrogators. They asserted that those tracks were only for calculation purposes, that in fact they had strict orders not to infringe Swiss territory, that they had got lost in cloud whilst navigating by dead reckoning. The truth was, of course, that they had known all the time where they were: over Switzerland.

Below cloud, the crew found good visibility. Also, in the north-west and almost hidden by hills, a 'largish' town appeared, towards which they flew, nursing their remaining engine. Without knowing it, they had discovered Berne, the Swiss 'capital'. It was only when passing abeam, hugging the eastern hills, that Wooll suddenly noticed that the grassy spot he had selected for his emergency landing, down in the valley, was in fact an airfield. This was Belpmoos. As a gentle turn on the live motor lined up the aircraft on what has now become runway 14, the roof was jettisoned. The available grass was then only 700m in extent (2,300ft). Coming into long finals at the safe speed of some 155mph (250km/h) prior to reducing to about 120 (190) in short, Wooll succeeded in arresting his single-engined twin within two-thirds of that length. Quite a feat, since, for all its glamour, the *Mosquito* was a demanding high-performance aircraft, 'not exactly a forgiving machine if one got behind the aeroplane', calling for precise airmanship, particularly at low altitude, 'on one' (engine), and with the bulky gear down.

AN (ALMOST) INTACT *MOSQUITO*

The wheels-down landing occurred at 1403hr, local time. Now, even though the King's Regulations said precious little about presenting an almost airworthy machine to a foreign power, the fliers immediately set about destroying their *Mosquito*. Meanwhile, armed guards from *Flieger Kompanie 10* had been alerted by the typical crackle of *Merlin* engines being throttled back, and were rushing to the road near which the aircraft had come to rest. Sgt Fielden had succeeded in exploding the built-in destruction charge in his IFF *R-3003* set, but attempts to set off the incendiary grenades meant to burn the wooden machine failed. The unnerved crew then resorted to firing revolver shots in the left tank, failing again to explode the 2,300 litres (506 Imp.gal.) of high-octane petrol still aboard.

Now the Swiss had a problem. To them, the *Mosquito*, their first Allied aircraft, was a war machine and as such was, like previous similar German aeroplanes, to be impounded, and the crew interned. This, however, was to prove somewhat more complicated.

Within an hour of their arrival, Wooll and Fielden were fed and rested at the aerodrome. Although their flying kits and revolvers were taken away, they had not been searched and, later, were able to hand over their escape kits to their Air Attaché in Berne, Air Commodore Ferdinand 'Freddie' West, VC. They were briefly interrogated[13] by Col. Ruedi of the Swiss Army, who reported to his supreme headquarters in nearby Gümligen, and later informed the British Air Attaché.

The wartime dedication of an Air Attaché in neutral countries was, among other less benign tasks, to insure the well-being of his compatriots and to ascertain that secret equipment did not benefit enemy intelligence.[14] In the case of a relatively intact machine such as the Berne *Mosquito*, West's brief was to make sure it was properly guarded against public curiosity and, if at all possible, returned to its country of origin.

TRAINING FLIGHT

This, West endeavoured to achieve. After meeting Wooll and Fielden on the very afternoon of their arrival, West questioned the Swiss prerogative to impound a 'non-armed aircraft engaged in a training flight'. The *Mosquito*, he asserted, was to be handed back to Britain, just as German training machines had previously been returned to their owners.

To this, the Swiss replied as early as 27 August. The *Mosquito*, said Col. Hans Bandi, commanding their aviation arm, was obviously a war-machine flying on long-range reconnaissance, complete with cameras[15] and the most up-to-date radio equipment. An aircraft able to clock up to 630km/h (400mph), added Bandi, with a slight exaggeration,[16] would not conduct training flights over enemy territory with vast amounts of petrol on board, and would not be subjected to repeated attempts of destruction by its own crew. The matter would again be scrutinised at diplomatic level, said Bandi, but meanwhile the aeroplane was to remain in Belp and its crew interned.

In so doing, the Swiss were only complying to international usage relative to war material ending up in neutral countries. Such equipment '... must be restored to the belligerent States whose property it is, after the termination of the war'. As for the combatants, they are supposed to be interned (a notion different from that of 'Prisoner of War') and repatriated at the end of the war, although some repatriations did occur before that. This was the case on 28 June 1940, just after the French collapse when the war looked like being over; the Swiss then allowed a batch of able-bodied German airmen to return to Germany from their secluded Kiental quarters. Later on, exchanges were to involve belligerents from both sides (see Chapters 5 and 18).

At the very moment, 1416hr (GB), when A/Cdre West was meeting the castaway crew, a flurry of aerial activity pervaded England. At Benson, the second *Mosquito* dispatched by 1.PRU from Benson had just returned to St Eval: it was

W.4059, one of the early PR.Mk.Is, the tenth *Mosquito* ever built, that F/Lt Van Damm had taken over the coast of France, all the way between Arcachon and the Spanish border. At bases all over the country, briefings were in the offing for a Bomber Command raid on Frankfurt, and at Oakington, 7 Squadron navigator, Joseph Antoine, carefully prepared his second Pathfinder sortie: he would never know that next morning his namesake would mourn him at Berzée, Belgium, and would later write about him.

SIGHTSEEING UNDER GUARD

For the time, however, Wooll and Fielden sat in peaceful custody at Berne, awaiting developments and a full-fledged moon eclipse. This they enjoyed as guests in the Bernese 'alcohol-free' Hotel Daheim, where the pilot's huge RAF-style 'handlebar' moustache created quite a stir.

On the 26th they were transferred to a 'camp' in Yens near Aubonne; here, awaiting further transportation, their guard, Wachmeister Brütsch, took them sightseeing on the lakefront. This, like a drink they had together while changing trains in Lausanne, shows how relaxed the situation was for the internees. A further proof is the friendship Wooll struck with the camp commandant, aristocratic Plt. Philippe de Weck.

On 18 December 1942, both men were released for repatriation to the UK. A quadripartite negotiation had resulted in their exchange against an Italian and two German flyers. By a strange coincidence, the latter's two Messerschmitt *Bf.109-F4Z*s had shared the same locked-up hangar as the *Mosquito*. Both had also landed at Belp, a few minutes apart, a month previously, on 25 July. Their pilots, *Feldwebel* Martin Villing and *Obergefreiter* Heinrich Scharf[17] from *4.Erganzungstaffel West*, had lost themselves during a ferry flight between Le Bourget and Erding. Berne, by the way, seemed to exert a special attraction on *Bf.109*s: two more were to land there on 20 August 1944, lost on another ferry flight between France and Italy. An Italian pilot was also included in the exchange: Alfredo Porta who, also lost in a ferry flight, had landed his Fiat *G.50* at Emmen on 21 September 1942.

In the early hours of the 18th, Fielden and Wooll, now clad in civilian clothes, left the US Bernese Legation at No.64, Kirchenfeldstrasse, chaperoned by Swiss sergeant Rico Kuhn. At Basle's Badischen Bahnhof, the trio met Plt. Gausi, who was the liaison officer in charge of passing them on to German customs. From then onwards, the fliers travelled first class with a Swiss diplomatic courier and a German officer with his batman. The party went through Baden-Baden, Strassburg, Paris, Bordeaux, Hendaye, San Sebastian and Madrid. From there the crew went on to Lisbon, and were flown to Whitchurch, the UK terminal for civilian flights from the south, arriving on 23 December 1942.[18] They were interrogated in London on Christmas Eve, exactly five months after they had left British soil.

Later on, Wooll test-piloted for a while at de Havilland's *Mosquito* factory at Hatfield. He returned to Canada on 4 February 1943, to be attached to DHC, the Canadian branch of the company, testing *Mosquito* bombers, which were by then trickling out of the Downsview plant in Ontario. One of the highlights of his tenure was, on 24 April 1943, bailing out at 17,000ft (5,200m) from KB.301, a *Mosquito* suffering from an engine fire. Gerald Wooll left DHC in 1947 to work on *Hudsons* for PSC, a photographic survey corporation. In 1979, Wooll had become managing director of Genaire Ltd in St Catherines, Ontario, a company making aircraft skis. He became the company's president in 1990.

As for John Fielden, his career is much less documented. To the delight of his friends in Benson, where he had been extremely popular,[19] he came back to navigate 544 Squadron PRU *Mosquitoes*. He had been awarded a well-deserved DFC and a commission as Flying Officer by the time he was killed, near Berlin, on 18 September 1944.

5

The Birmenstorf
Wellington

AIRMEN AND AIRCRAFT:
Pilot: Sgt James Avery
Navigator: Sgt William Shields
Air Bomber: Sgt Wilfred Boddy
Wireless Oprtr: Sgt Joseph Cash
Rear Gunner: Sgt Ronald McEwan
Wellington X HE.374, code SE°X, 431 Squadron

It was a very dark night that blanketed Switzerland and Southern Germany on the evening of Wednesday 14 April 1943. In the German skies RAF Bomber Command roamed in strength, 462 of its aircraft having been dispatched to attack the centre of Stuttgart.

The Main Force comprised the three types of current four-engined bombers: 83 *Stirlings*, 98 *Lancasters* and 135 *Halifaxes*, as well as 146 *Vickers Wellingtons*. This array of bombers reflected the slowly changing pattern of the Command's order of battle where the large, pre-war, twin-engined *Wellington* still equipped fifteen of the thirty-four Squadrons available to the Commander-in-Chief, Air Marshal Arthur Harris. The very dependable *Wellington*, with its characteristic geodetic construction would in any case launch its last bombing sortie on 8 October 1943 from England, and on 13 March 1945 in the Mediterranean front.

One of the Squadrons flying Mk X *Wellingtons* was a Royal Canadian Air Force unit, the 431 (*Iroquois*), based at Burn near Selby, Yorkshire. The Squadron was still part of Bomber Command's 4 Group, and it would not be until exactly three months later that it would join 6 (RCAF) Group.

Late in the afternoon of the 14th, the Squadron's CO, W/Cdr J. Coverdale[1] and his deputy, S/Ldr Mulford, who would be flying that night, had briefed twelve crews for the coming night's operation. Coverdale was not Canadian but a Briton like, at the time, many members of the unit. As the briefing developed, a coincidence fit for the previous chapter occurred down south, near Oxford. There, at Benson, landed a PRU *Mosquito* whose flight had duplicated Gerald Wooll's: a photo sortie to northern Italy. The crew had twice penetrated Switzerland's airspace – in full view of the prominent landmark that was Lake Geneva. Having made little of the standing orders not to overfly neutral territory, they succeeded in adding fuel to the quasi-permanent Anglo-Swiss confrontation arising from illicit overflights.

STINGING STUTTGART

The attack on Stuttgart, one of the eighteen major raids on this industrial city of Southern Germany,[2] was to prove a failure for the RAF. Twenty-three of its aircraft would not return: 5 per cent of the force engaged, a figure considered as a 'standard' loss rate in bombing operations.

In return, Bomber Command's results were only mildly indicative of the ferocity of the air war. The city centre where bombs were supposed to put out of action a large number of workers involved in the numerous local war industries, practically remained intact. 'Only' 393 buildings were destroyed while some 200 inhabitants lost their lives, a figure augmented by the death of 400 French and Russian working Prisoners of War killed in a single air-raid shelter.

Two of the crews being briefed at Burn would not return on the morrow: those of Sgt Denby, who would be killed near Koblenz, and Sgt Avery. James Avery was twenty-one and also a British citizen from Norton, where he used to be a bank cashier before joining the RAF on 6 March 1941. In fact, the only Canadian in his crew was the rear gunner, Sgt Ronald McEwan a twenty-seven-year-old efficiency expert from Verdun, Quebec. Their Vickers *Wellington X* serial HE.374 was one of a batch built at Chester and delivered to 431 Squadron prior to its initial operation, a mine-laying trip off the Frisian islands, on 2/3 March. Its code, SE°X, made it, of course, a natural victim of the obvious joke and the big twin was seldom referred to by its official designation, X for X-Ray.

The first operational sortie flown by Sgt Avery with the Squadron had been to Bochum in the Ruhr, on 29/30 March,[3] in an all-*Wellington* raid. 8 per cent of the force had been lost but Avery had to abandon the sortie, and landed at Oulton with a badly iced-up starboard engine. Icing was indeed the scourge of the *Wellington*, whose fabric skin was prone to ice accretion. On 4 April, Avery had again aborted a raid against Kiel, this time with another aircraft's defective supercharger. His first effectual operation with 431 Squadron had been to Duisburg on 8/9 April, when he had to land at Tangmere on return. On 11/12 April, Avery had taken the same SE°X gardening i.e. mine-laying, off Terschelling, one of forty-six aircraft sent sowing mines in German-controlled waters from Holland to the Bay of Biscay.

PRIMARY INDUSTRIAL AREA

The big smooth tyres of Avery's *Wellington* tucked neatly into their nacelles at 2108hr (GB) as the heavy aircraft laboured to gain height behind S/Ldr Mulford's machine. Tonight's target was a distant one and the navigator, Sgt. William Shields, reckoned on a seven-hour round-trip during which he would have to rely on dead-reckoning and the occasional star-sight in friendly galaxies, in order to fix his position.

Stuttgart was one of the most fiercely defended industrial targets in Germany. It had been bombed as early as 24/25 August 1940, and eight other attacks had since taken place. Exactly one year previously, just a week before Arthur Harris had become AOC Bomber Command, the city had been catalogued 'Primary Industrial Area' by the Air Ministry targeting section. The reason: it housed factories and workers of many important war industries such as the Robert Bosch magneto plant and the Bad Canstatt ball-bearing factories. So far, however, raids had been largely ineffective due to poor night navigation, poor weather and the existence of dummy targets. Tonight's raid would also be a failure compounded, as seen above, by the killing of hundreds of Prisoners of War in the north-east suburbs.

The attack was scheduled to develop from that direction with Bomber Command starting to experiment with a new technique. This was the so-called '*Modified Newhaven*' where five senior Pathfinder crews[4] using *H2S*-radar-equipped aircraft, marked 'blind' with target indicators and flares. This was to help conventional marker-aircraft and, in turn, the Main Force. On this night, the target laid in the clear, but red markers went down some three miles (5km) north east of the aiming point and, despite inter-aircraft instructions radioed to disregard them, Main Force bombing grossly undershot. The resulting 'creepback' of impacts was responsible for the bombing extending far outside the city boundaries. Avery's journey across Belgium and the German Eifel was to bring the aircraft on target from the north at about 0100hr, British time. The return trip would be on a westerly heading towards Nancy, then to Reims and the Channel.

Meanwhile, the crew did their utmost to make the sortie worthwhile under their captain's leadership. Although equal in rank to Avery, all recognised their pilot's expertise, particularly his ability to fly on dark nights devoid of starlight, with visibility not exceeding some 700ft (213m). Their skipper then put into practice the two months spent training to a high standard of instrument flying, beam approach and the like. Quite appropriately, also, the logical RAF policy heaved responsibility upon the pilot who thus became a captain whose skills, judgement and quick reactions meant life or death for crew and machine. Reaching the Rhine River, navigator Shields was able to pinpoint his position, near Speyer. Stuttgart lay in the distance, huddled in its peculiar punch-bowl and already ablaze. Shields, a twenty-three-year-old auditor from Willesden, had been through 20.OTU at Lossiemouth, like the rest of the crew. He now discussed where the target actually sat, with Sgt Wilfred Boddy, the bomb aimer: either towards the fuzzy horizon, or closer where yellow flares could be seen. In fact, these were dummies laid by the German defences between Karlsruhe and Heidelberg. Like the nearby decoy site at Lauffen, they were meant to attract and waste RAF bombs.

ENEMY FIGHTERS

In the case of Avery's crew, the dummies did not distract them from watching the very bright moonlit sky. Nearing the target, everyone was, as per instructions, intent on the look-out for enemy fighters: wireless operator Joseph Cash in the astrodome, Boddy watching the front right and Ronald McEwan at his rear gunner's position. This was actually where danger struck, when two Junkers *Ju.88* fighters attacked in a pincer movement; luckily a corkscrew evasive action saved the *Wellington*, whose return fire scored on one of the newcomers. Still, the fighters had hit the machine in the elevator, a considerable amount of fabric[5] being stripped off, thus rendering the aircraft sluggish to control.

Stuttgart was by now very close, and a turn to, approximately, the prescribed 190° heading was initiated for the bomb-run. It was while going into the target that the now rather weak ground defences managed to find their mark. A burst of flak violently threw the port wing up as SE°X was hit in the port motor. Boost and rpms[6] fell... Frantically, Avery, and Boddy, who also acted as assistant pilot, surveyed the damage and strove to hold the aircraft straight, maintaining speed at a safe 100 knots (185km/h) with 20° of flaps. Also, the airscrew had to be feathered on the defective Bristol *Hercules*. The thing had other intentions, however: it kept windmilling at some 1,700rpms. The pilot now faced his full accountability. Should he press on and keep trying to master his failing mechanical monster? Or should he right now give preference to saving the crew? The aircraft made the decision in going into a dreaded spiral dive.

Avery ordered his men to prepare to abandon ship. However, exerting all his skill and muscle power, he succeeded in regaining control of his heavy machine at 12,000ft (3,660m). He immediately rescinded the 'stand-by to abandon' order.

Avery pressed on with his one engine to bomb the railway station, jettisoning from an altitude of 10,500ft (3,200m) the mixed load of two 500lb (227kg) explosive bombs and the canisters of incendiaries. Below, a most fantastic pageant unfolded upon the doomed target. Dark shapes of bombers converged on cascading chandeliers spewing red and green stars. Adding to the illumination, flak bursts flickered, seemingly at random, high over the city. Bright fingers of searchlight beams added their millions of lumens to the radiant background. The ground itself changed into boiling purple clouds as high explosives churned the city into dust, obliterating the strings of whitish lights marking streets ablaze under the profusion of incendiaries.

In the *Wellington* it then became the turn of the bomb doors to act on their own: they would not close – Avery had to manually pump them shut. And now the remaining engine developed only partial power, reminding the pilot that at take-off the boost had been somewhat weak on that engine, and that its suction pump had failed shortly after leaving England. Worse now, fuel was leaking profusely.

The situation was rapidly deteriorating and to add to the mess, documentation was lacking for this new *Wellington X*, further complicating the process of decision! A hectic discussion took place in the noisy, cramped, vibrating cockpit, between pilot and navigator. It was indeed a strange sight to observe their bulky figures, their faces distorted by the rubbery snout of oxygen masks, eerily illuminated by moon and phosphorescent dials, trying to reach a decision from which might depend their future, if not their lives and those of the others.

BLACK-OUT IN SWITZERLAND

The two young men reckoned the situation would only allow half an hour's flight time. It was thus decided to remain on a southerly heading to reach Switzerland, and force-land there. The crew again prepared to abandon the aircraft, and the navigator detonated the Gee-set, the wireless operator doing likewise for the IFF.

The crippled *Wellington* crossed the border over the western tip of Lake Constance, the large body of water darkish in the blacked-out landscape of the neutral territory. It was 24 minutes past midnight, Swiss time. In April 1943, Switzerland still enforced the black-out that had been initiated on 7/8 November 1940. In diplomatic circles the measure was contested by the British Foreign Office, at the instigation of Sir Charles Portal at the Air Ministry, and of Air Marshal Douglas Evill, vice-chief of the Air Staff. Their view was that violations of Swiss airspace would be reduced if crews could clearly identify the country.

The Swiss countered that leaving their cities illuminated could ease navigation for the belligerents and that Axis protests would follow, with Germany and Italy claiming that Swiss lights allowed RAF bombers to navigate more easily towards targets close to the borders. And in any case, said the Swiss, tongue-in-cheek, Zürich had been bombed by the RAF well before the black-out had been enforced! Ironically, it was generally not known that, in 1943, south-east Germany was not blacked-out before 2300hr!

The subject of Swiss black-out remained a touchy political subject for the duration. As it was, the decision of 7/8 November 1940 would be confirmed on 25 August 1943, and the ban was only lifted on 12 September 1944, after Allied forces had reached the Swiss borders.

Black-out or not, Avery's moves were plotted with some accuracy by the Swiss observers corps. His *Wellington* was flying a rather erratic course in and out of the sinuous Swiss-German border, cruising around apparently aimlessly. The *Wimpy* was notorious for showing poor single-engine performances: Avery did his best – and failed – to keep a steady heading while maintaining the safety speed. The machine crossed the border near the Schaffhausen bulge, returned into Germany, flew back in Switzerland to Zurzach and Laufenburg, and finally turned south-east to Zürich. The crew later told the Swiss interrogators that they were flying between two layers of cloud, making dead reckoning uncertain. Eventually, navigator Shields observed Lake Zürich, where, 'lights [probably the railroad station] and then the lake and a river [the Limmat] allowed a pin-point'.

DEFECTIVE PARACHUTE

In the near distance, the crew saw the bleak fingers of searchlights probing the hazy opal: they belonged to a flab battery stationed near Oberrohrdorf, Canton Aargau. The *Wellington* was now 40km (25mi.) inside Switzerland, passing 7,500ft (2,287m), descending. On the look-out for a spot where to land, Avery flew north-west, away from built-up districts and along the river. Then, unable to find a suitable field, he had a couple of red flares shot and ordered 'abandon ship'. This unfulfilled sortie – his fourth – would place Avery just below the five-operations average survival rate of Bomber Command's aircrew. Fortunately, he and his men were not destined to became part of the terrible statistics that would eventually entail the loss of 55,573 aircrew![7]

The *Wellington* was now nearing Wettingen, very close to the industrial city of Baden, and only 16km (6.2m) from the nearest German territory. Jumping last, Sgt. Avery had time to notice a flame under the fuselage of the ponderous *Wellington* which was now turning on its back. This passing glimpse was quickly forgotten as he vainly tried to open his parachute. Free-falling in the dark, he had little time to reflect on his rapidly oncoming fate. The brown parachute pack was of the chest type so he quickly struggled to open it by hand and pull out the ropes.

'Never,' said he later, 'did I work so fast with my hands...' Fortunately, the bailing-out altitude had not been low; even so he did not float down for long before crashing into a roof. Here the silk had barely collapsed when a man appeared underneath, swinging a rifle. It took a long discussion in French for Avery to convince the German-speaking character that he was an English flyer and not a burglar. Avery was eventually allowed to come down from his perch, near the Ziegeli tile-works, in the hilly, forested area of Meierhof, south of Baden, and just 24km (15mi.) away from Zürich's town centre.

The pilot was then given a meal, still under rifle cover, before being handed over to the police. True to form, they investigated the means of support of the new immigrant. They discovered him to be the proud owner of 10 shillings, overlooking the contents of his escape box which they did not open: 750 French francs, a sizeable sum meant to support eventual evading enterprises. Not surprisingly, once the initial excitement of the last hours had somewhat subsided, Avery's thoughts were for his sister Rita, to whom he had promised to be best-man at her forthcoming marriage!

The first man to bail out had been rear gunner Ronald McEwan. He had clipped his 'chute on, swung his turret aside and pushed himself into the void. The Canadian's sinking, swinging motion stopped in a forest clearing, where he rested until morning. He had ascertained that he was well within Switzerland by reading an inscription on a roadside crucifix but even so he kept awake most of time due to excitement

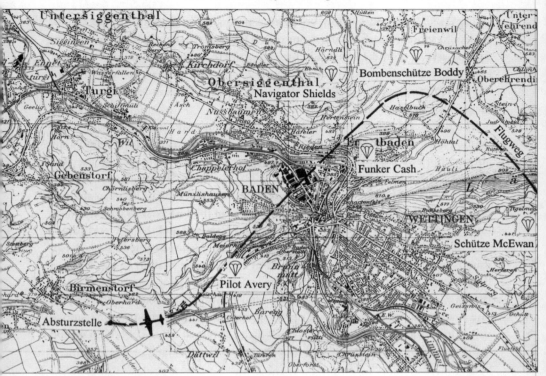

Approximate track of the Birmenstorf Wellington's *final flight path over Baden, north-west of Zürich. (courtesy Theo Wilhelm)*

and wariness of his surroundings. McEwan was actually east of Wettingen, near the isolated Eigi farm, and about 8km (5mi.) from where his pilot landed.

A LONG WAY TO ABERDOUR

Meanwhile, the *Wellington* and a string of three more parachutes had plotted a tightening left spiral. Sgt Wilfred Boddy was next out. Quite appropriately for this former agricultural engineer, he came down in a copse. There, he huddled in the silk of his parachute till morning, thinking of his new wife Babs, and his child in Aberdour, Scotland, and also of Hanna Roth, a family acquaintance in Teufen... only 20km (12.5mi.) away as it was! A boy discovered the air bomber at daybreak and took him to the Swiss police who were concluding a field night. Boddy had landed halfway between the villages of Freienwil and Oberehrendingen, whose unlikely name he forever proved incapable of pronouncing!

From that point of view, William Shields was better off, ending down near Baden, in the hamlet of Ebnihof. This was also wooded and hilly country, and the navigator found himself enmeshed in an hazel tree. After a difficult extraction, he saw a light and went to a house where, again, the telephone rang for the local police.

The *Wellington* had by now completed its first spiral, right over the city of Baden. Sgt Joseph Cash tumbled out over Ennetbaden, slightly hurting his right foot on arrival on the rocky 'Hill of the Goats'. He hobbled down to the suburb, ending in a garden whose owner promptly telephoned the harassed police. They discovered that the former clerk of the 'Bird-in-Hand' hotel in Mobberley, whose name was Cash, had on him £2 6s in cash.

The deserted *Wellington* swished over a forest south-west of Baden, stalled and crashed nose-first in a lonely spot. The time was 0043hr (CH). Had it remained airborne for two more miles (3.2km), the aircraft would have crashed at the very spot of the future Birrfeld aerodrome.[8] The doomed *Wellington* came down south-east of the village of Birmenstorf, punching three small holes in the soft sediments of the Reuss River. Nothing remained of the first RAF bomber to drop into Switzerland, apart from small debris thrown around and the few odd papers such as Shields' new *Air Almanac* and his *Astronomical Navigation sourcebook*. A few rounds of ammunition were also recovered and sent for analysis to the Bernese 'Eidgenössische Waffenfabrik', the Swiss federal weapon factory comparable to the British Aldershot facility. The right engine buried itself in the dark earth, the port one shattering on impact. In the morning, only a puny plume of white smoke would mark the point of impact towards which converged dozens of cyclists gaping at the outline of wings, motors and nose etched on the ground.[9]

FROWNING ON FRIENDLINESS

The novelty and drama of the crash made headlines. The local press keenly reported the friendliness of the locals towards the British outsiders. Such publicity was, however, frowned upon by officials such as Col. Ruedi, the head of intelligence with aviation troops, who feared such a penchant for the RAF might be exploited as an excuse for Nazi leverage on his country.

By morning, Avery and Shields had been taken to the Civil Guard headquarters in Baden. They were interrogated about personal particulars, but were not asked questions of military relevance.[10] This, however, came later in the day, at the Aarau military compound, where, said the crew, 'a Swiss Air Force officer interrogated each of us separately'. There were actually three interrogators: Lieutenants Walder and Schaub of the Armeeflugpark (Air Force material section), and J. Rolf Lécher, a twenty-six-year-old Oberleutnant (1st Lt.) who had learned to fly in Cleveland, Ohio, before the war. Now a Swiss military pilot, Lécher belonged to the air force intelligence unit headed by crack Captain Gottfried von Meiss.

Thus, on 15 April 1943, Lécher conducted his first questioning of Allied airmen. He did not fare badly at all. His twelve-page report on two of SE°X's crewmembers is a monument of information on subjects as varied as the *Wellington* performance, training, operational methods, bombs, briefings, nightfighters, and much more than the classical 'Name, rank and serial number' supposed to be the only information disclosed by stranded airmen.

No wonder Lécher would later be chosen as chief interrogator of Allied air-crews. Of course, Avery and company knew they were in neutral country and, having escaped injury in their ordeal, could be excused for being rather more voluble than expected. One ploy used for extracting information while in Aarau might also have been the detention of the airmen with three Dutch refugees. It has not been found out whether this was on purpose or accidental.

POCKET MONEY

On 17 April, the crew was sent to Berne, to the office of the British Air Attaché, Air Commodore Freddie West. They were outfitted with civilian clothes and lodged for four days in the 'Pension Herter', being allowed out under guard. Regulations allowed them to mail one letter[11] and a postcard per week, but phone calls were forbidden.

Allied personnel in Switzerland received 'pocket money' directly from their Legations. This was on top of their normal pay accumulating at their respective bases. In March 1944, for instance, the Americans received, irrespective of rank, 3 Sw.Frcs per day if officers, and half that amount if enlisted personnel. For the British, the amount varied according to ranks: 10.36 Sw.Frcs for a full colonel, down to 2.16 Sw.Frcs for the lowest 'other rank'. For comparison purpose, one Sw.Frc amounted then to 0.23364 US dollar.

At this stage of the war, Swiss policy towards aviators landing in the country fol-lowed the *Mosquito* experience: after initial internment, they were exchanged against Luftwaffe personnel. Less fortunate were evaders whose aircraft had been downed over enemy territory, and who had managed to avoid capture and reach the Swiss border. These were interned for the duration, a process which meant spending months or years under guard in the comparative cosiness of otherwise deserted Swiss hotels.[12]

An example among the 319 identified recipients of that distinction was that of Canadian S/Ldr Fletcher Taylor, the pilot of a 420 (Canadian) Squadron *Wellington* shot down in France, near St-Quentin, on the very same night as Avery.[13] Taylor reached Switzerland on 30 April and was caught at Lausanne. He escaped intern-ment, reached Geneva and the French border on 8 January 1944, found assistance with the Avons and Blanc families in nearby Frangy, and succeeded in entering British soil at Gibraltar, reaching England on 24 February.

Swiss policy towards escapers, i.e. military personnel having slipped away from German or Italian hands, was more liberal. The Swiss felt they could not be 'more royalists than the king', that is if the Germans did not succeed to hold them, why should they put them behind bars! Accordingly, those escapers who managed to cross into neutrality were not even interned and were allowed to leave if they wanted to. After the war it would be known that Switzerland had been haven for a total of 4,852 escapers of all ranks from the British Commonwealth and 24 from the US forces, from which respectively 76 and 12 were flying personnel. There would also be the 319 evaders, including 136 RAF personel, 147 USAAF and 36 others, mostly Belgians.[14]

REPATRIATION OR EXCHANGE

The Swiss repatriation policy in force in 1943 was in accordance with international usage, namely the 1907 Hague Convention, and Red Cross procedures. Here the basic criterion to be accepted for repatriation was that the physical condition of the individual would not ever allow him to return to military duty. This had not always been the case. Due to the pressure of events, namely the arrogance of a Third Reich becoming master of practically all of western Europe around the country, Switzerland was compelled in June 1940 to release the 17 Luftwaffe airmen it detained.

As the war wore on, several exchange sessions took place involving RAF (see 'Aftermath'), and later USAAF, personnel. For instance, on 3 March 1944, six American pilots (Martin Andrews, William Cantwell, Alva Geron, Donald Oakes, Stephen Rapport, Sam Turner) and a navigator (Robert Titus) went home, as well as seven German airmen interned at Davos.[15] There were also the 'medical cases', involving belligerent personnel unfit for further duty. Typical examples were five unrelated American aircrew (Vance Boswell, Vincent Hayes, Roy Homer, Louis Loftiss and Charles Page) who had landed in Switzerland in 1943 and 1944, and were sent home in December 1944.

In accordance with article 13 of the Hague Convention, seventy-five escapers were also released on 13 September and 4 October 1944, soon after Allied forces had reached the Swiss border near Geneva. This was, of course, outside the actual exchanges of internees, and so were the hundreds who 'illegally' fled internment.

In February and March 1945, near the end of the war, a mass exchange was organised for American (586) and British (43) internees against Germans. The latter (1,288) were from ground forces and the ratio of exchange was established at one USAAF or RAF airman being sent home against two Germans... a case of some being more equal than others.

* * * * * * * * *

Returning to Avery and company, they left Berne on 21 April 1943, bound for the Polish internee centre at the Grand Hôtel in Vevey. They spent three days there on the shore of Lake Geneva and were eventually displaced inland, to Corseaux, at the pension 'Beau-Site'. From this lofty abode they would gaze west to England, unaware that just below, the Vevey cemetery would in time become the ultimate resting place for thirty-four of their fellow RAF comrades.

BLISS AND BOREDOM

In Corseaux, the days went by with a peaceful atmosphere, far different from that of squadron life, under the supervision of consecutive English-speaking Swiss military policemen. The last of them was to be Edward Forster[16] whose double

Swiss-British citizenship made him the perfect choice for the job. It was he who, browsing through the paperwork relating to the transfer to Corseaux, noticed an hilarious mistake: the orders issued by the *Heerespolizei* qualified wireless operator, Sgt Joseph Cash, as being a '*liveless* [sic] operator'!

A sample of how the internees fared in order to break the monotony of the days is worth reviewing; the 'standard fare' of the almost daily walks in the immediate vicinity are here omitted:

- 18 April: Sunday service at the Anglican church in Berne [later in their sojourn near Lake Geneva, it would be in Territet]; afternoon walk in company of Major Herbert Fryer, Assistant British Military Attaché, enlightened by a 'Zvieri' drink, in restaurant Dählhölzli
- 19 April: end afternoon at the cinema 'Capitol' showing *For which we serve*.
- 21 April: at British legation to draw clean uniforms; A/Com. West gives Avery 100 Sw.Frcs as pocket money for the crew. The men are then sent to Vevey with a couple of guards: Sgt.Baumann and App.Gysin
- 26 April: Planting potatoes, a chore that will go on for several days
- 28 May: travel to Lausanne to buy civilian clothes at the PKZ store
- 29 May: gardening and visit to Dr Bettex in Vevey for the benefit of Avery and Shields
- 31 May : picking cherries; hairdresser session
- 1 June: more cherries and doctor in Vevey plus reception at Mrs.'Peter' Norton's, the British Ambassador's wife
- 2 June: Shields, Avery and McEwan brought to 'Grand Hôtel' in Vevey for disc plinary confinement [undisclosed charges; they were released on 7 June]. Walk in countryside [Boddy and Cash only]
- 4 June: cherries again; tossing hay; bathing in lake; books from Mrs.Scott [British resident on the Swiss 'Riviera']
- 9 June: French lessons; visit of British clergyman; afternoon tea;
- 10 June: evening: one beer in Corseaux café
- 13 June: lunch in 'Hôtel du Lac', Vevey, sponsored by British Legation, A/Com. West attending
- 17 June: in civilian clothes [including the two guards], early departure to catch train in Vevey going to Hotel Bären in Berne; meet Major Fryer at Legation prior to exchange process.

GOING HOME

By 17 June 1943, arrangements had indeed been completed for returning the Avery crew to England. Counting the crew of the 'Pioneer *Mosquito*', they were the second exchange of flyers taking place through Swiss mediation; their German counterparts were the four occupants of two Fieseler *Storche* who had landed in Samedan on 19 March 1943.[17]

Very early on 18 June, the RAF crew moved to Basle. Here, a Swiss civilian courier — Mr Vuillemin from the Swiss Political Ministry — joined them as neutral protection during their journey to Spain. For the trip across occupied Europe, a German captain and an interpreter also went along. From Basle, the group proceeded to Baden-Baden, Nancy, Paris, Tours, Bordeaux and Irun on the Spanish border. Minus the Germans, they were then entrained to San Sebastian and Madrid, from where they left for Gibraltar on 25 June, arriving the day after on the Rock. After two days, passage was secured on a flight to the UK; they landed at Lyneham on 29 June 1943.

Their round trip to Stuttgart and back had taken all of seventy-six days! Subsequent to their return in the UK, the crew was given a couple of weeks' leave, McEwan returning to Canada to become a gunnery instructor. As for the British airmen, it remains unclear if Cash and Boddy ever flew again in operations: they left the service in November 1945 and February 1946 respectively. Their two other mates were to be killed in air operations. Pilot Avery was instructing at 15.OTU on 1/2 March 1944, when his clapped-out *Wellington* suffered a complete electrical failure and crashed attempting to land at Harwell. As for Shields, he lost his life just three weeks later, on 24/25 March 1944, aboard a 78 Squadron *Halifax* which crashed in England after raiding Berlin. His luck had run out, contrary to his namesake, also a navigator, who, very much of a Canadian, would be downed and evaded in France, on 10/11 June 1944.

6

Badge's Bouveret Barrier

AIRMEN AND AIRCRAFT:

Pilot: P/O Horace Badge
Flight Engineer: Sgt Robert Wood
Navigator: F/Lt Arthur Jepps
Bomb Aimer: Sgt Arthur Wright
Wireless Op: Sgt Edward Higgins
Mid-upper Gunner: Sgt James Spence
Rear Gunner: F/Sgt Ronald Brett
Lancaster Mk.I, ED.412, code EM°Q, 207 Squadron

By mid-July 1943, two British aeroplanes had touched Swiss ground without causing any casualty. Their crews, safe and sound, had had it rather easy in Swiss hotels and were by now repatriated. The spell was dramatically shattered on the night of 12/13 July when two Lancasters crashed in the Canton of Valais in south-western Switzerland.

There were no survivors among the fourteen crewmembers and, tarnishing the Swiss image with the Allies, the disaster was claimed by the Swiss anti-aircraft artillery. True, there remains room for controversy about the claims, but in any case the deeds of the flab gunners collapsed the fable of leniency towards Allied aircraft attached to the Swiss defences.

SOFT ITALY

At dusk on Monday 12 July 1943, the first of nearly 300 RAF *Lancasters* took off from England. Their target: Turin in northern Italy. The raid was Bomber Command's seventeenth against this distant town, some 1,100km (685mi.) away inside Europe. Turin, with its sprawling Fiat works, represented, like Milan, Genoa and La Spezia,[1] a particularly attractive target for the Air Staff and crews alike.

Politically, the bombing was also expected to destabilise the rather weak morale of the Italian population. Indeed, Sicily had just been invaded and it was felt the raids could help to topple Mussolini's Fascist Italy. By the end of 1942, British bombs from England had been directed to Italy whenever the weather there was more favourable, rather than for bombing Germany.

Turin had first been attacked on 11/12 June 1940 by a small force of *Whitleys* staging out of the Channel Islands (see 'Why the RAF?'). Since then, the city had been targeted sixteen more times with increasing numbers of bombers participating. Before September, when the Allies would cease considering Italy as the enemy, three more raids would take place, the last one on 16/17 August 1943.

On the night of 12/13 July, 297 *Lancasters* left England in another show of the amazing flexibility of the air arm, striking remote targets all over Europe; 253 of them would bomb, 13 would be lost and 31 would turn back due to various human or mechanical shortcomings. Originating from bases of 1 and 5 Groups near Lincoln and York, and of 8 (Pathfinder) Group in East Anglia, the number of aircraft dispatched was to be the peak of the whole Italian campaign.[2]

'EASY' DESTINATIONS

Italy was a welcome relief for the crews who had lately been subjected to the fierce defences of the Ruhr. For the newcomers among them, the long trips provided excellent navigational experience. All in all, Italian targets had a reputation of being 'easy' ones. It is true that they were distant, sorties lasting around nine cold, noisy, nerve-straining hours. Also, facing the Alps was a chief hazard, particularly in bad weather. But on the other side of the ledger, the routes in and out across France were relatively free of defences, and opposition over the targets was generally weak to non-existent at night. This was because the Regia Aeronautica, like the Swiss air arm, was practically unacquainted with aerial night fighting.

The Italian campaign lasted three years before the country changed sides in the war. It was, with its fifty-two raids, to cost Bomber Command, 103 aircraft missing i.e. 2.85 per cent of the forces dispatched.

On occasions, however, losses were comparable to those sustained during raids on Germany. That the sorties were not exempt of danger is illustrated by the disappearance of S/Ldr John Nettleton, Victoria Cross, of the Augsburg raid fame.[3] He would go missing on this very night when his *Lancaster*, as the two which tragically ended in Switzerland, was one of the thirteen four-engined aircraft which would not return, adding up to 4.4 per cent of those taking off.

Another Victoria Cross had, by the way, been earned posthumously over Turin by F/Sgt Rawdon Middleton of 149 Squadron, for his deeds on 28/29 October 1942. Another, for extraordinary heroism and again over the same city, would be won exactly one month after the Bouveret drama, on 12/13 August, also by a *Stirling* pilot, F/Sgt Arthur Aaron of 218 Squadron.

LONG-RANGE TARGETS

Raids to Italy were near the extreme range of the aircraft and furthermore, the formidable alpine barrier had to be overcome by heavily laden, sluggish machines. Just prior to reaching Turin, Mont Blanc – the highest European summit – towered menacingly at 15,771ft (4,807m), at three quarters of the operational altitude of the *Lancaster* raiders. Fortunately, Bomber Command planners in their infinite wisdom had routed the penetration track around the giant of the Alps.

That night, the attackers crossed the English coast at Dungeness to reach the enemy shore near Cayeux. The stream then flew a 148° magnetic heading direct to Lake Annecy. This is 100mi. (160km) north-west of Turin and the target could now be attained by skirting the right side of Mont Blanc and overflying mountains of 'only' 13,000ft (3,963m) thus allowing a rather safe altitude margin.

Zero hour – that is time on target for the first wave – was initially to be 0040hr British Time, but was revised to 0135hr. This was after the decision had been taken at HQ Bomber Command, to scrub the *Halifax* and *Lancaster II* components of the raid, i.e. 182 aircraft which were to make up two of the six waves of attackers. One reason was a lack of protective cloud cover foreseen on the penetration route. As will be seen this forecast grossly erred, which greatly complicated the task of the crews.

The weather briefing had indeed warned them about a front closing over the Alps which should be of little importance during the penetration. The cold front was however there and quite so. Its cold air colliding with the local warm layers engendered the massive thunderstorms that proved to be the decisive feature for an upcoming tragedy.

TURNING POINT ANNECY

Of course, the principal reason for making Annecy a compulsory navigation feature was that it allowed circumnavigation of Switzerland. Unfortunately for neutrality and safety, on that night many crews were to erroneously identify Lake Geneva and even Lake Neuchâtel, both in Switzerland, for the Annecy body of water. The Pathfinder aircraft ahead of the main force were to mark the turning point in the region of Annecy. They did indeed: from their high-perched observation post in the Jura mountains north of Geneva, Swiss flab gunners noticed red parachute flares dropped somewhere south. They surmised this was near Mont de Sion, a low pass between Annecy and Geneva, not to be confused with the Swiss town of Sion which will appear in the next Chapter.[4]

What the Swiss gunners could not see over the turning point was the concentration of bombers. Nor the inherent risk of collisions such as the near-disaster that scared stiff an 83 Squadron W/Cdr, John Searby. Over Annecy, an anonymous machine came, as he said, 'within an ace of colliding with [us. It] literally brushed us with its tail plane…!'. That near-miss averted a terrible waste of life and talent: if a collision had put an abrupt end in Searby's career he would not have been

'Master of Ceremonies' – again over Turin, on 7 August – to initiate a new tactic of directing raids from the air, a responsibility that was to be fully exploited at the Peenemünde rocket laboratory on 17/18 August 1943.[5]

The postponement of Zero Hour caused tactical changes. The initial plan had been for a standard turn to Italy over Lake Bourget (Chambéry) but the revision brought the turn closer to the Swiss border, over Lake Annecy. Furthermore, first light came early at this time of the year and the postponement would deny the bombers one hour of protective darkness. To offset the potential advantage this would give to nightfighters, the return leg did not, by far, retrace the penetration track: the *Lancasters* were routed back along a quite unconventional course.

ATLANTIC RETURN

From the Alps, the bombers would steer west, descending across France to a spot in the north of the Bay of Biscay, 185mi. (300km) west of Noirmoutier island. Over the Atlantic, the returning aircraft would pair for mutual protection and the navigators would give their captains a heading suitable to skirt Brest and its formidable defences. The detour was to produce surprising encounters. For instance, pilots Walter Thompson and Maurice Chick, both of 83 Squadron, spotted U-boats serenely surfaced, sunning themselves on a calm sea. It would also be off Brittany that Nettleton's demise occured. He possibly fell a victim of *1. Seeaufklarungsgruppe 128* whose pilots claimed five *Halifaxes* off Brest around 0630hr Of course, briefings could not have foreseen such interceptions when they specified that landfall was to occur at Lizard Point in Cornwall. Flying to base would make the round-trip a 2,250m (3,600km) voyage. If short of fuel, aircraft could land at Exeter, and then proceed to their respective airfields.

Not everyone would make this intermediate landing. For instance, F/Lt Florent Van Rolleghem, a Belgian in 103 Squadron, came back directly to Elshalm Wolds after eight hours and thirty-seven minutes in the air. Not so for W/O. Breckson, whose *Lanc* ED.701 had its outer starboard *Merlin* burst into flames over Lons-le-Saunier on the way out. The pilot elected to press on but, unable to climb the Alps, had to jettison his load and return on three engines. He was one of sixteen crews to turn back before the Alps and it is interesting to note his position at the time the engine quit, since this probably entailed the jettison over Switzerland (see Chapter 17).

Breckson was slightly left of track, heading smack into Switzerland's Lake Geneva. Why risk an infringement of orders and once more raise diplomatic turmoil? A navigational error can probably be ruled out: ground witnesses stated that waves of bombers flew the same route. Still, navigation this far out of England was far outside Gee-range[6] with its fair accuracy. Navigators were by now working on dead reckoning, aided by pin-point visual observation, if available, or by *H2S* reading if this radar aid was on board.

OVER LAKE GENEVA

A deliberate shortcut avoiding the Annecy detour is another possibility. This would save some slight mileage for fuel-conscious pilots and flight engineers, and provide fighter-free travel over Swiss territory.[7] Most probably, in view of the weather conditions, cloud cover and/or terrain prevented the observation of the PFF marking while holes in the cloud undercast allowed the sighting of a large body of water. Thus, Lake Geneva could just – if only part of it could be seen or observed on *H2S* screens – be mistaken for Lake Annecy. They are distant by only 18mi. (30km) although their shapes, sizes and bearings are different... if seen in daylight and good weather.

Indeed, weather over France was terrible. Large cumuli build-ups with their associated electrical storms loomed up to 23,000ft (7,000m) on the route, with moderate to heavy clear ice forming inside them around 20,000ft (6,000m). A number of captains must thus have been induced to skirt the weather, altering course to their left. After all, they could always – and many did – claim their concern for safety, or blame electric storms for having disturbed their instruments.

In any case, the Swiss reported that between 0004hr and 0051hr, around 100 foreign aircraft penetrated the northern Swiss border below 3,000m (9,830ft). Reports sited them in three areas: across Lake Geneva, or on a line running from Neuchâtel to Sion, or as far east as a line joining Porrentruy to Berne to Bellinzona, a track which, incidentally, points to Milan rather than Turin.

By 0105hr, Swiss skies were again clear of foreign interference. After the attack, a single aircraft was plotted re-crossing Switzerland, flying to the north-west just east of Geneva – perhaps a turn-back who did not cross the Alps or a cripple running the gauntlet of exposure at daybreak to Continental defences. It takes only a mild stretch of imagination to see this lonesome raider as being Breckson's aircraft mentioned above.

SWISS FLAB

The Swiss–French border in the western part of Switzerland draws a tormented line around Geneva, longitudinally across the lake and then south along high summits towards Italy, then east again from Mont Blanc. It is therefore quite normal for a flight to cross and re-cross the border several times as it proceeds from France to Italy. It is only north of Geneva that the borderline runs rather straight on the medium-altitude ridges of the Jura range.

Here, in 1940, dramatic confrontations took place between Swiss fighters and the Luftwaffe. This was where the Swiss had erected a number of flab batteries in the Jura mountains, having observed that they were being overflown by RAF raiders to Italy.

On 12 July 1943, *Flab Detachment 150* of Major Wyss' anti-aircraft *Gruppe 10* had its three 75mm batteries pointing up near the Marchairuz pass, north of Geneva. The guns were of a French pre-war design, manufactured in Switzerland under licence from Schneider-Le Creusot. Directed by a Hasler 'Gamma' Kommandogerät, they could in theory fire from fifteen to twenty rounds a minute, each shell weighing 6.5kg (14lb); they were said to be lethal between 2,000 and 16,000m (6,560 to 52,500ft). Before the night was over they would have fired about 400 shells at the RAF. The guns, supplemented by four searchlights, were set up at an altitude of some 1,400m (4590ft). This offered excellent observation of Lake Geneva to the south and east, of Geneva proper towards Annecy in the south-south-east, of Mont Blanc and the towering Alps, and north-west to France, towards Dijon and Besançon.

As seen earlier, the country had, at the time, 170 such tubes spread over her northern borders, as well as 900 20mm guns, about 120 of 34mm bore, 44 gun-laying 'Gammas' and a dozen of searchlights.

ENTERS HORACE BADGE

One of the aircraft flying east of track was *Lancaster* ED.412 flown by Horace Badge, a twenty-year-old Sergeant from Camelford, Cornwall. The son of farmers, the blue-eyed, good-looking Badge had been educated at Shebbear College in Devon; there he was remembered as a calm, studious young man excelling in the choir and at playing violin. Badge had joined the RAF in 1941 and been sent to Canada for training. On 20 June he had been posted to 207 Squadron from 1654. Heavy Conversion Unit, where he had gathered his crew.[8] The very next evening he was supposed to have been be 'broken in' with an experienced pilot flying to Krefeld. Then, a last minute change replaced him by another rookie, Sgt Cook.

So, Badge's first operational sortie was with his own crew: a trip to Cologne on 3/4 July 1943. No doubt the young man had known that foreboding feeling most flyers – and more so the wartime aircrew – experienced when looking at the night rising from a grim eastern horizon. As it was, that night in July was to go down into history as being the one when enemy nightfighter tactics turned to Wilde Sau,[9] and cost the RAF thirty aircraft, a 4.6 per cent loss rate. Badge again went to Cologne on 8/9 July, coming back on three engines, and to Gelsenkirchen the night after.

This night, July 12/13, was Badge's fourth sortie, and his commission to Pilot Officer had just been announced although Squadron records still report him as Sergeant. His aircraft, a comparatively new Mk.I, with 108 hours of flying time, had been delivered to 57 Squadron in December 1942 and passed on to 207 Squadron in May. Wearing the code letters EM°Q for 'Queenie', it had lifted off from Langar, west of the Wash in Nottinghamshire[10] at 2235hr British time. Aboard were a crew of seven and 2.5 tons of a less than standard load allowing better climb capabilities; this included one 4,000lb (1,816kg) HC (high capacity, explosive) *Cookie*, plus two SBC containers for 90 4lb (0.9kg) incendiaries and three SBC of eight 30lb (13.6kg) similar fire-raising bombs.[11]

AN EXPERIENCED UNIT

The *Lancaster* was carrying two trained navigators. One was F/Lt Arthur Jepps, aged twenty-nine, husband of Fanny Watson, of Forres in Scotland: he had been with 207 Squadron for just a couple of weeks. The other, Sgt Observer/Bomber, Arthur 'Burt' Wright, was, at thirty-two, the oldest member of the crew. A carpenter in civilian life, he was married to Winnifred of Llanhilleth in South Wales; they had three children. Wright had, like all aircrew, volunteered in April 1941, and had been at pilot training in South Africa, then re-mustered into the navigator/air bomber trade. He had been awarded his 'Observer' half-wing brevet[12] in mid-1942, staged into the 1654 Conversion Unit and arrived at 207 Squadron on 18 June 1943.

On this night, the Squadron mustered ten *Lancs* against Turin; it had a solid experience of raids over Southern Europe, having taken part in most attacks on Italy and also the famous low-level dusk raid on the nearby Schneider factories in Le Creusot, on 17 October 1942. Soon after, on 8/9 December, the commanding officer, W/Cdr Francis Bain, had been lost and killed over Turin. Again, on 25/26 May 1943, the Squadron had lost another CO, W/Cdr Thomas Parselle,[13] in a raid to Düsseldorf.

Flying over the Channel, Badge had altered course to Annecy, 370mi. (595km) inland. As usual with Bomber Command night operations, each aircraft in the stream was steering its own course in darkness. There is little doubt that some crews elected to take a shortcut on the assigned route. Indeed, a straight line drawn from Troyes – about halfway inside Europe – to Turin, intersects Lake Geneva about 30km (19mi.) inside Switzerland, and goes on to Mont Blanc and Turin.

AROUND BAD WEATHER

A western detour to avoid neutral territory could have been flown, but this would entail two hypotheses. First, that a visual fix on the lake was obtained in time to change course, which seems unlikely because of the unexpected prevalent cloud cover over France. Second, that the captain was willing to run the gauntlet of bad weather and penetrate embedded cumulo-nimbus with their associated heavy turbulence and icing. One can surmise that Badge chose to weave around the cumuli cells reported over the mountainous French-Swiss border, and found himself, knowingly or not, over Swiss ground.

Whatever the reason, pilot and crew were now to pay the ultimate price. By 0045hr (CH), ED.412 was getting clear of the thundery build-ups over France, and holes in the clouds allowed a pin-point on a lake far below. However, the improved conditions – ground observers reported a 7/10th cloud cover with base near 2,500m (8,200ft) – also allowed the flab gunners below to spot vapour trails left by the bombers and illuminated by the half moon, at an estimated height of about 4,500m (14,760ft).

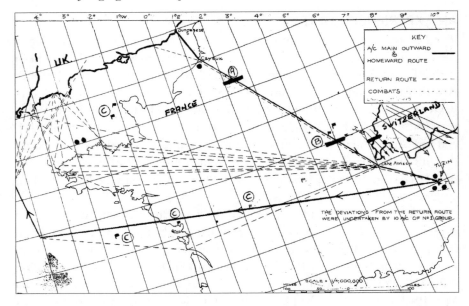

Raid tracks to Turin, 12/13 July 1943, showing (plain line) the briefed penetration route and (dotted lines) the deviations from the return route as undertaken by ten aircraft. Black dots indicate crashes and heavy black lines, where flak was encountered. Combats with nightfighters occurred near Amiens (A), abeam Le Creusot (B) and other spots (C). (PRO via Pascal Blanchard)

Those gunners were rather wary, having heard of the experience of colleagues from *Flab Detachment 110* at Staubikon in eastern Switzerland, three weeks earlier. That had been on 20/21 June when one of the *Lancasters* shuttling to North Africa after bombing Friedrichshafen, had machine-gunned the searchlights that had caught him.[14] Intent to avoid the same treatment, the Jura gunners only switched on their supporting searchlights just before the flab batteries began firing, their shells set to explode between 4,000 and 6,000m (13,120 to 19,680ft).

HEAD-ON CRASH

What exactly happened inside ED.412 shall forever remain a mystery, but *Detachment 150* would soon claim it destroyed. They had seen a plume of black smoke issuing from a bomber above, and later noticed a violent explosion some 60km (37mi.) away, at the other end of Lake Geneva.

Over there, next day at Villeneuve and Le Bouveret on the south-eastern shore, Capt. Max Wuest from HQ, *Aviation Regiment 2*, interrogated many witnesses. They had noticed 'numerous aircraft towards Lausanne [to the west, mid-lake and not far from the flab batteries] much lower than usual'. Over there, 20km (13mi.) to the west and in quasi-clear sky, bombers were milling around, they said, as if trying to regain altitude prior to crossing the Alps. Taking for granted the accuracy of such observations, one could make a parallel with a similar situation that had occurred on the afternoon of 24 October 1942. Then, some thirty-five *Halifaxes* had been spotted, gathering near the lake prior to heading to Milan.[15] Tonight, in the July sky, it appeared to ground observers that the bombers were wandering between cloud base and the lake surface. Whatever their altitude, the aircraft were to clear Mont Grammont, a southern-shore mountain, 2,172m (7,125ft) high, plunging almost vertically, close to the water. The Dents du Midi towered at 3,257m (10,686ft), 30km (19mi.) further south, and still further on, the last barrier which was also the Italian border, would have to be cleared at no less than 4,575m (15,000ft).

Low-flying aircraft, if any, could avoid Mont Grammont and the Dents du Midi by slipping into the relatively narrow (5km (3mi.) wide) north–south Rhône River valley, and there initiate a climb to the Italian border. But to fly there, a pilot needs visual contact with both sides of the gap and this was far from being the case in the electrical storm raging on this south-eastern shore of Lake Geneva.

OVER THE RHÔNE DELTA

On the awful weather, witnesses agreed, but otherwise, their observations differed quite a lot. For some, Badge's aircraft had circled confidently over the Rhône delta prior to flying into the Grammont cliff. For others, engines had been acting erratically while the machine circled on and on, parachute flares being dropped, illuminating the cloud-strewn scene. Some theorised that this could have meant that a stricken ED.412 was preparing to ditch. Another witness, Jeff Morphew, was just as credible. He was a South African fighter pilot who, after evading from Italy, was temporarily interned in the Hôtel d'Angleterre in Vevey.[16] With fellow grounded flyers he watched 'a small light moving overhead [which] grew… suddenly dropping towards the Savoie mountains'.

Surprisingly, the most important observer of the drama was to be a teenager who, like thousands all over Europe, was a keen youth burning with curiosity at the extraordinary events that were shaking the world. Leo Clerc lived in Les Evouettes, a tiny hamlet near the merging of Rhône River and lake, and a mere 3km (less than 2mi.) south-east of Mont Grammont where Badge and crew were to end their life. It was past midnight when the almighty thundering of storm and aircraft engines drew Leo outside. To the north, across the lake, the wailing of sirens added to the dramatic atmosphere. As he looked up towards the east, huge flashes of lightning suddenly turned the dark overcast into an illuminated saucer. For a fleeting second the fiery background exposed the outlines of a couple of aircraft flying on a northerly heading, parallel to the Rhône River. They were fairly low, perhaps at 1,000ft (304m) above Rennaz, some 4km (2.5mi.) away to the east. What looked like fire was visible – but was it just exhaust flames? – on the first one whose engine(s) ran rough, perhaps as would *Merlins* sputtering at reduced power, in landing configuration. The other machine was showing a landing light. Flares slowly came down. Then over the lakeshore the first machine started a left turn, on a westerly course.

A FOUNTAIN OF BURNING PETROL

Investigating the drama many years after the events, one can come to a most probable conclusion. It is that Badge's aircraft had been forced downwards by a flab hit and that, flying roughly on his initial south-easterly course, it had come out of cloud in time for the pilot to notice peaks in the eerie light of the storm. Reacting swiftly, he had veered left to avoid them and had simultaneously spotted the flat Rhône delta, a surface he deemed suitable to attempt an emergency crash-landing. Being too high, Badge would have elected to go around and lose altitude in a 360° turn, still to the left. This would have been when Leo spotted him.

Young Leo never, of course, reflected on the question, not least because within a minute a tremendous explosion erupted, covering even the prevailing pandemonium. The aircraft had smashed into the mountainside above Le Bouveret. Again, one can surmise that Badge had either been blinded by another thunderflash or, on the contrary, be surprised by the sudden cessation of lightning. Continuing in his left turn he had flown into 'stuffed cloud', the mountains hidden in the mist.

Inside the cockpit, the nervous tension must have reached a tremendous level. Imagine a twenty-year-old youngster struggling to keep control over a thirty-ton flying machine; a machine disabled by anti-aircraft artillery which had started a fire in or near an engine; a youngster in charge of six lives beside his own; a young, too young, pilot frantically trying to muster all the vital actions that not many hours of training and still less operational time had, hopefully, drilled into his senses – all that in the darkest of nights in a nightmarish environment of thunder and blinding flashes annihilating the night vision so vital to hold in leash the big *Lancaster*; a crippled bomber replete with its full load of explosives, now loseing altitude in the fiery night, descending towards an unfamiliar country studded with treacherous peaks. The pressure on Badge must indeed have been overwhelming! Another riddle arises here. Why, if he was attempting an emergency landing, did he not jettison his lethal load, including such a temperamental brute as the *Cookie* known to go off at the slightest invitation? Were the hydraulics-operated bomb doors stuck shut? Was the starboard inner engine (No.3) supplying power to operate them, disabled by Swiss flab? Those questions, like so many others in wartime, shall never be answered.

DISCOVERING THE SCENE

At dawn, with little sleep behind him, Leo set out with several other youths to investigate the crash. Access roads were shut off by the Army but the boys knew the mountain well. Climbing on all fours, *en châble*, up the steep and deserted Bellossy ravine, guided by the acrid smell and the shouts of soldiers already on the spot, it was not long before Leo found the site of the crash. The scene was apocalyptic as seen through the eyes of a sixteen-year-old not weaned from the distressing sights of war. Over the years, an image remained etched in his mind: that of a red-headed dislocated body hanging from the shrubbery with a deployed parachute, some 20m (20 yards) east of the point of impact. The location fits with Leo's witnessing of the doomed aircraft turning from east to west in its final seconds, and indeed the sole body identifiable was that of the aircraft's rearmost occupant.

The terrific explosion shattered the *Lancaster* at about 0055hr Swiss time, on Tuesday 13 July 1943. The life of seven brave men was being snuffed out in a savage, lonely spot known to the locals as 'Prés-Dessus'. A dark-red fountain of burning petrol swished upwards for ten seconds. When it subsided shrubs were afire, soon to be doused by the rain. The aircraft had hit the mountainside some 900m (3,000ft) up the cliff, above the Swiss village of Le Bouveret and only 4km (2.5mi.) from the French border. Had he been the same distance away to the east in tightening his turn, Horace Badge would once more have missed the mountain and descended into the Rhône gap! As it was, the explosion triggered a rock slide which buried much debris, some engines included: these were not discovered for three days. One had however been noticed some distance away by an early rescuer who was quick to conclude he could manhandle it down the slope. This he did on a sled, hiding the *Merlin* in his barn… until suspecting soldiers came to retrieve the booty!

RESCUERS UPSLOPE

There was no hope of finding survivors. Rescuers from the village led by fireman René Curdy, reached the scene after two hours of strenuous climbing. Earlier, Curdy had heard an aircraft low near the village. He had jumped from bed to draw his baby's crib away from the window, just in time for his week-old daughter Danièle to escape broken glass shards.

On the mountain, the rescuers' torches only illuminated grim remains. As in many such crashes, the tail gunner's body was the only one recognisable. He was Sgt James Spence, twenty-one; once a clerk in Althorpe, Lincolnshire, he had died in the scree near the severed tail and his parachute. The high-capacity blast *Cookie* had scattered the remainder of the aeroplane in small debris thrown over a square kilometre! Men from a local Army unit found few items that could prove useful for analysis at the *Armee Flugpark* in Zürich: a parachute pack, another draped over shrubs, a propeller, parts of Badge's armoured seat, some eighty incendiary phosphor bombs, escape rations and – as with the Birmenstorf *Wellington* – an item seemingly indestructible: the navigator's astronomical almanac.

At dawn, the remains of the crew were gently manhandled down in Army tents by three men of *Detachment 31, Compagnie de Fusiliers LwII/3*. At the Deaf and Blind asylum, they were subjected to a difficult identification with Capt. Mariethod, the local doctor who was also physician for *Arrondissement Territorial 10* of the Swiss Army. Besides the pilot, rear gunner and two navigators, there was the flight engineer, Sgt Robert Wood who was twenty-one, and twenty-four-year-old Sgt Edward Higgins, the wireless operator, both from Glasgow. Finally, there was the mid-upper gunner, F/Sgt Ronald Brett a twenty-seven-year-old Australian from Mount Bute, Victoria.

RE-MUSTERED INTO AIRCREW

Wood, the flight engineer, had in 1938 been a teenage apprentice auto mechanic in Scotland when he expressed his desire to join the RAF. His father firmly opposed this, only to be overruled later on. Bob Wood thus joined in March 1940, training as a motor mechanic at St Athan in South Wales. He had served for a couple of years in 75 (New Zealand) Squadron before re-mustering as aerial engineer; he had been posted to 207 Squadron about a month previously. As he was entering Switzerland, Wood had been shuffling figures, logging engine temperatures, boosts and the like in order to achieve fuel economy. Over Lake Geneva the exercise suddenly turned quite futile, with the crew intent on saving the aircraft and their own lives.

Their remains were taken to a temporary mortuary in the Bouveret's school.[17] The burial of the crew took place in nearby Vevey two days later, in bright and sunny weather, with full military honours and in front of hundreds of sympathisers. Also buried there and then were the seven victims of another *Lancaster* downed the same night as recounted in the next Chapter.[18]

In the village, all windows facing the mountain had been blasted. This and other damage was to make Badge's crash the most expensive of all RAF accidents in Switzerland: it was to cost Britain a total of 7,447.40 Sw.Frcs in compensation.

FLAB AFTERMATH

The Swiss badly wanted some anti-aircraft results for political reasons, but at first it looked as if they would be robbed of the claims. Indeed, on 16 July, when Col. Ruedi, Head of Aviation Intelligence, wishfully stated that Swiss flab did shoot down the two *Lancasters* crashing in Switzerland on 12/13 July 1943, he was soon contradicted by at least two reports from the *Armee Flugpark* investigators, who stated on 17 July that, 'so far [there is] no [apparent] indication that flab hit [the aircraft]' (Major Gerber) and, 'in bad visibility the aircraft flew blind [IFR] against the cliff' (Capt. Wuest). Furthermore, on 20 July the Commandant, *Armee Flugpark*, concluded his report by saying, 'As far as can be ascertained by the state of debris, there is no indication the crash was due to flab.'

The writer's belief is that Badge's machine down at Le Bouveret was indeed shot down by flab and weather. In any case, the flab version prevailed and soon afterwards the reported downing of the two *Lancasters* served the interests of the Swiss defenders well. Indeed, the flab arm had, a month before, ordered 400 new 20mm Bofors guns. The decision had been criticised in Switzerland's Parliament, where it was felt the order could have been better placed with the Zürich arms firm of Oerlikon, whose products had been giving sterling service in Germany.

On the political scene, the Chief of the Swiss Département Politique Fédéral, Mr Pilet–Golaz, had earlier complained that in view of the repeated violations of Swiss airspace, the country 'ought not just to make noise [at the RAF]'. Actually, the flab had already, in co-operation with Swiss fighters, downed a foreign aircraft early in the war: a German Messerschmitt *Bf.110* on 8 June 1940. Swiss guns had again fired against German machines near Frauenfeld on 10 April 1943, and on numerous occasions against RAF bombers. The mid-July episode was, however, the flab's first success against the latter, and Pilet-Golaz could now counter German accusations of Swiss leniency in favour of the Allies.

MORE OF THE SAME

Large aeroplanes flying head-on into cliffs were a rather rare occurrence in the Second World War. One, undocumented for a very long time, was the crash of another four-engined bomber, an American *B-24 Liberator* operating over China on 31 August 1944. The plane hit a 1,800m (6,000ft) high cliff with the loss of the ten men aboard. The wreckage, hidden in the undergrowth of a remote area, was not discovered before 1996, contrary to the 207 Squadron *Lancaster* whose fiery demise drew the attention of thousands at the eastern end of Lake Geneva.

Badge's unfortunate saga would be concluded with a trio of subsequent tragic aerial occurrences that were to happen near Le Bouveret. After the war, three light aircraft flew to their doom in this 'crash corner', killing eight people and a dog. Two Piper *Cherokees* hit in bad weather near the *Lancaster's* point of impact: one just west on 23 March 1980 and the other in the east on 9 March 1988. Then, on 3 September 1989, it was the turn of a *Cessna 172*, to the west again. In two of the cases the accidents were attributed to pilots trying, in bad weather, to grope their way into the Rhône valley – not perhaps unlike the situation that befell the unlucky Horace Badge.

7

High-Altitude Crash

AIRMEN AND AIRCRAFT:
Pilot: F/O Graham Mitchell
Flight Engineer: Sgt Benjamin Evans
Navigator: F/O Harold St George
Bomb Aimer: F/O Walter Morgan
Wireless Operator: Sgt John Maher
Mid-upper Gunner: F/Sgt Anthony Terry
Rear Gunner: Sgt Hugh Bolger
Lancaster Mk.III, ED.531, code PO°T, 467 Squadron RAAF

As Horace Badge's crew met a brutal end near the eastern end of Lake Geneva on 12/13 July 1943, another doomed Lancaster already flew deep in the Swiss Alps. This was ED.531, labouring much further east and captained by F/O Graham Mitchell. The flight was indeed one of the easternmost violations of Swiss airspace that night.

FOUR SORTIES

Australian F/O Graham Douglas Mitchell was a twenty-year-old from Tusmore, South Australia. He had enlisted in the RAAF on 7 May 1941 and, after gaining his wings, had left his native sub-continent almost exactly a year before, on 26 July 1942. Passage to the UK had taken nearly three months. The young bomber pilot then had had to go through more training, particularly on blind approaches, indispensable for operations in British weather. He had, meanwhile, gathered his crew and on 18 June been posted to No.467 Royal Australian Air Force Squadron[1] at Bottesford. He was to live just twenty-six days at his new base.

Mitchell had but four completed sorties under his belt; as such he would add to the statistics showing a vast number of aircrew 'getting the chop' in the early stage of their mandatory tour of thirty sorties. He had started pre-operational flying in the moon period on 20 June, but of course not against Friedrichshafen[2] and the long shuttle flying illegally across Switzerland to North Africa. Instead, as a freshman, he had been detailed on a Bullseye trip, a night-affiliation sortie during which he had been illuminated by searchlights and intercepted by a friendly *Mosquito* nightfighter – all this in the framework of the extra training given to pilots who had not been through the three-year-long pre-war curriculum.

Mitchell had his first taste of Germany on 21/22 June. This had been over Krefeld, as second dickey (pilot) to the more experienced F/Sgt F. Dixon.[3] On the 24th he took off as captain to Wuppertal but was late to set course and had to return without completing the task. Mitchell also failed to complete a Gelsenkirchen operation on 25/26 June, but on the 28th he went to Köln in what proved to be the city's worst attack of the war. He and his crew were there again on the night of 3/4 July when the innovative German 'Wilde Sau' tactics claimed thirty RAF heavies, none of which were from Mitchell's unit. Gelsenkirchen and its synthetic oil plants had seen Mitchell's crew amongst 400-odd raiders attacking on 9/10 July. The Squadron then stood down until tonight this night.

AUSSIES

Mitchell's crew was of mixed RAAF and RAF origin. As often, due to the scarcity of the trade within the RAAF, the flight engineer was British: Sgt Benjamin Evans. Also RAF-trained was the bomb aimer, F/O Walter Morgan a twenty-four-year-old from Rumney near Cardiff.

Morgan had had an untypical Service career. As a member of the police force he had not been permitted to enlist before 1941; he was then sent for pilot training in the USA, at Pensacola, Florida, but did not make the grade and was shifted north to Canada. Re-mustered in the bomb aimer trade, he had returned to the UK aboard the fast *Queen Elizabeth*. Late in 1942, a practice flight had ended in disaster, and he was the only survivor of the crash. His luck was to run out on13 July, the day he was supposed to go on leave and meet his brother Derek, who was also in uniform.

All the other airmen in ED.531 were Australians.[4] F/O Harold Raymond St George, twenty-two, hailed from Indooroopilly, Queensland; he had undergone pilot training in Canada, and had been washed out to become a navigator. His pre-operational career is representative of the world-wide training scheme that turned out the thousands of aircrew needed in the huge air-arm wielded from Britain. Sgt John Martin Maher was the wireless operator, from East Malvern, Victoria. Like most of his fellow crew members he had enlisted in 1941, their training taking at least fourteen months.

The two gunners were Sgt Hugh Burke Bolger, a twenty-year-old former under-training accountant from Auchenflower, Queensland. Olive-skinned Bolger was typical of the thousands of young lads who, at the time, saw in volunteering for the Services a way to adventure and to escape dull junior positions. He had trained at wireless, bomb and gunnery schools in Australia and Rhodesia. He was Mitchell's mid-upper gunner.

His mate behind the quadruple Brownings in the tail was to be F/Sgt Anthony David Terry, a twenty-two-year-old born in London to a family that later emigrated to Williamstown, in Victoria. Prior to enlisting he had been a workman, earning a difficult life in salt mines. Always smiling and helpful, Terry had exchanged positions with Bolger for the Turin raid. It would never be known if either gunner had ever fired their Brownings in anger, nor if their three-second bursts had ever repelled an enemy fighter.

FINAL FLIGHT

It can be surmised that the machine flew steadily south-east from Amiens, probably bearing east to avoid the unexpected thunderstorms drifting across France. Mitchell would then have entered the Swiss sanctuary around Porrentruy-Neuchâtel, altered his heading to Turin and then started over-flying the alpine wastes south of Fribourg, droning over the elephantine rock formations of the Sanetsch pass, to emerge over Sion and the Rhône valley, on course to Italy.

A remote possibility could also be that the *Lancaster* had – like Badge who crashed at Bouveret – steered more normally further west and been hit by Swiss flab when arriving in sight of Lake Geneva. Crippled, he would then have flown a crooked and unlikely course, first to the eastern end of the lake, avoiding Mont Grammont, and then heading south-east towards the Diablerets mountains. He would have cleared these above 3,210m (10,532ft) while descending to reach the Sion area. Here, he would have proceeded for a landing on the aerodrome. But why then did not he chose Geneva aerodrome when hit, this being much closer and also appearing on RAF maps?

As it was for Badge, what really happened to ED.531 will never be known for certain; again, there was no survivor who could attest to the flight's last hectic moments.[5] It remains this writer's opinion that Mitchell's *Lanc* was damaged by either fighter or flak over France,[6] the crew then electing to press on to Italy across central western Switzerland.

In any case, approaching Sion, probably with a fire gnawing at his right wing, the captain must have judged the situation urgent enough to warrant a forced landing on the town's aerodrome. However, landing with the big 4,000lb (1,816kg) *Cookie* bomb aboard was a dangerous operation, the missile being well known to be unstable. Also, even if against all odds the landing succeeded – in unknown territory, at night and in a damaged aircraft – defusing the highly sensitive bomb would require skills that the Swiss probably would not have. The crew thus elected to get rid of the most lethal part of the load over a deserted rocky spot. This explains why the aircraft started orbiting over the valley's south rim, and why the temperamental *Cookie* was released in deserted expanses further south.

LONG-RANGE SORTIE

At 2249hr (GB) on 12 July 1943, Mitchell's *Lancaster III* ED.531, coded PO°T for 'Tare', had flown out of Bottesford, an airfield close to Langar which had seen Badge's take-off fourteen minutes earlier. The machine was a 230-hour veteran acquired new by the Squadron on 26 January; it had since flown ten operational sorties. Like Badge, Mitchell was part of the large force performing the deep penetration to Turin and back.

Tonight's 2,250mi. (3600km) sortie made it one of the longest-ranged tasks ever attempted by Bomber Command. The extra amount of petrol needed entailed a proportional reduction in bombs carried. Therefore, ED.531's load was similar to that of the seventeen other *Lancs* sent aloft by the Australian Squadron: one *Cookie*, the outsized oil drum filled with almost 2 tons of high-explosive. Also behind Mitchell were rather more incendiaries than 207 Squadron had allowed Badge to carry: he was taking along forty 30lb (13.6kg) bombs and 450 4lb sticks.

Labouring for altitude, PO°T had broken cloud, emerging in full view of a magnificent sunset. But as always, however, the elation had soon been quenched by the knowledge of incoming operational anguishes. By 0102hr Swiss time, on Tuesday 13 July, Mitchell's *Lancaster* had reached Sion, deep inside Switzerland. With fair weather prevailing outside the building thunderheads, visibility was good. The half moon shone on snowy patches over the highest peaks, and down below in the darkened Rhône valley, a still darker area could be made out: Sion's grass aerodrome.[7] There, by co-incidence, at a time when raiders to Italy were active above, aviators remembered the morrow was to be the 30th anniversary of the first flight across the Alps. Indeed, the route flown then from Berne to Milan – Talledo by Oscar Bider and his flimsy *Blériot*, had been practically that of tonight's stray *Lancasters*.

In town, numerous witnesses watched the heavy machine. It had been one of the last to overfly the valley but much lower than its brethren. Also, the engines seemed to be running at a different tempo. In Sion, the lady owner of the railroad station restaurant had just died. That night her young kitchen hand, René Rosset, was sitting up with the corpse. Hearing the drone of aircraft engines fairly close, he rushed outside in time to see 'a torch stabbing the dark sky from the north-east'. This indication of a fire aboard in an aircraft arriving from that direction, strengthens the hypothesis of previous damage incurred outside the range of the Marchairuz flab batteries.

SPARING SION

The aircraft veered left somewhere south of the valley, and red and yellow flares were seen prior to bombs being jettisoned. The aeroplane flew south, losing altitude, clearing several peaks around 2,500m (8,200ft) and flying a couple of racecourse patterns over the Val d'Hérémence. On the return leg of one, the load

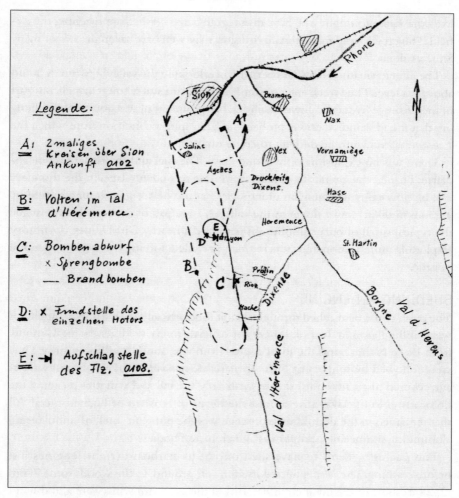

A Swiss-German conscript drew this sketch depicting the final minutes of F/O Graham Mitchell's Lancaster ED.531. With the possible intention of performing an emergency landing on the local airfield, the aircraft circled twice at 0102hr over the city of Sion (A) in the Swiss Alps. It then went over the high ground in a racetrack (B) that terminated in a fatal flat spin at 1308hr (E), just after the starboard engine dropped at D. Bombs had been jettisoned at C. (Swiss Army)

was jettisoned on the mountain. The *Cookie* exploded on an overhang just west of the hamlet of Riau,[8] removing some 50m³ (65 cubic yards) of rock and destroying a field of rose-bays. Some incendiaries also burned harmlessly nearby.

Suddenly, short of completing a last simulated standard landing pattern, the *Lancaster* broke sharply left in a steep turn which brought it from west to east towards a clump of chalets nesting on a crest. This was Thyon, altitude about 2,100m (6,900ft), a hamlet that has since grown into a renowned ski resort.[9] The time was 0108hr (CH). Had it not gone over the mountain to dispose of its war load, the *Lancaster* might well have disintegrated and crashed approaching the airfield. The crew's unselfish ultimate decision may well have saved the life of many Sion residents![10]

The aircraft smashed on a flat overhang overlooking the valley, 2,575m (8,500ft) above sea level. The wreck cut a power line, missing a water tower which was part of the Dixence hydraulic power facilities. No ground trail was noticeable, indicating that it had slammed down, probably in a flat spin, a condition from which the *Lancaster* is known to be difficult to come out of.

There was no explosion, only a loud crash. The fuel and the remaining incendiaries burned the aircraft to cinders from nose to mid-fuselage. In the thundery and by now rainy darkness, an orange glow could be seen for hours from Sion, 1,530m (5,000ft) lower down in the valley. A large pall of dark smoke rose while the typical smell of burnt aluminium pervaded a nearby Girl Guides' dormitory. Exploding ammunition and pouring rain prevailed, forcing them not to venture outside.

SHEDDING AN ENGINE

The crash could be reached through abrupt footpaths and soon a dozen shepherds were milling around. It took longer for officials to arrive: a gendarme Genoud, from Basse Nendaz and the local guards from Vex, another village nearby. They were followed by soldiers of *Swiss Territorial Kommando 10*. The burned wreckage covered just a fifty-yard square, with only the tail and wingtips escaping the holocaust. No one was alive amidst the heaps of crushed or burned metal. All that remained in the dour rainswept scene was the pungent smell of smouldering aluminium, simmering phosphorus and cremated bodies.

The *Lancaster* seems to have shed one of its starboard (right) engines just before crashing. The *Merlin* buried itself in soft ground, in the woods some 700m (2,300ft) short of the main crash site. Bits of the starboard wing were also discovered some distance away, at the rear and to the right of the main wreck: a section of the main spar with an engine mount, 190m (625ft) away, the dinghy which had come loose from its wing stowage, again on the right side, and a main wheel (probably the starboard one) that had rolled 70m (240ft) downhill.

Hence, there are reasons to believe that the machine had suffered mechanical damage some time before impact.[11] Again, the truth shall never be known. One can, however, fairly safely surmise that a fire broke out in the right wing, which then subsided or had been extinguished. The crew could then have elected to press on, RAF-style. When the fire broke out again, the decision may have been taken to jettison the load and attempt a landing in the relatively obstacle-free valley west of Sion. Then, as the fire ate away at the wing and the machine became uncontrollable, the captain would have ordered his crew to bail out.

The rear gunner almost made it: Bolger's twisted body was found protruding from the turret which he had been rotating to port in a belated attempt to escape.[12] In the emergency, Hugh Bolger had evidently gone through the lengthy, life-saving process of opening his turret's 'back doors', grabbing the stowed parachute he had no room to wear amongst his four Browning breeches, clipping it on, turning his cupola sideways into the howling slipstream and – too late – starting to slide out of it.

Jeanne Ometz, an employee at the nearby girls' dormitory, was the first civilian to reach the scene. Bolger's face, she said, was, 'peaceful, he looked like someone I knew'. In the deeply Catholic community where he died, it was not long before Bolger became a sort of fallen angel: he was wearing a rosary[13] around his neck and his well-worn prayer book witnessed that he, too, was a fervent Catholic. F/Sgt Terry, the mid-upper man, was recovered in his smashed turret. He was twenty-two and from London. The five others were found charred beyond recognition. However, Jeanne Ometz remembers noticing the remains of the pilot still clutching the control wheel, as if striving to the last to check the desperate situation.

BURIALS

The remains of Mitchell's crew were taken to Vevey's cemetery at the eastern end of Lake Geneva, rejoining their Bouveret comrades they would never know. A large throng of sympathisers gathered there on 15 July, swamping the official ceremony. In attendance were the British ambassador in Berne, Sir Clifford Norton; Air Commodore West, the ever-present air attaché; many Allied delegations; the Aga Khan who happened to be on holiday nearby and, last but not least, a group of British aircrew evaders who had previously managed to reach the Swiss safe haven after being shot down.

To this day, the carefully kept graves of the crew of ED.531 grace Vevey's St Martin cemetery, just across the lake from Le Bouveret and overlooking the spot where Horace Badge and his fellow airmen met their death. They are not alone. The cemetery shelters the graves of thirty-four Commonwealth airmen who died in Switzerland during the war. The British plot also contains the graves of nine Second World War soldiers and one sailor, and of eighty-four British and Dominion military personnel who died in the First World War.

A sad aspect of the two tragedies in Valais was that it took almost four months for the Swiss to obtain particulars of the identities of the crews killed in the two *Lancasters*. Information had been requested from the Foreign Office on 25 September 1943, after attempts to identify the remains of most aviators had failed. The FO, which had received the telegram on 28 September, passed it on to the Air Ministry, only on 9 November, and obtained an answer on 3 January 1944! The fourteen death certificates relating to the Badge and Mitchell crews eventually reached England via the diplomatic bag on 17 July 1944, a year after the airmen had died.

The wreckage of *Lancasters* ED.412 and ED.531 were brought down their respective mountains. From Thyon, no fewer than twelve truckloads of badly twisted or burned components went to the Dübendorf airbase. There the Swiss endeavoured to piece together the various items. They wanted to study what they could of the *Lancaster* and succeeded in compiling two large volumes of data on the four-engined monster of the time. Only then did they load their accidental prizes on freight trains to be shipped to the Chippis aluminium smelter near Sion.

RAID RESULTS

Switzerland later submitted bills for damage or services (see Chapter 19). To some extent the country had good reasons for claiming compensation, particularly when it came to other events that occurred on 12/13 July 1943. No fewer than five large high-explosive bombs and more than 250 incendiaries had peppered her country-side, as recounted in Chapter 17.

Was the raid on Turin successful? Over the town at around 0200hr British Time, visibility had been fair with little or no cloud. Most aircraft bombed from around 17,500ft (5,335m). At debriefing, crews reported very weak Italian flak, wavering searchlights and, overall, little opposition. That is except for the weather over France, on the penetration leg: that part of the journey had been mostly in cloud with severe icing encountered over the Alps.

S/Ldr Alfred Raphael who, aged twenty-seven, was in command of 467 Squadron, stated he 'could not imagine any loss due to enemy action'. He, too, was to lose his life next month over Peenemünde. Sterling marking by the Pathfinder force, the PFF, had done much to ease route navigation and was again praised over Turin. Pathfinders were, like the Main Force raiders, late on target. Here, the bombing concentrated on the north-western parts of the town where 792 people were killed.

Next day, 13 July, photo reconnaissance brought back pictures showing fifty fires still raging and much damage to the Fiat factories. Also hit were rail facilities, textile and steel mills, and the arsenal.

In England, most aircraft had returned by 0730hr (GB), and by the time of the last landing at 0955hr – a 207 Squadron machine on three engines – a tally could be made. The raid had cost the RAF thirteen *Lancasters*, a particularly notable loss being, besides the two 'Swiss' *Lancs*, the twenty-six-year-old recipient of a Victoria Cross, W/Cdr John Nettleton (see preceding Chapter).

* * * * * * * * *

Once more, as near Le Bouveret, the site of the *Lancaster* crash almost became, post-war, the scene of a repeat operation. On 5 February 1955, just 6km west (3.7mi.) a Piper *Warrior* smashed at dusk against the mountainside, killing its four occupants.

8

Smith's Sihlsee Spin

AIRMEN AND AIRCRAFT:

Pilot: P/O George J.A. Smith
Navigator: P/O Basil T. Medcalf
Bomb Aimer: F/O Herbert J. Benson
Wireless Operator: F/Sgt Eric Hiley
Flight Engineer: Sgt George Beevers
Mid-upper Gunner: Sgt Arthur Truscott
Rear Gunner: F/Sgt Ronald Carr
Lancaster Mk.III, ND.595, code HW°V, 100 Squadron

Late on the evening of 13 November 1940, an unmanned German Dornier Do.17 Z–3 crashed on a slope overlooking lake Sihl in central Switzerland. Returning from a raid on England, the bomber had been abandoned over Germany.[1] Three years later, by coincidence, a British Lancaster *was to come down at practically the same spot.*

The ill-fated machine was ND.595, brand-new with only 23 hours of flying time and coded HW°V by 100 Squadron on whose inventory it had been for just two weeks. The aircraft had left Waltham-Grimsby on the evening of 25 February 1944 on its way to Augsburg. Besides bombing this southern target, it was detailed to act as wind- and path-finder. The *Lanc* was one of 12 *H2S* radar-equipped aircraft[2] dispatched by 100 Squadron; only eight were to be effective: one being lost and three more aborting for human or mechanical reasons.

AUGSBURG BY NIGHT

The raid was a 'maximum effort' mounted against the industrial city. Factories and the old town were to suffer extensively in this, the first and only Main Force attack mounted by the RAF against Augsburg during the war. Altogether, 594 aircraft comprised the Force sent out in two waves, bombing respectively at 2245hr and 0145hr (GB). 'V'-Victor was part of the second wave.

At this time the RAF Bomber Command was able to send some 600 aircraft almost each night, helped by *Gee*, *Oboe* and *H2S* navigation and bombing aids enabling the crews to locate and hit targets with reasonable accuracy, even in bad weather. This night, over Augsburg in clear starlit weather, the attack was to drop 2,076 tons of bombs, destroying 29 per cent of the built-up area in the old imperial city sprawling under its snowy mantle. Aerial reconnaissance by 541 (PRU) Squadron on 16 March was also to disclose extensive damage to industrial buildings, the MAN factories for instance. These were Germany's main source of submarine diesel engines and were so important that a force of the earliest *Lancasters* had been sent out against them in daylight two years before. Other factories in the north and north-east of Augsburg were damaged as well, including the Schmittner aircraft-component workshops at Lechhausen.

ND.595's contribution to the conflagration consisted of a load of high explosives only: 4.3 metric tonnes of them. The aircraft was one of thirty PFF supporters[3] which would contribute to send flak gunners and firemen scurrying for cover – and inefficiency.

The suburb of Haunstetten, birthplace of throngs of Messerschmitt fighters, escaped the wrath of Bomber Command; it had, however, been hard hit a few hours before the RAF raid, by 196 *Fortresses* belonging to the UK-based 1st Division, US 8th Air Force. From this contingent, a 92nd Bomb Group *B-17* (serial 42-37755, pilot Lt. Clifford Beach) had found refuge in Switzerland, landing at Dübendorf military airbase. Other American heavies had also been involved in raids on Southern Germany, amongst them 15th Air Force *B-24 Liberators* out of Italy. One of them, a 450th Bomb Group machine (serial 42-52148 flown by Lt. William Cranston), had been abandoned by its nine crewmen. It had crashed at Kirchberg, just 35km (21mi.) north-east of Lake Sihl.

150 MEN LOST

The night would see more casualties: twenty-one four-engined RAF bombers[4] with some 150 men, most of whom would rest forever in foreign soil. *Lancaster* ND.595 was one of them. The black-undersurfaced *Lanc* had left England at 2125hr (GB) flown by George ('Bish') Alistair Smith, a recently commissioned Pilot Officer from Southsea, Hants. Smith was flying a replacement aircraft, a new Mk.III. His own regular machine was JB.289 'T'[5] which sported the 'Bishop' cartoon illustrating one of the pilot's nicknames. It was undergoing an engine change after the preceding night's trip to Schweinfurt, an eight-hour affair in which Smith had taken a sprog crew to the capital of the German ball-bearing industry.

George Smith had been a police officer in Hastings. He had joined the RAF on his twenty-second birthday, on 25 April 1941. As could be expected, his name was to complicate more than one administrative cog and, furthermore, his nick-names also did their best to confuse a number of friends. Officially he was George although his family knew him as 'Jock'. His crew and other friends, however, called him 'Bish'. After the war, living in a Southsea road with no less than eleven Smiths, he changed his name to Alistair Crowley-Smith, a move that did not ease things when it came to trace him!

'Bish' had trained as a pilot in Canada;[6] he had returned to the UK at the end of 1942 and married Myriam, who had already given him a small daughter by the time he arrived in Switzerland. The twenty-eight-year-old Bish Smith had picked most of his crew at 28.OTU Wymeswold and Castle Donington, fly-ing *Wellingtons*. They went on to 1662.Heavy Conversion Unit at Blyton, Lincs. Here they acquired their seventh comrade, Sgt George Beevers, who was just twenty, and had been a joiner in Huddersfield. Now his flight engineer trade was needed aboard the large four-engined *Halifaxes* or *Lancasters* they would have to fly. Beevers thus became a member of a 'family', a close-knit, trusting group where everyone acted for the safety of all.

In mid-October 1943, the crew had been posted to 100 Squadron at Waltham, practically in sight of Grimsby and the North Sea. Some of the crew flew on operations in November, but this was not to be for their pilot: he had dislocated his right index finger playing rugby! The mishap explains why, on 26 November, his wireless operator made his first trip, to Berlin, with another pilot. His rear gunner, Sgt Frank Diggle from Nottingham, also flew his first sortie on the same night, only to be killed outright near Postdam.[7]

NEVER AN EASY TARGET

December 1943 marked the height of the Battle of Berlin and on the 16th, for his first operational sortie, Bish Smith was treated to the relative delights of the 'Big City'. Upon returning in foggy weather, as often occured in winter in those parts of England, Smith almost collided with another *Lancaster*;[8] he nevertheless managed a perfect landing at nearby Binbrook. Altogether before being downed, Smith had taken part in twelve raids, making the Berlin run seven times. Indeed he was far from being favoured with 'easy' targets in his operational life. His other sorties were equally distant ones: Magdeburg, Leipzig, Schweinfurt and Frankfurt, involving up to eight-and-a-half hours of wintry night-flying time. Augsburg was thus Smith's 13th operation, a forbidding omen.

Contrary to early operations in 1940-1942, RAF tacticians now sent the bomb-ers in 'compact' streams at pre-determined altitudes and timings, and through routes conceived to avoid as much as possible fighter and flak opposition. Furthermore, diversionary raids and intruder sorties also added to the difficulties of the German nightfighters. For all its benefits, the bomber stream tactics were not devoid of dan-gers, including the risks of collisions or of being hit by bombs falling from above; flying very high as Bish Smith did that night alleviated this hazard.

The first thrust at Augsburg had reached the city and bombed after a circuitous route via Le Tréport, south to Saarbrücken and then direct to Lake Amersee before veering north to the target. By the time it bombed at 2245hr (GB), the second wave was on its way, reaching the enemy coast north of Antwerp, Belgium. Its penetration routeing differed completely: it went through Liège, to Malmédy, straight south-east to the tip of Lake Constance and up to the Amersee, also reaching the target from the south.

The return route for both waves was to be west to the vicinity of Epinal and back to Le Tréport and Eastbourne. Bish Smith never arrived this far. On the way out, the stream had exited broken cloud past Liège, and was now flying in clear sky. Smith's new aircraft, V-Victor, had climbed quite well and was steadily cruising at 23,500ft (7,165m). From their vantage point, the crew forward could see the blaze developing over the target from as far as Saarbrücken, 300km (190mi.) away. The night was fantastically clear, with snow sharply etching the ground. Such conditions were a mixed blessing: good visibility eased navigation and reduced the risk of collision within the stream of bombers but at the same time it made the crew uneasy, for clear nights were indeed nigthfighter nights. As it was, various diversions and the two-pronged attack scattered the fighters all over Europe, resulting in comparatively light losses.[9]

HIT BY FLAK OR FIGHTER?

Smith had passed Strasbourg when he had to reduce speed to 140mph (225kmh) after noticing they were pushed ahead of schedule by stronger than expected winds. The aeroplane must have reached the Black Forest, plodding along between Tüttlingen and Freiburg on the 142° heading requested by navigator Basil Medcalf, when disaster struck. What the crew construed as being 'a burst of heavy, radar-directed flak' seems to have exploded below and forward of ND.595. There had been no warning, no previous burst seen in the distance and no searchlight indicating the region was defended. Later analysis hinted that there must have been an undetected nightfighter below, which peppered the nose with bursts from its *Schräge* upward-firing cannons. Such tactics were common at the time, with German nightfighters sliding unseen under the undefended belly of most RAF bombers, taking time to aim through their upwards-looking sight and letting go at the soft underside of their enemy. It took a year for RAF tacticians[10] to realise that scores of unexplained losses were actually due to upwards-firing weapons. The irony is that the system had been invented in Britain for use in the RAF during the First World War!

Instantly the aircraft became very difficult to control, the starboard inner engine was rendered useless, flames broke out in the radio compartment gradually filling the fuselage with smoke which unwound in a long trail behind the aircraft making it most conspicuous in the clear night.

Four men up-front received slight wounds. The fifth, P/O Herbert 'Jack' Benson, the bomb aimer, was not so lucky. Blue-eyed Benson, whose parents lived

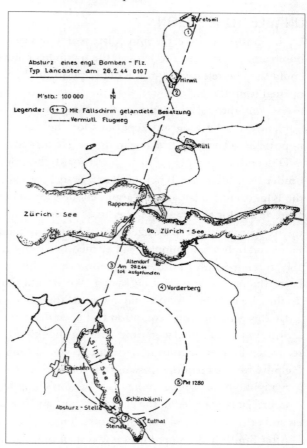

Absturz eines engl. Bomben – Flz.
Typ Lancaster am 26.2.44 0107

M'stb.: 100 000

Legende: (1 + 7) Mit Fallschirm gelandete Besatzung
— — — — Vermutl. Flugweg

'Bish' Smith and his Lancaster ND.595 (HW°V) flew in from the north of Lake Zurich to explode near Einsiedeln, on Lake Shil. Circled figures indicate where the seven crewmembers parachuted. Post-war research indicates the aircraft first circled south of Lake Zurich's shore (between figures 3 and 4), before proceeding further south to Lake Sihl. (Swiss Army)

in Romford, Essex, was twenty-two; he had been promoted from sergeant a week earlier, just before Smith's own promotion. His luck ran out because somewhere over Germany the *H2S* radar set had developed a malfunction. Benson, who so far was helping the navigator inside his compartment behind the pilot, thus went down in the nose in order to get visual fixes. The burst of 'flak' caught him there, severely wounding him in the abdomen and one leg. He fell unconscious.

When hit, the *Lancaster* was probably nearing the southerly turning point, near the western tip of Lake Constance. This was only some 20km (12.5mi.) north of Switzerland, and once more the RAF had routed its stream close to neutral territory. The inevitable spread of aircraft would again cause border violations: by daybreak Capt.Pista Hitz at Swiss intelligence reported nearly 100 foreign penetrations.[11] Amazingly, he correctly guessed that the attack involved from 400 to 700 bombers (there were almost 600). Hitz was however mistaken when he stated that, as had been the case on 20/21 February against Stuttgart, the bombers had been sent overflying Switzerland in order to develop the attack from the south.

UNABLE TO JETTISON

Up in Smith's machine, the immediate worry was to keep the aircraft steady. The bomb aimer was unable to jettison the bomb load due to his incapacitation. Nor could they be released from the pilot's position, the bomb doors refusing to be opened from there. Adding to that, the control column was virtually useless and it was only through the tail trim that a degree of control could be maintained. Somehow the heading was kept but soon the captain realised it was becoming impossible to keep the *Lancaster* in the air. He turned south, to Switzerland.

Descending in a gentle turn to starboard, the bomber probably crossed the border over Stein-am-Rhein where a branch of Lake Constance empties into the Rhine. Here, a last-minute argument developed between pilot and navigator. Were it not for the tragedy in being, it could seem farcical! When the flak hit, the navigator estimated Switzerland and safety as being some ten minutes away. However, only a few minutes had elapsed when the aircraft became unmanageable, forcing Smith to order to abandon ship. This was when rear gunner Carr heard the navigator protesting, saying, 'We are not there yet [over Switzerland].' To this, the unfazed Smith coolly retorted 'You still have to go.' And they went.

By this time Benson's condition had been discovered. His wounds were most serious with multiple lacerations causing shock by loss of blood. He, however, recovered long enough to understand he would soon have to use his parachute. Helping him to snap the brown pack on the harness was not easy in the eerie grey nightlight prevailing in the nose. Benson's limp figure, bulky in his bloodied clothing, laid entangled in the clutter of gun- and bombsights, bomb release panels and other hardware seemingly protruding at random.

After Smith had ordered his crew to bail out, the men came down in a long string some 19mi. (30km) long. Three came out the rear door jettisoned by the wireless operator, Sgt Eric Hiley, who jumped first. He landed at Bettswil, a hamlet near the village of Bäretswil, east of Zürich. Hiley had been a wool salesman before volunteering for aircrew duties. He had acquired his trade at No.4 Radio School, Madley, early in 1943, and graduated with 'average' marks before meeting his crewmates at 28.OTU.

DOWNED ON HIS SECOND TOUR

The tail gunner, F/Sgt Ronald Carr, came out second. A brewery worker in civilian life, he had joined the Service in July 1941 soon after his nineteenth birthday; posted to 150 Squadron he had done a full tour of thirty operations[12] on Wellingtons, acquiring in the process gilt crowns promoting him from sergeant. He then had been rested as instructor at 30.OTU Seighford before joining the Smith crew to replace Frank Diggle, the rear gunner lost with another crew on 26 November. In that position, that of the crew's loniest man, Carr was to fly seemingly suspended outside the aircraft.

He was thus on his fortieth sortie when he landed unhurt in a tree barely 3 miles (5km) further south than Hiley, at Hinwil. He waited until daylight, 'to find out which country I was in', smelling wood smoke as he descended a forlorn track to a chalet. As he was cautiously edging his way across a clearing, an old man carrying a bucket suddenly came out. Carr said:

> I do not know who had the biggest fright, him or me... I walked towards him and, pointing to the ground, asked, 'Deutschland?', to which he replied, 'Nein, Schweiz.' When I said 'RAF' I was warmly shaken by the hand. Inside, two very excited ladies gave me food. To their two boys I showed where the parachute was and after that was ushered into a nice warm bedroom where I took off my outer clothing and went to sleep.

The awakening came as a shock. Someone in a grey uniform, wearing a German-style helmet, prodded him with the barrel of a rifle! Carr thought he had been tricked. He was actually victim of an illusion common to many – including the author – who first came in contact with the Swiss military: he thought he was in Germany. He soon realised he was facing an elderly Swiss soldier who motioned they were to go. Off they went – first the gunner, followed by his proud 'captor' and the two boys pulling a sledge with the parachute and Carr's gear. The strange caravan (what a picture this could have been!) made it to the local police station 3km away, just a room in an ordinary house at nearby Hinwil.

HELPED OUT

Third man out was the crippled Benson. He seemed fully conscious and quite able to pull his 'chute's ripcord. Still, Beevers the flight engineer elected to fit the wounded man with the static line provided to help casualties out. The procedure was not helped by the restricted space in the nose. Having released the escape hatch, he struggled to put Benson's feet in the aperture, facing aft. The injured bomb aimer then slid out into the freezing air.[13]

Beevers followed him. Wallowing and burning, the *Lancaster* was by then gliding over Rapperswil where a dike cuts Lake Zürich in two halves. Soon after this, the stricken machine had lurched to port and begun a left turn over the northern end of Lake Sihl. Beevers thus floated down in the Vorderberg, the hills south of Altendorf near Lachen. In the last few minutes of controlled fear and excitement he had twice acted as an airborne good Samaritan: for Benson first, then as per regulations, for his pilot. Indeed, leaving his station near Smith, he had clipped on the pilot's parachute; what he did not know was that in the dark, he attached it over Smith's oxygen line, a mistake that would soon prove scary for the recipient!

Sgt Arthur Truscott, the mid-upper gunner, escaped next. He had been an electrician in Plymouth in 1940 and had joined the RAF that August, serving in a balloon unit. Later, when his parents were killed in a German raid, he had wanted to avenge them as aircrew. This night he was obliged to extricate himself from his high-perched Frazer-Nash dorsal turret, to stumble for a couple of yards in the dark, vacillating rear fuselage to reach his parachute stowed near the gaping hole of the entrance door.

Meanwhile, the plane had circled round Lake Sihl, near Einsiedeln. This small town was renowned for its convent and its huge baroque church whose twin towers could have been seen protruding from the layer of fog hiding ground and lake alike. It is doubtful, however, that any of the tense airmen did spot them as by this time the smoke-filled *Lancaster* was swaying wildly, initiating another left spiral and descending fast with four tons of high explosives inexorably drawing the doomed machine to earth.

IN FOG AND SNOW

After hanging for what seemed a long time in the cold void, Truscott sank into the fog. The next thing he knew, he was sitting in deep snow. He would later learn he had landed near Willerzell, some 900m (1,850ft) above sea level. Still swinging in his parachute, he had heard the mighty explosion of ND.595 blowing up nearby. The gunner thought the fracas must have alerted every soul for miles around. It had. At nearby Steinbach, the three Lienert sisters had spent a tiring evening in their country restaurant, the Rössli. Upstairs, the cold was intense, augmented – it seemed – by the fog that strangely enough engulfed only the ground floor. Maria Lienert was first to notice the hum. She had been baking dessert for the forthcoming day and when the noise of engines became alarmingly loud, she ran upstairs to wake up her two sisters. Rushing to the windows, the girls gaped at the flying machine throbbing louder and louder, clearly visible as it circled ever lower. It seemed so low that guards of *Territorial Kommando 9a* in the adjacent woods thought it was going to crash on the restaurant!

Inside, the girls retreated to their beer cellar, lying on the cold floor in their nightgowns. Then it came. A terrific detonation over the lake. When Hedy Lienert emerged from her hideout, the Rössli had lost all its front windows. Upstairs, where the sisters had slept, a jagged piece of foreign metal rested on the floor. They had little time to ponder over their luck, good or bad. Within minutes, a strange-looking character materialised in the smashed doorway. He carried a package of white silk, so odd that Alice, the younger sister, thought this was hardly a time to peddle women's underwear! The intruder, a small man, was dressed in warm and bulky clothing; behind him appeared a couple of the soldiers stationed nearby.

TOLD TO GO TO HELL

The stranger was not a salesman after all but an airman freshly rounded up by the steel-helmeted guards. He inquired with a funny accent, 'Hier Berne?' and was told this was rather Schwytz Canton, to which he mumbled some German words indicating he knew someone in the federal city. He was Basil Medcalf, the navigator. Parachuting just before his pilot, he had landed in the hills across the causeway spanning the lake. An insurance clerk from Southend-on-Sea in Essex, Medcalf

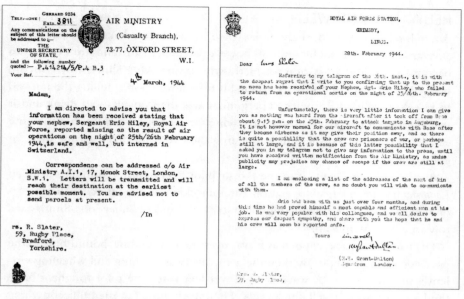

Two official letters received within a week by Sgt Eric Hiley's next-of-kin after he was shot down in Switzerland. The one on the right (28 February 1944) is typical of the dreaded 'failed-to-return' message. No doubt the 4 March Air Ministry letter did bring much relief in Bradford; it was, unfortunately, an exception, and in most cases the postman was the messenger of a tragic announcement. (Hiley family)

had joined the RAF in the early days of 1941, aged eighteen. He had spent very little time falling in the dark: his 'chute had barely had time to open when he hit the high ground north of Euthal, across the lake from the Rössli. Tumbling in jagged rocks, he scratched his neck, adding to a facial scar caused by a shell fragment. Groping his way down he came upon a house, knocked at the door and was promptly told to go to hell by the owner. He knew enough German to understand that. Soon after, he was discovered by alert Swiss guards; after walking with them across the causeway, he became a late customer at the Rössli.

Meanwhile, the wandering Truscott had met a couple of soldiers who had emerged out of the milky darkness. They harboured cocked rifles, sported German-looking helmets and spoke German. Truscott was to say later: 'They thought I was German and I thought they were!'. His newly found companions were in the process of taking him to the 'Rössli' on the west shore, when a small van overtook the trio, stopped and gave the men a ride. The driver, Arnold Kälin, a young plumber from nearby Gross, was one of the hundreds of people shaken awake by the explosion. He knew the commotion had occurred on the southern end of the lake, where his girlfriend Hedy lived. He had set out forthwith but fog slowed him on the two-mile journey along the shore – fog and the sudden ghost-like appearance of two soldiers and a bundled figure.

HEDY ALIVE AND WELL

A much relieved Arnold barely spoke when he saw Hedy, shaken but very much alive among strangers. The reunion however cemented a friendship that was to become a lifelong association for Hedy, who is now Ms Kälin. As for Truscott, with only his own life to worry about, his first move upon reaching the inn was to kneel in front of a crucifix. The gunner was then given a stiff drink and it may have been him who insisted on paying for it with a 100 French-franc note extracted from his escape pouch... adding the exquisite silken escape map for good measure.

A third man also made it to the Rössli: pilot Bish Smith. Exiting his disabled *Lancaster* had been a freak operation. After checking on the intercom that everyone else had left and undoing his safety straps and mike connections, Smith tried to vacate his seat. In vain!

His parachute pack, clipped as it was over the oxygen line, bound him to the port side of the cockpit. By then the aeroplane was lurching and wheeling violently in a steep dive. A wave of cold wet fear rose. The pilot fought it back, thinking, 'If I panic, I will not survive'. He forced himself to methodically tear at the soft rubber end of the oxygen tube entering the mask, then reached down in the dark behind his 'chute, found the crocodile clip attaching the line to his harness, undid it and pulled the strong, wire bound hose from under the parachute.

He was free. But Smith, who still had to squeeze his legs between the engine-control pedestal and the maze of flap and trim handles, came to the conclusion he did not want to escape through the top canopy hatch. He therefore had to crouch near the engineer's folded seat, and claw his way down the tunnel to the open, life-saving, front escape hatch. All that within sparse seconds of time, fighting the blast of upcoming freezing air and trying to keep some sort of balance within a wavering aircraft. All that also in the semi-darkness of a fuselage frightfully illuminated by the orange glow of a fire gnawing away at the aircraft's vitals.

UNCONSCIOUS UNDER HIS PARACHUTE

Smith's luck held. He was barely out of his machine and pulling the parachute's ripcord, a few hundred feet above the fog, when V-Victor blew up. The petrol fumes within the fuel tanks had detonated, exploding the bombs and shredding the machine as if it were an oversized grenade. A fountain of burning petrol erupted, rapidly quenched by the explosion − Fragments hurtled everywhere, fortunately missing the hapless pilot knocked unconscious by the blast under his lifesaving canopy. Below, an engine went straight through the 20in-thick ice covering the lake. The outer starboard *Merlin* flew away, and landed in the hills to be found many days later. Two more broke up on impact with the ice, leaving a mess of oily pistons, rods and crankcases. Some seven acres (3 hectares) of virgin ice and snow were churned into a smudged, broken jumble. Black, burning bits shot away from the impact of a flaming wing, leaving dark streaks much like the coronas around moon craters. Apart from a propeller or two, no other large fragments were found.

Other objects preceding Bish Smith on the ice were his own flying boots, jerked loose when the parachute opened. This was a common occurrence with low-legged American A-6 boots, but even the long-legged RAF model was not immune to parting from its owner on deceleration. When he came to his senses again, Smith was sitting on his parachute in the snow, trying to light a cigarette. A shaking hand was bleeding and, unknown to him, a couple of minute splinters had embedded themselves in his head.

Near him stood a pair of not-so-young soldiers. Noticing the German-looking helmets, Smith fell victim of the usual phantasm: was he in Germany? He then saw the red armband with a white cross and understood he was safe from the PoW stockade. His rescuers then proceeded to prevent his feet from freezing, one of the guards even putting the pilot's hands inside his warm tunic. Later on, Smith was lent a pair of Swiss Army boots, which he had to return next day when his own had been retrieved on the ice. Smith was helped ashore and across the same causeway which Medcalf would tread a few minutes later. He reached the Rössli first. The new stranger was soon to present his pair of long leather flying gloves to Hedy, who remembers him as 'tall and blonde'.[14]

HANGING IN A TREE

Meanwhile, in the Hinwil police premises, Carr was facing 'two men in Gestapo-like long black leather overcoats and wide-brimmed trilby hats', getting nowhere in questioning him. The situation was relieved by the arrival of a car with Eric Hiley, the wireless operator. They soon were on their way to army barracks in Zürich.

Within a couple of days, the survivors were reunited. They had meanwhile been interrogated by their captors and later, at Dübendorf, by specialist aviation officers under Oberst Karl Högger.[15] Only six airmen had been rounded up and hopes that the wounded Benson could be at large soon faded. On the afternoon of Monday 29 February, he was discovered by Leo Notter, a young man from the isolated Luegeten farms on the south shore of Lake Zürich. 'Jack' Benson was dead, hanging from his parachute draped over a 25m (80ft) pine tree. He had fallen in the Schwandigässchen, a maze of trails within the wooden Vorderhof hills, some 5mi.(8km) north of the crash site. Covered in his parachute,[16] the body was taken on a sledge to the closest village, Pfäffikon, where Dr F. Höfliger performed an autopsy.[17] Loss of blood, shock from his wounds, exhaustion and exposure[18] had killed him, one month after his twenty-second birthday.

Coffin and flowers were quickly provided in Pfäffikon, where the body was laid in state in the communal house. This was a last-resort location chosen by Capt. Gamma, the gallant officer in charge of the proceedings, after access to the Catholic chapel had been denied. The morning after this distressing incident, bell-ringing and a guard of honour saluted Benson's coffin as it was driven out to Vevey for interment in the British plot. Today, the unlucky navigator rests in the quiet cemetery overlooking Lake Geneva, along with thirty-three other RAF colleagues killed in Switzerland during the Second World War. His tombstone bears an appropriate epitaph: 'Let me feel the wind on my temples when I answer the last great call'.

The survivors of *Lancaster* HW°V were taken from Dübendorf to Berne to be quarantined for three weeks at the Hôtel Gurten Kulm, a secluded spot overlooking the city and the aerodrome where the PRU *Mosquito* had landed eighteen months earlier. The Smith's crew was granted permission to attend Benson's funerals at Vevey: 'hard going for us' said Carr who, like the others, reflected on how twists of fate mean life for some and death for others.

GOING HOME

Later, duly kitted out in essentials by a member of the British legation who had taken them out shopping – in uniform as all internees were – they transferred to the Hôtel 'Bären', which was rather like an internment 'camp' at Adelboden. Here they met other RAF outcasts and, as Truscott noted, 'hundreds of American aircrew who [must have] come into Switzerland by the Squadron'.

On 12 May 1944, dressed this time in civilian clothes, they started on an official and rather unusual repatriation journey; this will be covered in Chapter 19, since the experience does not lack flavour. The crew transited in Gibraltar whence a BOAC *Dakota* took them to Whitchurch on the evening of 24 May:[19] for them the Augsburg raid had lasted three months. The men were given three-weeks' repatriation leave, going their separate ways.

Eric Hiley, the wireless operator, was to experience a tremendous career as a specialist radio man after returning to England. Reassigned to Ferry Command and the more balmy No.113 South Atlantic Wing in the Bahamas, he spanned practically the whole world ferrying a wide variety of aircraft. Arthur Truscott went to 206 Squadron, flying anti-submarine patrols in Coastal Command's *Liberators*, an experience he considers, 'a bit hectic at times but nothing to compare with Bomber Command'.

As for Bish Smith, the RAF Central Medical Board grounded him as well as Basil Medcalf. After six weeks of combined sick and survivor's leave, he was posted to Air Sea Rescue. He wound up his RAF career in May 1946 as Commanding Officer of the ASR unit, operating launches out of Ponto del Gado in the Azores. After the war, Bish twice returned to Switzerland, in 1960 and 1989, visiting Hedy Kälin, the site of his violent arrival and the grave of his unfortunate friend, 'Jack' Benson. Bish rejoined Benson and countless Bomber Command colleagues when he passed away on 7 May 1994.

9

Sam Atcheson's Death

AIRMEN AND AIRCRAFT:
Pilot: P/O Samuel Atcheson
Flight Engineer: Sgt Brian Thomas
Navigator: P/O Anthony McCall
Bomb Aimer: F/Sgt Jack Greenhalgh
Wireless Operator: Sgt Frank Weaver
Mid-upper Gunner: Sgt Kenneth Reece
Rear Gunner: Sgt James Naylor
Lancaster Mk.III, JB.474, DX°F, 57 Squadron

The early hours of Thursday 16 March 1944 shone bright and crisp. Over the Swiss Jura mountains clearings and fir patches sparkled in snowy splendour, contrasting with the sense of gloom pervading the silent crowd. Hardly anyone spoke in the small group gathered close to the isolated Chaumont farms near Saignelégier. When they did, it was only in muffled tones.

Edi Gyger and other villagers had good reasons to mourn. They were witnessing Swiss *Supernumerary Company 1043* gathering the pitiful remains that only hours before had been six young and healthy British airmen.

ONE SURVIVOR
Nearby, only four miles (7km) away, a lone, dazed survivor had just been rounded up. He was Sgt Kenneth Reece, a *Lancaster* mid-upper gunner. A fair-haired, good-looking youth, the nineteen-year-old aviator was the eldest son of a family in Roughton, near Bridgnorth in Shropshire. He had been a Cadet in the Air Training Corps, before joining the RAF where he had qualified as an aerial gunner. In September 1943 Reece had been posted to 57 Squadron at East Kirby, Lincolnshire – Base 55 shared with 630 Squadron, and known to radio

operators under its callsign 'Silksheen'. The unit had been one of the earliest *Lancaster* squadrons in Bomber Command.

His crew of seven, as for all heavies in the RAF,[1] was captained by another youth, a twenty-four-year-old Irishman, P/O Samuel Atcheson. The son of farmers in Envaugh, Sam had been a bright scholar and had served for six years in the Omagh Post Office, County Tyrone, Northern Ireland. After volunteering for aircrew duties, he had trained as a pilot in Canada.

On 8 November 1943, by then a Flight Sergeant, Atcheson had been posted to the Squadron from 1661 Heavy Conversion Unit at Winthorpe. After a lengthy acclimatisation period spent on various chores including 'Y' training,[2] he had his first taste of operations. This had been a sortie as second pilot to Modane, bombing the strategic rail tunnel on the French–Italian border on 10/11 November 1943. His mount for the occasion had been *Lancaster III* JB.233, a fairly new machine that was to disappear in mysterious conditions on Christmas Eve. Atcheson then had to await the night of 22/23 November to take his own crew out as captain. This had been on a trip to Berlin from which he returned early, after an instrument failure. The 'Big City' did not, however, deter him again – he was to visit it ten times in the next three months!

Sandwiched into the so-called Battle of Berlin were trips to Leipzig, Stettin, Braunschweig, Stuttgart, Augsburg and Schweinfurt. All were long assignments lasting up to eight hours of icy flying in winter darkness. Altogether, pilot and crew had logged nineteen effective sorties by the time they took off to Stuttgart on the evening of 15 March 1944. Such a figure had taken them all past the halfway mark of the thirty raids needed at that time to complete a tour of operations.

ON LEAVE AND A DFC

Meanwhile, Sam had returned to Ireland in early March. He had just been commissioned and it was a proud Pilot Officer who had been on leave. He visited Drumquin to see his father, and spent a couple of days in Dublin and Leicester. Back at base, the young man was quite surprised to find he had been awarded a DFC. The citation read:

> This officer has completed 19 successful attacks on strongly defended targets in Germany, including Berlin… displaying outstanding courage and devotion to duty… and by his determination, set a fine example. On 19/20 February when carrying an attack on Leipzig his airspeed indicator became unserviceable shortly after take-off due to icing. However, he continued the sortie and delivered an accurate attack on time (showing) outstanding airmanship and skill.

The fighting Irishman proudly quoted the citation in full in his last letter to his father. He then shyly added, 'now don't mention it to a soul… I feel my success is entirely due to you'. The faithful son never had a chance to show the decoration to his father. Two days after writing the letter he was killed in action, just inside Switzerland.

At 1858hr (GB), in the twilight of Wednesday 15 March 1944, Sam Atcheson pointed his *Lancaster's* nose into the wind over the runway's white line, and pressed shut the brake lever. Then as the control tower flashed 'his' green light, he released the brakes, noticing the peculiar hiss of compressed air. In complete radio silence, Sam then eased forward the throttles of *Lancaster* JB.474.

The machine was the crew's old acquaintance, each man having performed his own station's daily inspection prior to taking her up in the afternoon for the ritual of a short test flight. Indeed, they trusted old JB.474: in the 154 hours of her flying lifetime, she had taken them once to Berlin and also on the last four raids. Alongside Atcheson, the flight engineer Brian Thomas, sat on his folding seat assisting his pilot. Momentarily acting as second pilot, he retracted the landing gear and flaps, controlled the fuel booster pumps and fuel pressure, monitored airspeed and a host of other parameters. Like his captain, he was ready to face any take-off emergency; he was even trained and ready to fly the aircraft straight, level and on course.

For both men, perhaps more than for the rest of the crew, the intensity of the task at hand freed their minds of the apprehension. Like all aircrew who in the morning had seen their names slated for tonight's operation, covert anxiety had been their lot. Now that they were airborne, their thoughts were all on per-forming the demanding business of flying a 65,000lb (29,510kg) four-engined machine. Not even with them any more was the diffuse uneasiness felt at dusk by so many pilots flying towards darkness. The night was raising from the east, from the North Sea and from enemy territory, but they had confidence in the big aircraft they were mastering and in their own skills.

H2S EQUIPPED

Their *Lancaster*, coded DX°F, was equipped with a ventral blister housing the *H2S* downward-looking radar. Stuttgart laid indeed beyond *Oboe*[3] range, and thus, *H2S*, although less accurate for marking and bombing, was a prerequisite in lead aircraft such as this one. Furthermore, most front-line aircraft in the Command would soon sport that most valuable belly bulge.

Having departed earlier than the main force, the crew was to act as wind-finder, like Smith of Sihlsee fame three weeks earlier. Along the route over France, the wireless operator, Sgt Frank Weaver, was to broadcast for the benefit of head-quarters Bomber Command, the values recorded by the navigator, P/O Antony McCall. The winds thus obtained from various aircraft would then be averaged and re-broadcasted to the main force in coded form at half-hour intervals.

Weather over the Continent was surprisingly varied. Heavy cloud and haze over the Normandy coast would cause the abandon of operation 'Alexander', a *Lysander* clandestine pick-up.[4] At Amiens, however, visibility was termed moderate, but a dense, low overcast cloud prevailed in the Metz area. The same conditions were found over Munich-Schleissheim, foiling a 605 Squadron *Mosquito* nuisance intruder, while colleagues operating over other airfields at Florennes, Belgium and Boblingen, Germany, met with suitable weather. Over Stuttgart itself, the bombers would fly in the clear, arriving late after encountering high winds.

The bomb load carried by JB.474 amounted to 8,840lb, four metric tons – much more than what the vaunted *B-17 Flying Fortress* could take over Germany. The cavernous entrails of Atcheson's *Lancaster* held the traditional drum-like heavy *Cookie*, some squat amatol-filled 1,000lb (454kg) medium-casing explosive bombs, 88 Mk.IV 30lb. (136kg) incendiaries and a myriad – 1,050 of them – of 4lb (18kg) incendiary sticks. With all that burden, the *Lancaster* had climbed well and reached its bombing altitude of 21,000ft (6,400m) over France. The route planners in the 'Hole' at High Wycombe had headed the bomber stream south-east towards Switzerland. Short of the frontier, over the Vosges-Jura gap near Belfort and Basle, the 847 four-engined attackers were to proceed north-east to Stuttgart.

AGAIN INFRINGING NEUTRALITY

As it turned out, the southward momentum of the main force caused it to 'bounce' over neutral Swiss territory, 'as often observed when an RAF attack develops from the south', Swiss intelligence Capt. Loderer would sternly remark at dawn. Loderer[5] was also to report a peculiar occurrence near Frauenfeld, north of Zürich, where 7.5cm Swiss flab guns were in action. Two parachutes were observed in searchlight beams but since there is no record of them having landed in Switzerland, it must be surmised that their unhappy proprietors ended the war in Germany just 14km (9m) distant. An unidentified and agressive four-engined aircraft was also reported at a mere 500m (1,500ft) over ground, firing red flares and shooting up a Swiss 20mm flab battery.

The Swiss radio-intercept station at Basle had heard the Luftwaffe reporting '300 Kuriers' (bombers) heading from Nancy to Stuttgart. The second force, equally strong, ventured much further south, infringing the north-western Swiss frontier between Le Locle and Basle. Swiss plotting, drawn the morning after, thus showed a dense grid of penetration lines running west to east and passing as far south as Thun in central Switzerland. One plot even showed a lone raider heading imperturbably over Brig, crossing into Italy, overflying Ticino and suddenly veering north-east over the Grisons peaks to rejoin the fray in Southern Germany!

Over there, life was not easy for the defenders either. Electrical storms and snow grounded all but the ninety-three best nightfighters of *Jagdkorps I*. Also, the German controllers erred in assessing the RAF intentions. The 7th *Jagddivision* responsible for the defence of Southern Germany vectored the *Bf.110* nightfighters of *Nachtjagdgeschwader 6* too early out of Mainz-Finthen and Stuttgart-Echterdingen. Dispatched to Nancy and beacon 'Kuli' near Metz, they succeeded in downing three heavies, perhaps five, but lost five, possibly seven, of their number through lack of fuel. One casualty was Major Heiwick Wohlers, *NJG. 6*'s *Kommodore* with twenty-nine victories, who went down south of Stuttgart.

A MESSERSCHMITT GUEST

Another German loss that night was an impromptu visitor to Switzerland: Messerschmitt *Bf. 110-G*, Werknummer 5547, coded 2Z+OP. Flown by *Oberfeldwebel* Helmut Treynogga, a thirty-year-old former baker from Königsberg, it had taken off from Base 701 at Echterdingen at 2105hr German time. His radar operator, Heinz Schwarz, also from Königsberg, had just acquired a contact when they were hit by a *Lancaster*'s alert gunner, who in the dark sky confused the shape of the prowler with the silhouette of a friendly fellow bomber. Treynogga could not even fire his two 20mm (.79in) cannon nor the four 7.8mm (.31in) machine guns. When the port engine died of fuel starvation due to the feed line being cut, the crew radioed base for a QDM bearing. RAF radio countermeasures rendered the answer incomprehensible, and soon the crew became lost.

Later, searchlights materialised so that the pilot believed he was over Germany but actually the lights belonged to the Frauenfeld flab battery. When the crew fired red flares to request directions, red perimeter lights were switched on further south. Those, Treynogga wrongly identified as belonging to Munich-Riem, Base 709 of the Luftwaffe. Soon he proceeded to a smooth landing on the snow-covered airfield which proved to be Dübendorf. Switzerland thus acquired a very good example of the mainstay of German night defences, and its air force lost no time in examining the hitherto unknown Telefunken radar, an *FuG. 202 Lichtenstein BC*. A still better specimen of a *Bf. 110* fighter was to arrive on 27/28 April, but that is another story.

Twice at the end of February and on the first night of March, Stuttgart had already suffered at the hands of Bomber Command. Twice, the cloud cover had scattered the attack. Tonight the town was once again hidden in cloud, although above, the night sky was clear: Stuttgart would again escape lightly. The weight of the raid fell 6 miles (10km) south-west of the city centre, in woods near Sindelfingen and its Mercedes factory. The 2,735 tons of bombs dropped resulted mainly in two large fires which, as their light reflected on the overcast, were seen from as far as Switzerland. Next day one could, for instance, read in *L'Impartial*, a local newspaper, about 'a raid of hitherto unknown might... that started an enormous conflagration'. Disappointed by the results, Bomber Command did not relent; before the end of the war in May 1945, six more major raids were launched against Stuttgart. Altogether, twelve such large attacks were aimed at that industrial town, showering it with 21,246 tons of bombs that destroyed 46 per cent of the buildings.[6]

SERIOUS LOSSES

This night, results or not, the RAF was again to pay a serious toll: forty-two bombers, almost 5 per cent of the force involved. No doubt the tally would have been even more tragic had it not been for several diversions which contributed to spread the German defences: 140 heavies attacked the marshalling yards at Amiens-Longeau. Twenty-two other specialists from 617 Squadron were sent for a precision attack on the Metz-Woippy aero-engine works, only to return with their bombs after finding the weather unsuitable for bombing near friendly civilian housing.

There were not many crews at this time to do ten ops before being lost. That Atcheson was an exception underlines the mixture of skill and luck he was endowed with. Many of the Stuttgart losses occurred in the target area, and at least sixteen *Lancasters* and *Halifaxes* also crashed on the long route across France. A total of 267 young airmen were lost outside Britain on the raid.[7] F/Sgt Victor Perry of 166 Squadron was more lucky. Stuttgart was his first raid and for his introduction to the perils of Europe, he was attacked seven times by an enemy fighter, which succeeded in killing his rear gunner, Sgt J.H. Riddle, and in wounding the mid-upper. But Perry's good fortune did not hold: eleven nights later, this writer was to witness his demise at Pry, Belgium, on his return from Essen. Another freak incident had, meanwhile, occurred over Stuttgart, when *Lancaster* F-Freddie from the same 166 Squadron and flown by S/Ldr Sewell, was 'bombed' with 'friendly' incendiaries from another aircraft and managed to return safely.

Apart from the occasional shudder generated by the slipstream of an aircraft ahead, nothing untoward happened aboard Atcheson's JB.474 over France – at least until navigator McCall reported they were nearing the German frontier. He had barely spoken when the *Lancaster* seemed to stop dead. Immediately, the petrol tanks exploded and the whole aircraft was aflame within seconds! Unseen by either gunner, a nightfighter must have sneaked under the undefended belly. Visibility in the moonlight was about 1,500ft (457m) but the foe remained unnoticed. He let loose a deadly salvo from its slanted *Schräge Musik* guns. Once more, as in so many cases at the time, the crew never knew what hit them. The adverse nightfighter tactics of slipping undetected under their prey had not yet been 'rediscovered' by the RAF (see Chapter 8). Sgt Reece, like most survivors who were victims of the same predicament, simply believed the aircraft had been hit by flak, albeit 'in a region where no flak concentration had been reported'!

VICTIM OF THE *SCHRÄGE MUSIK*?

The time must have been 2230hr Swiss time, one hour ahead of British time at that period. The position: just south-east of Belfort, where nightfighters gathered around another of their beacons, *Bella*. Fuelled by hundreds of gallons of petrol, oxygen tanks and incendiaries, the conflagration turned the *Lancaster* into a fiery meteor.

Startled, blinded by fire and smoke, Atcheson must have let the blazing machine bank right. By the time he could regain some sort of control, *JB.474* was heading south across the French–Swiss frontier above Lugnez. Here, bombs were jettisoned, the pilot probably applying the emergency procedure in case of fire: bomb doors open, jettison, dive. Four bombs exploded in the forest near Coeuve, breaking windows in the village, and in nearby Porrentruy; another, a dud, was left for the Swiss army to destroy later. The mean 4,000lb (1,816kg) *Cookie* impacted between Epiquerez and Essertfallon, digging a large crater and damaging a power line.[8] Two more missiles fell ten miles (16km) further south, across the river Doubs. In the river itself, some incendiaries burned in an eerie greenish glow. Above, parachute flares illuminated the snowy countryside. Further on fluttered some 200 incendiaries and small parts of the aircraft. The tally does not fit with the full load so part of it must have remained aboard to burn in the ensuing crash.

Mid-upper gunner Reece jumped just after the second attempt at jettison, near Montfaucon.[9] From the high perch of his turret overlooking the whole of the aircraft, he had seen the wings bursting into flames. When the pilot gave the order to abandon the *Lancaster*, he was ready to let himself fall in the fuselage and lost no time, groping in the smoke and flames for his parachute near the exit door. Drifting east in the moonlight, Reece landed unhurt on a hill covered in thick snow. He then elected to walk down into the valley to find a road. Instead, he stumbled upon a railroad track and promptly sought cover by slipping under a small wooden halt built on stilts off the ground. This was La Combe, halfway in the hills between Montfaucon and Lajoux. Believing he had landed in Germany, Reece hid there for hours. Cold, lonely and feeling unwelcome, the gunner vainly waited for a train to come along in which he could hide and be taken back to France.

STARTLING THE STATION MASTER

He had lost a flying boot on the way down and the biting cold convinced him to surrender to the halt master who now could be heard walking on the flooring above. Gunner and railroader were equally surprised by the meeting. The latter, by discovering the eerie figure on his doorstep: a pale, unshaven and amazingly clad RAF representative. The gunner, by learning that luck had made him land a mere 4km (2.5m.) inside the safety of Switzerland!

That same night, Reece was in Berne, the Swiss capital, beginning the now standard 'quarantine' at the Hôtel Gurten Kulm, already patronised by Alistair Smith's crew and others. It was here that one day Reece got the surprise of his life when the one boot he had lost in parachuting was returned to him full of carefully wrapped eggs!

Ken Reece had left the burning *Lancaster* at around 5,000ft (1,500m) just as it went completely out of control. By a grim quirk of fate, the aircraft was then overflying the mountain village of Les Enfers (The Hells), only 2,000ft (609m) below. Possibly at the same moment, another airman also exited the aircraft: his opened parachute was found on the ground, caught in the remains of the vertical stabiliser. This could well mean that the parachute belonged to the rear gunner Naylor, and was blown open when the aircraft exploded on the ground.

For Naylor, in any case, over were the long, lonely and sickening hours spent in the cramped confines of his rear turret, a device that reversed all natural physical reactions to motion. Indeed, for a rear gunner sitting backwards some 20m (65ft) away from the pilot, a dive of the aircraft meant he was facing up at the stars. In contrast, a climbing machine had him overlooking a void thousands of feet deep. And that said nothing of the constant weaving nor of the violent corkscrewing maoeuvres – the safety banking search for enemy fighters – when the turret practically laid sideways.

Half a minute and 6km (3.7m.) after Reece had jumped, the machine plunged into snow-covered pastures. The *Lanc* hit and exploded in an inverted position, burying itself 3m (10ft) deep in snow and soft ground. Large panels of the starboard wing were thrown clear, the outboard section coming to rest upright to show the red and blue RAF roundel. A rudder flew away, also ending upside down, ramming vertically into the snow as a forlorn signpost to the scene of desolation.

SIX CASUALTIES

The remainder of the aircraft, apart from the elevators and the rear fuselage aft of the mid-upper turret, was reduced to scrap to be either buried or thrown in a forward arc 100 yards wide. Amongst debris and the pathetic remains of the crew, the local residents discovered personal letters and photographs, an unopened parachute pack and a shredded tunic dangling in the shrubs, complete with the decorations of its unfortunate owner. Those sad mementoes of a once eager crew were handed over to the Swiss military.

Edi Gyger was, however, one of the first people on the spot and was able to retrieve a few small items. These included a crash axe and the remains of an escape pouch with a silken map which to this day graces a wall in this writer's workplace, a poignant reminder of what it cost to fly for freedom.[10]

The rear turret was yanked loose and rolled away, killing its occupant, the nineteen-year-old, ever smiling Sgt James Naylor from Bradford. Gendarmes Simon and Krummenacher, who gently laid him in the snow, found him in possession of an escape kit complete with French, Dutch and Belgian money and, amongst other odds and ends, a pair of trouser clips, indicating the young man rode a bicycle at base.

The terrific impact and the subsequent fire could not be survived. So, near Saignelégier[11] and close to the Chaumont farms, ended the young lives of Sam Atcheson and four of his comrades in arms. The charred bodies were painfully identified by Dr Baumeler, summoned from Noirmont. They were the remains of: F/Sgt Jack Greenhalgh, aged thirty-one, the bomb-aimer from Oldham, Lancs; P/O Anthony McCall, aged twenty-eight, the navigator from Aberdeen; Sgt Brian Thomas, the flight engineer who hailed from Leigh-on-Sea and missed his twentieth birthday by five weeks; and Sgt Frank Weaver, the wireless operator from Leicester. Weaver and Greenhalgh had been identified by daybreak. The pilot, whose identification stemmed only from a name in a tattered leather helmet, was at first reported as being a Lt Atheotos.

SWISS PRECISION

True to their well-known precision, the Swiss determined the exact moment of the crash: 2242hr (CH) (2142hr GB time at that period), on 15 March 1944. On Tuesday 21 March the six airmen were buried at Vevey, by Lake Geneva, alongside comrades from earlier accidents. This time, however, the Swiss only organised a private ceremony as their neutrality compelled them to prevent throngs of sympathisers from turning the burials into a pro-British demonstration. The authorities remembered only too well how such a display in July 1943 had been frowned upon by Germany.

In attendance, together with the local officials led by the syndic (mayor) Mr Denereaz, was a delegation of Swiss airmen with the British Air Attaché, Air Commodore Freddie West, with the survivors in Smith's crew as guards of honour in RAF uniform. Vevey's Anglican minister, Walter Legg,[12] also attended, as well as Polish and American internees and officials. Last but not least was Reece, the sad but very lucky survivor. Today, his six comrades rest together in Vevey cemetery. There, as in the dozens of British Commonwealth and Empire final resting places dotting Europe, one can meditate on the terrible waste of life brought about by international rivalries. One will ponder also over the sibylline message adorning the pilot's gravestone: 'Peace Perfect Place'.

Kenneth Reece was of course interned and spent his months of leisurely custody in several hotels in Berne, Adelboden and Lausanne. Here, at the quaint little Hôtel Le Chalet, he eventually met a W/Cdr Jones, who suggested he leave Switzerland to meet the advancing US Army in France. This he soon did, recrossing the border to the Pays de Gex, north of Geneva. He returned to England on 5 November 1944. Soon after that, a happy Reece was visiting his favorite pub in Bridgnorth, when he bumped into the same W/Cdr Jones[13] who had so thoughtfully counselled him in Switzerland, where he was the Assistant British Air Attaché! A last and grim coincidence relates to Ken Reece: he died in March 1994 and his funeral took place on the 16th, the fiftieth anniversary of the death of his crew.

10

Glide to Golaten

AIRMEN AND AIRCRAFT:
Pilot: F/Lt Walter Blott
Flight Engineer : Sgt G. Mattock
Navigator: F/O Cedric Nabarro
Bomb Aimer: W/O John Millard
Wireless Operator: Sgt Gordon Gill
Mid-upper Gunner: Sgt William Forster
Rear Gunner: Sgt Denis Murphy
Lancaster Mk.I, W.4355, code LS°A, XV Squadron

*One hour after Sam Atcheson's doom as related in the preceding chapter, another of his col-
leagues arrived in Switzerland, practically over the same route he had followed. Fortunately,
contrary to the tragic fate of the Atcheson's crew, F/Lt Walter Blott's did survive the ordeal.*

A twenty-three-year-old former insurance clerk from Bedford, Blott had joined
the RAF in June 1939. After initial training he went through 82.OTU at
Ossington and then converted to four-engined *Stirling* bombers at 1651.HCU,
Waterbeach. OTUs (Operational Training Units) prepared pilots, navigators,
air bombers, radio operators and gunners to work together as a crew. All were
already proficient in their respective trades. All would furthermore benefit from
the experiences of tour-expired 'old-timers' acting as OTU instructors. The next
step prior to being posted to an operational Squadron were the HCUs (Heavy
Conversion Units), where pilots and crews got acquainted with four-engined
bombers.

EARLY AND UNCLEAR CAREER
Blott's career remains unclear up to the first day of 1944 when he was posted
to 15 Squadron with his navigator, both arriving as Flying Officers from 3.LFS,

the Feltwell *Lancaster* Finishing School. Since the Squadron had been operating *Stirlings* until December 1943, it could very well be that Blott did fly them on operations, or as an instructor before converting to *Lancasters*, or that he had been assigned to other duties or units.

It seems that his bomb-aimer, twenty-two-year-old Warrant Officer John Millard, was new to the rest of the crew, perhaps a replacement, as neither Blott nor his navigator F/O Cedric Nabarro could remember his name at the post-crash interrogation. One can surmise that Millard had been summoned at the last moment to fill in for Blott's sick regular bomb-aimer. In any case, one can expect that the crew looked upon Millard with a jaundiced eye: it was indeed dogma that a fine way to 'get the chop', i.e. being shot down, was to have a 'spare bod' aboard. As for the wireless operator, Sgt Gordon Gill, he had, like his pilot, been a clerk in Bedford before joining up in 1941; both had followed the same service progress. Gill was now on his second war sortie, like all the others. That is except for their pilot who had been out on an initiation sortie before them. As for Millard, with twelve operations behind him, he was by far the most experienced of all aboard.

Blott had been promoted to F/Lt on 19 January 1944. His initiation trip had been on the night of 24/25 February 1944, as second pilot to P/O Amies. They flew to Schweinfurt in *Lancaster* LS°G, serial R.5904, an old machine that was to attain the then considerable flying age of 504 hours before being downed on 21 July in Holland.[1] The following night, Blott aborted his sortie to Augsburg owing to a port inner engine failure in *Lancaster* ED.473. This occurrence, one of many similar incidents at that period, could reflect either poor maintenance or the age of the machines allotted to 15 Squadron. Likewise, to the chagrin of the historian, the Squadron's Operations Record Book was at the time far from being a model of perfection, lacking data such as bombing times and loads carried.

STUTTGART IN BAD WEATHER

On the night of 1/2 March, the Squadron dispatched to Stuttgart 17 of the 557 aircraft sent out for more than eight hours flying in atrocious weather. F/Lt Blott was first off and he safely brought back *Lancaster* W.4355 LS°A. This was the same machine he was to use against the same target a fortnight later, to unwillingly dump it in Switzerland.

On this night, 15/16 March 1944, Blott had lifted off from Mildenhall, Suffolk, at 1915hr in the gloom of an early darkness that was quick to swallow the field's Drem lights. His brief: again attack Stuttgart, in the second wave of bombers hitting the town. Old LS°A for 'un-Able' was, to paraphrase the crew, an 'absolutely worn out machine', a Mark I that had seen service with 97 Squadron and 1661.Heavy Conversion Unit prior to being allotted to 15 Squadron: altogether it had spent the highly respectable total of 795 hours in the air.[2] In its chequered career the aircraft had logged at least thirty-nine sorties, as witnessed by the rows of bars painted in a quite unusual spot – on the rear fuselage, near the crew entrance door.

The weary *Lanc* had crossed the enemy coast at its cruising altitude of 20,000ft (6,100m). At the controls, besides having to cope with the tension of night-flying into hostile skies, Blott was wondering what the weather conditions would be upon returning. He was still smarting from the weather experience he had faced upon coming back from the earlier Stuttgart raid. Indeed, at this time of the year it was not uncommon for early morning fog to rise, obscuring the East Anglian airfields. Finding an aerodrome and attempting a landing in fog or in clouds with bases on the deck then became as dangerous an operation as fighting the enemy; numerous 'cold losses' thus occurred in Britain[3] involving returning aircrews, sometimes flying in damaged machines but always exhausted by operational demands.

DISASTER NEAR VESOUL

Blott's *Lancaster* had been plodding along for two hours when disaster struck. Navigator Nabarro had just reported their position as being near the three white ground markers dropped by the Pathfinders to indicate the turning point east[4] – close to Vesoul, France. At briefing the crews had been instructed not to overshoot the spot in order to cross the Rhine and into Germany between Strasbourg and Basle, thus avoiding Switzerland.

As had been the case a few minutes earlier for Atcheson and his comrades, the attack came without any warning, also after crossing the Rhine north of Basle. At the last moment, the engineer standing watch in the astrodome – Sgt G. Mattock, a twenty-two-year-old married former welder from Winchester – saw the single-engined Messerschmitt *Bf. 109*. The fighter had slipped from behind and below, unnoticed by the rear gunner Sgt Murphy, and was sweeping up in a left turn.

Cannon-fire from the *109* holed the port-wing tank, disabled the left inner *Merlin* engine, made the intercom unserviceable and the blind-flying panel useless. Glass shards, oil, smoke and petrol burst into the cockpit. Walter Blott felt a severe blow on his left elbow: a metal fragment had hit him, rendering the arm useless. At the same time, the aircraft began shaking with terrific vibration and started to fly sluggishly with the port-wing low. Owing to the thick smoke, Blott was unable to see the instrument panel, which was smashed anyway. Blott thought he had got the chop.

Then, adding to the confusion, the call-light appeared on the emergency intercom. In 'normal' conditions this is a signal from the rear turret to start an evasive manoeuvre. Instantly, Blott threw his heavy *Lanc* into a corkscrew dive: control wheel fully banked, full bottom rudder same side-killing lift. The aircraft fell like a brick and nearly stalled. Shocked as he was by the spectre of brutal extinction, Blott nevertheless managed to right the machine, losing some 7,000ft (2,100m) in the process.

TOWARDS SWITZERLAND

The incendiary load was jettisoned and he instructed his crew to stand by to bail out, endeavouring at the same time to turn the machine towards Switzerland. Within minutes, they could see the lights of a Swiss town. By then they had unknowingly cleared the high, bald Chaseral mountain poised to snare them with its 1,607m (5,300ft) height. When he felt on the verge of losing control, Blott gave the 'abandon ship' order. The two gunners in the rear acknowledged the injunction, the mid-upper man beating everyone in jettisoning the back door, to be followed by the wireless operator and his mate from the tail. Up front, the bomb aimer, navigator and engineer preceded their pilot into the void.

In the faint, nocturnal light, the northernmost parachute came down near the Métairie de Prêles, east of Lignières, in the snowy Jura mountains north of Neuchâtel. Below the white life-saving canopy was Sgt William Forster, the mid-upper gunner who, prior to enlistment in March 1942, had been a clerk in Hexham, Northumberland. He landed about 12 miles (19km) away from the German-held French border, beyond which he would probably have become a Prisoner of War for the duration. Where he landed was also at an equal distance south of where Atcheson had lost his life forty-eight minutes earlier. Forster did not notice the smoldering wreckage.

The gently descending *Lancaster* spilled its crew on a straight south-easterly line towards the small Lake Biel which sat much lower down in the plain. Prior to reaching it, two more men bailed out in the frozen hills: Mattock and Millard. The local guard at Lamboing promptly arrested Mattock. As for Millard, who as a newcomer had been true to form in bringing bad luck to his mates, he was suffering from a serious perforation of the lung: he was rushed to Cadolles hospital in Neuchâtel.

The disabled machine then left the mountainous area, passing near where, on 1 June 1940, Swiss *Me.109*s had shot down a German Heinkel *He.111* near Lignières. Another wounded man was the rear gunner Denis Murphy. By chance, he had been slow at jumping, remaining poised at the rear door, thus allowing the aircraft to clear Lake Biel where he could have drowned or died of exposure. As it was, he landed south of the lake, on the verge of the Grosses Moos plain. When found, he was sent to Aarberg hospital by the Swiss local guard who reported him as only eighteen years of age. Gordon Gill landed unhurt in the same neighbourhood, on soft ground. He had jumped a second before Nabarro, who broke a leg upon meeting the rich earth of Kallnach. He, too, went to Aarberg.

IN THE GARDEN OF SWITZERLAND

The last man out and the fourth airman wounded was pilot Walter Blott. He had put the *Lancaster* on autopilot, extricated himself from the web of restraining intercom connection and oxygen hose, slipped in the nose as per drill and left the orbiting machine quite low over the woods of Kallnach. From where he landed, he could observe the glow of his burning aircraft.

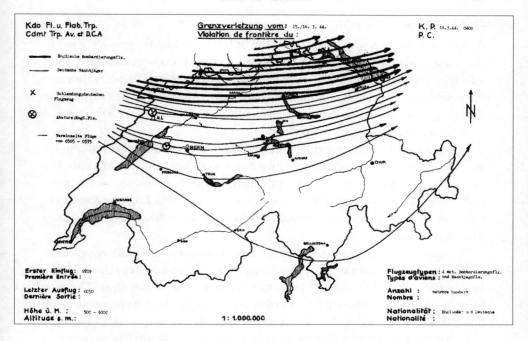

Kdo Fl. u. Flab. Trp.
Cdmt Trp. Av. et D.C.A

Grenzverletzung vom: 15./16. 3. 44.
Violation de frontière du :

K. P. 16.3.44. 0400
P. C.

Englische Bombardierungsflz.

Deutsche Nachtjäger

X Notlandung;deutsches
   Flugzeug

⊗ Absturz:Engl.Flz.

Vereinzelte Flüge
von 0505 - 0535

Erster Einflug: 2219
Première Entrée :

Letzter Ausflug: 0050
Dernière Sortie :

Höhe ü. M. : 500 - 6000
Altitude s. m.:

1 : 1.000.000

Flugzeugtypen : 4 mot. Bombardierungsflz.
Types d'avions : und Nachtjagdflz.

Anzahl : mehrere hundert
Nombre :

Nationalität : Englische und Deutsche
Nationalité :

Swiss Air Force plot of multiple penetrations over Helvetic territory on 15/15 March 1944, between 2219hr and 0050hr (CH). The overwhelming majority was attributed to British bombers, but some German nightfighters also joined the proceedings, one of them – Obfw Treynogga's Bf.110-G of 6/NJG.6 – landed at Dübendorf at 2347hr Note the stray aircraft way down in the Alps. (Dübendorf archives)

Circling lower over the flat, vegetable-growing Seeland region, the *Lancaster* had attracted a lot of attention in the 'garden of Switzerland'. In Kallnach, a gathering of Swiss soldiers at the Sonne restaurant quickly concluded that the unknown aircraft was trying to land. To them, the only possibility seemed to be the arrow-straight road in the level 'Moos' land between Sisselen and Aarberg. Led by *Panzerkanonier* Ernst Beletti, they had started to proceed there when they heard the crash, south of them across the woods. The abandoned *Lanc* had maintained its gentle descent. East of Golaten hamlet, it clipped a row of tall trees and dipped towards the village.

A large farmhouse sat in its path. Herr Siegenthaler, the owner, was out, and alone in the premises were Alice Remund, her sister and her mother. They had heard 'three waves of bombers high in the night sky' before a lone machine came orbiting, noisy and rough. Then tearing noises followed by a formidable rending shattered the night, quickly followed by the acrid smell of burned rubber and metal, carried by the northerly wind. The aircraft had skimmed the ground just sixty yards short of the farm, cutting a larger and larger swath in the soil. The blind monster had ploughed its way to just outside the outer building, scattering debris over 200 yards before being stopped by a cluster of pear trees. It exploded forthwith. That night at 2330hr Swiss time, luck had indeed been with the Remund family!

FORSTER MISSES FORSTER

A mile away, burly young Emil Rieser was at home cutting firewood. He ran to the scene, dodging exploding ammunition, picking up maps and sundry papers which he later had to surrender to the official *Territorial Kommando 2*. Another of the neighbours converging on the Remund's backyard was Robert Forster who, examining the smashed rear fuselage, never imagined that its former tenant had been his namesake, William Forster!

At the wreck Emil Rieser met young, good-looking Alice, who was also his age. She had barely escaped becoming the first Swiss victim of an RAF crash. The averted disaster was to prove useful to them: Alice and Emil were to marry at the end of the war, the second Swiss couple to meet because of a *Lancaster*. They went on to successfully run the farm where W.4355 once laid in fiery fragments amidst a burning orchard.

The spot was soon cordoned off by the local *Ortswehr* soldiers following orders issued by the chief of *Armee Flugpark*, Oberst Karl Högger, soon after the Bouveret crash when a complete *Merlin* engine had disappeared from the scene. The men were quick to report the aircraft's correct serial number and, surprisingly, a still unexplained figure '51' on the other side of the fuselage.

Its skipper, F/Lt Blott, had been serenely descending in his parachute, believing he was still some 4,000ft (1,200m) high. Actually the ground was 560m (1,800ft) above sea level at that spot, and *terra firma* was rushing up in the dark. Blott landed heavily on his back, adding another injury to his numb left arm. He found a hut in the woods and rested outside for half an hour, wrapped in his parachute and using his Mae-West as a pillow. He did not know that local guards were then searching the region for 'two or three men' falsely reported as fleeing from the wreck. Blott then walked down a path, came to a road and in the prevalent darkness was startled by a clock striking the hour. Turning back, he knocked at the door of the first isolated house he came upon. An old woman appeared, and Blott inquired in bad French about her nationality.

HURRY UP TO THE PUB

After introducing themselves to each other, she fetched a farm worker who lost no time in taking the pilot by the hand, and rushing him along the road to the village pub. This was the Sonne, where Beletti and his partners had the surprise of their life to see the tall, limping airman appearing in the doorway.

Blott, whose back was by now in considerable pain, was given a bed. Next morning, 16 March, he met Swiss military policemen who were taking Murphy and Nabarro to hospital. Later in the day, they brought Gordon Gill who, after burying his 'chute and Mae-West in snow, had proceeded south. By 0700hr, Gill had reached Sisselen, unaware that he was in Switzerland. He was soon arrested while walking through the village, and was brought to the Sonne to meet his pilot.

The two men were taken to Aarberg hospital, which Gill left almost immediately, to go to Bienne. After a cursory interrogation he met Forster and Mattock at the station, and the trio proceeded to Berne. Here, after a well-earned night's rest in a hotel, they were interrogated by a Swisss Air Force officer who could have been either Lt Rolf Lécher or Chase Achard. The Swiss were keen to learn about navigational matters and radio equipment: today, it is most surprising to find in their records an amount of information departing widely from the mere 'name-rank-serial number' aircrew were supposed to proffer to foreign parties!

In Aarberg hospital, the wounded airmen were visited by the assistant Air Attaché, W/Cdr R.D. Jones. He was instrumental in having forwarded to England – via cipher or diplomatic pouch – the information that all the crew were safe in Switzerland: by 27 March the families could be notified. The most seriously hurt remained in the Aarberg hospital, but Blott soon moved to Berne. By the end of March he was at the Gürten-Kulm Hotel where he met Bish Smith, his fellow pilot from 100 Squadron, and several American airmen. He was eventually rejoined by Forster, Gill, Mattock and Ken Reece, the lone survivor from the Atcheson crew. In mid-April, the stranded Britons were displaced to the large Adelboden internment area, where about 600 Army personnel[5] and 500 Americans whiled away their time. Being the only RAF members there, they lived with American aircrew whose contingent was steadily increasing. On 16 March, for instance, the day after Blott's arrival, it had been augmented by forty-nine US airmen survivors from seven four-engined daylight bombers.

GOING HOME!

On 6 May, Blott and his wireless operator, Gill, were released to Berne, given a passport, civilian clothes and the extraordinary news that they were soon to be repatriated! In a wartime Switzerland replete with refugees of all conditions stretching the available food, the country was not averse to getting rid of its uninvited guests.[6] Accordingly, as seen in previous Chapters, specialist aircrew were exchanged against an equal number of Luftwaffe Angehörigen.

Blott and Gill's journey to Spain via Paris took place with George Smith and others (see Chapters 8 and 19). By the end of May, they were safe and sound in England. It took a while longer for their fellow crewmembers, who had to wait for the tide of Allied armies to reach the Swiss borders. The wounded Murphy and Nabarro were repatriated in early October 1944; Mattock, a month later. Forster returned on Christmas Eve and Millard, on the last day of the year.

11

Good Friday
Watery Crash

AIRMEN AND AIRCRAFT:
Pilot: S/Ldr Michael Negus
Navigator: F/O Arthur Gapper
Mosquito VI, NS.875, code UP°R, 605 Squadron

*The most mysterious of all the RAF arrivals in Switzerland was to be a machine of the
same type as the 'Berne* Mosquito' *which had been the first Royal Air Force aircraft to
land there as seen in 'Pioneer* Mosquito'. *Now at eight minutes past midnight on the
night of 6/7 April 1944, the Swiss corps of border surveillance reported 'loud engine noises'
over Lake Constance, north of Romanshorn.*

Three minutes later, the sound ceased abruptly. Silence reigned once more over
the vast expanses of water separating northern Switzerland from Germany. The
lake, 40 miles long and about eight miles wide (65km by 12km), made an excellent navigational checkpoint in clear weather.

FLAK NEAR THE LAKE
The landmark had a serious drawback: its northern shore was strongly defended
by the German 26th Flak Division. Guns, mostly of 88mm calibre, were laid thick
to protect the sensitive industrial area round Friedrichshafen – F'hafen for short
– the 'Zeppelin City' active in producing submarine, tank and radar parts (see the
Chapter 12).

The night of 6/7 April was cloudless, with visibility reported as good at ground
level under a full moon; it is probable that the lake fulfilled its role in easing
navigation for a number of night-flyers. Several unknown machines were indeed
reported by Swiss observers near Romanshorn. At least one crossed their shore
over Altnau one minute after midnight, Swiss time. Sweeping left at around

3,000m (10,000ft), it departed neutral territory seven minutes and 18km (11mi.) later, to the south-east, over Arbon.

Combat activity of an unspecified nature was also reported round F'hafen just before an aircraft crashed into the lake at 0012hr, about 4km (2.5m.) off Uttwil, a fishing village between Altnau and Romanshorn. There had been no Bomber Command sortie over Southern Germany on this night preceding Good Friday 1944.[1] Fighter Command, however, was mounting several intruder flights over the Continent.

NUISANCE OPS

Intruders were a rewarding and inexpensive, albeit dangerous, RAF activity, which sought targets of opportunity on enemy aerodromes, canals, railways and roads, and made a general nuisance of themselves to Germans and Italians alike. 'Six-O-five' was one of the units intruding in darkness over Germany. The Squadron flew out of the 'splendid isolation' of Bradwell Bay near Clacton-on-Sea but was scheduled to move on the morrow, Good Friday, to Manston, south of the Thames at the very eastern tip of England. There would also be a change of Commanding Officer: one-eyed ace W/Cdr Bertie Hoare, DSO, DFC and bar, and possessor of a huge RAF 'handle-bar' moustache, was to be posted to 100 Group three days later.[2] He would relinquish command to W/Cdr Norman Starr, DFC, an intruder pilot just back from Malta. Starr would eventually take over 142 Wing in Belgium and 'rest' with No.276 Air-Sea Rescue Squadron before being killed on 8 January 1945, in particularly distressing circumstances. The mishap was to happen over Dunkirk when the *Anson* he flew to his wedding would be shot down by defenders of the German pocket remaining within liberated territory.

At Bradwell Bay, 605 Squadron flew *Mosquitoes* but a few Douglas *Havoc* were still on strength, two of which would be lost this April, as well as two *Mossies*. Tonight 605 Squadron was sending out three sorties. Two were deemed 'training' runs to France: one went to Coulommiers and the other to Châteaudun and Rennes.

The third was to patrol the area between Strasbourg and Lake Constance, with particular attention paid to Baltringen airfield further east.[3] The aircraft involved was a *Mosquito VI* coded UP°R, serial NS.875, up at 2247hr (GB). A fighter-bomber, 'R-Robert' carried four 20mm cannon and as many 0.303in machine-guns in the nose. Although it was capable of taking along four 250lb (113kg) bombs in belly and underwing positions, these were, tonight, replaced by long-range tanks. The machine was the third 'R-Robert' owned by 605 Squadron; it had been on strength since 1 March, having rolled out of de Havilland's Hatfield factory on 20 February. The first 'R' aircraft had been HJ.790, lost on 22/23 September 1943 in a sortie against Ardorf airfield; the second, HX.968, had gone missing on 21/22 February, when F/Lt Richard Pickering, with F/O Ernest Edwards, did not return from a Dinard-Avranches patrol.[4]

LONG-RANGE FLOWERS

Flying the new UP°R was S/Ldr Michael Negus.[5] By now a most experienced pilot, Negus, whose home was in Dunmow, Essex, had joined the RAF on 7 March 1940 and soon been granted a Pilot Officer's permanent commission as 'acting pilot on probation'. Each subsequent anniversary had seen him promoted until he had reached his present rank on 7 March 1943. By then he had joined 605 Squadron where he had been appointed Flight Commander as an acting Squadron Leader on 17 February. Negus had been awarded the coveted DFC barely one day before his demise, on 5 April; this was in recognition of his three certain, and two probable, air victories in a difficult night environment.

His navigator, with whom he had flown most of his previous sorties, was F/O Arthur Gapper, who was twenty-eight years of age, from Mitcham, Surrey. He had been granted a commission as P/O on probation when coming out of training on 19 February 1943, and promoted to Flying Officer (War Substantive) after six months.

Many of Negus's sorties had been long-range ones. In the first two months of 1944, he and Gapper had been on twelve missions. In March, Negus had flown five more, all of them with *Mosquito* UP°R: *Flowers* to Laon, France, to Gilze-Rijen in Holland and towards Schleissheim in Bavaria. His previous raid had again been to Southern Germany: on 30/31 March 1944, to Crailsheim and Ansbach in support of Bomber Command's ill-fated raid against Nuremberg.[6] Negus had not flown operationally since.

FOREVER A MYSTERY

What happened to Negus and Gapper on the night of 6/7 April 1944 shall forever remain a mystery. At 0012hr (CH), their aircraft disintegrated upon striking Lake Constance, practically at the spot where Swiss Lt G. Suter had stalled his Me-109 fighter on 7 June 1939.

At first light on Friday 7 April 1944, fisherman Imhof from Romanshorn and his motorboat *Hecht*, helped the Maritime Inspection to locate and take aboard the few sparse items floating on a 4km (2.5mi.) stretch off Uttwil.[7] Some of the debris bore traces of human remains, indicating that at least one airman had perished. The material brought ashore included a wheel with its oleo leg, two oxygen bottles, a rubber fuel tank, the wooden entrance door and a piece of rudder showing the RAF fin flash. Also afloat were parts of a wooden wing and a piece of rear fuselage on which, stencilled red on a medium sea-grey background, could be seen the figure '75' which was part of the serial, as well as a shattered letter 'U'. The flotsam was all that was left of the new *Mosquito* and its crew.

None of the debris recovered bore any trace of shell strikes but one can nevertheless put forward some speculation as to what brought about the aircraft's demise. Negus' ultimate target had been Baltringen airfield in the Dürnach marshes, south of Ulm and 47 miles (75km) north-east of Uttwil where the crash occurred. One might surmise that the *Mosquito* reached the target area, finding no suitable prey. The crew could then have decided to fly further south, hoping for better luck near Ravensburg and Lake Constance. They would then have been shot up by a nightfighter or been hit by flak, then electing to try and reach Switzerland in order to land or bail out without fear of becoming Prisoners of War. They would eventually have recognised Lake Constance, and crossed into Swiss airspace near Altnau, scrutinising the moonlit silver ground for a suitable place to crash-land, unless they were considering ditching close to the shore.

SPECULATIONS

Circling left, passing over or near Amriswil, they would have re-crossed the shore, outbound near Arbon, still in their left turn and descending fast with Gapper calling out the height to his pilot. Such a description fits in well with reports from the Swiss Observer Corps. Then the aircraft would perhaps have become unmanageable, possibly owing to structural damage or simply because it reached stalling speed.[8] With a crash foreseeable, did the crew try to bail out? The entrance door was found separated from other pieces of wreckage; this could perhaps indicate that it had been jettisoned or at least that it was being opened by Gapper, who sat close to it in the cramped cockpit.

Another possibility could be an accidental crash owing, for instance, to a faulty altimeter setting. Here it should be remembered that the only reliable settings available were those obtained some two hours earlier at the far away UK bases, deriving from observations made even much earlier over the Atlantic. True, they could, at best, stem from data obtained either over the Continent by the weather spies of 1409 Meteorological Flight, provided such a recce had been scheduled, or from ground measurements forwarded by the *Beagle* resistance ring in Belgium.[9]

It is doubtful, however, that data from the latter could be of immediate use in view of the delay between observations and transmission in the field, reception and processing in England, and forwarding to operational units. It could thus well be that an inadequate altimeter setting would have given the pilot a false sense of security while descending in the dark towards the glassy grey surface of water. Here, in passing, it is of interest to point out another trap for the unwary: the lake surface does not show the usual white foam cresting the wave tops that crews were used to seeing at night on each and every crossing of the often choppy sea.

WATERY GRAVES

A third possible circumstance is much simpler to explain. The night of 6/7 April was cloudless near the lake and visibility termed good but, even so, judging one's height over calm waters is difficult in daylight and even more at night. The pilot, hard-pressed as he perhaps was by difficulties in controlling his machine, could easily have been lured into believing that he was higher than he actually was over the featureless water surface.

Finally, one can also consider the turn over Switzerland and the lake, as a 180° manoeuvre intended to return against a target, aircraft or train, spotted when overflying the north shore. Descending to attack at low level he then would have hit the water for one reason or another. The assumptions are many and those listed above are not exhaustive.

In any case, the sudden impact must have come as a thunderbolt in a blue sky. Abruptly the rending crush of wood must have mixed with the gurgle of inrushing water, drowning the engines as deceleration suddenly put an end to lives and *Mossie* alike… Negus and his friend Gapper had found a watery grave, some 655ft (200m) deep, virtually on the Swiss–German border line.

Their remains would not be alone too long as Lake Constance seemed to magnetise many aircraft into oblivion! On 18 June 1957, Swissair's *DC-3* HB-IRK was lost in the lake with nine lives. On 11 January 1989 a Swiss Bölkow *117.A3* helicopter came down at almost exactly where Negus' *Mosquito* ended, also killing its two crewmen. It was soon followed, on 23 February, by another twin-engined aeroplane, an Austrian Gulfstream *690D Commander*, which came down in fog 1,000 yards (1km) off nearby Rorschach, killing its eleven occupants. Two earlier accidents had been less tragic. The first happened on 17 July 1982, when a hot-air balloon, appropriately coded HB-BAD, dunked across the lake near F'hafen; the four aeronauts were rescued. The second was on 30 May 1987 when a single-engined Rockwell *112B* was lost, nearby again, whilst taking off from Altenhein; within a minute, the four aboard had been safely fished out. And closing the litany relating to 'Bad Luck Bodan'[10] there was, on 24 January 1994, the loss of five people and a dog in a twin Cessna that came down, again off Rorschach but in German waters.

12

Alpine Adversity

AIRMEN AND AIRCRAFT:
Pilot: W/O Bertram Noble
Flight Engineer: Sgt Ronald Bridges
Navigator: F/O John Burton
Bomb Aimer: F/O Hubert Prowse
Wireless Operator: Sgt William Anderson
Mid-upper Gunner: P/O Oscar Albrecht
Rear Gunner: Sgt Francis Bathmaker
Special Operator: Sgt Maurice Smith
Lancaster Mk.I, LL.750, code SR°P, 101 Squadron

The night of Thursday 27 April 1944 was to prove the most eventful as far as RAF air-crew arrivals in Switzerland were concerned. It also heralded a turning point in the delicate balance of forces between Switzerland and the German Luftwaffe. On that night, three Lancasters *ended up under Swiss jurisdiction, while the impromptu landing at Dübendorf airfield of the latest in German nightfighter technology was to stress relations between the neutral country and her ruthless northern neighbour almost to the breaking point.*

ZEPPELIN CITY

Tonight's target was Friedrichshafen (F'hafen). This small residential town with a population of 25,000 was part of Bomber Command's 'South-Eastern Complex' of targets.[1] After the decision taken earlier in the day by Bomber Command's Air Chief Marshal, Arthur Harris, and staff in their High Wycombe bunker, the town became the destination of 323 RAF bombers. The armada brought over the target 549 tons of high explosives and 480 tons of incendiaries. The attack was backed up by various diversions, including raids on the Montzen and Aulnoye marshalling yards, both in or near Belgium and adjoining the main force route.[2] On the previous afternoon, 27 April, Bert Noble's responsibilities had been to air-test his aircraft, to iron out some trouble with his crew's loading list and, just as important, to send a telegram to his son Raymond, whose eighth birthday it was. Little did he know that another telegram would soon follow with the terrible news that he had not returned from operations. For his brothers, however, this did not come as a surprise: they had visited him a short while before with their children, including Bernard,[3] who to this day remembers clearly that Bert was very pessimistic about his chances of completing his tour of thirty-three operations.

MULTIPLE INDUSTRIES

F'hafen was known to host aircraft, tank-engine, gearbox and radar war factories, namely *Dornier Werke*, the *Maybach Motorenbau*, the *Luftschiffbau Zeppelin* and the *Zahnradfabrik F'hafen AG*. Furthermore, it was supposed to be one of three cities (with Peenemünde and Wiener-Neustadt) where the final assembly of a new German weapon took place: the *Aggregat A-4* rocket – one of the *Vergeltungswaffen* later to be known as the *V-2*. In fact, production was by then phased out of the nearby village of Raderach and concentrated in one great underground factory at Nordhausen, deep in the Harz mountains of central Germany.

F'hafen's position, 500 miles (800km) from the UK bases on the northern (German) shore of Lake Constance, made it not only a distant target but also a touchy one in view of the proximity of the neutral Swiss shore. Only three days earlier, the US 8th Air Force had sent 243 *B-17 Flying Fortresses* to the same target, more precisely to Dornier facilities: GY-4758 in the suburb of Löwenthal, near the airfield, and GY-4755 in Manzell village on the western outskirts. This was a follow-up raid to previous missions on 16 and 18 March.

The RAF itself had once been involved with the town. On 20/21 June 1943, with 'Operation Bellicose', sixty of its *Lancasters* had performed a precision attack before proceeding unmolested to Africa in the first shuttle raid of the war.[4] That night, German flak firing at the *Lancasters* flying south across the lake, killed three people watching the fireworks from the Swiss shore. A freak event also occurred at Arbon (see preceding Chapter) when an unexploded 88mm dud went through the ceiling of a room where young Werner Hanselman slept. Unhurt, the boy did not even wake up!

On the night of 27/28 April 1944, the raid proved successful, even if a last-minute change of zero-hour did raise some questions amongst participants. The combination of accurate initial marking with an efficient 'Master of Ceremonies'[5] set the town ablaze within fifteen minutes. A total of 1,029 tons of bombs[6] devastated 67 per cent of the built-up area, killing 136 civilians.

MARÉCHAL PÉTAIN SUNK

More importantly, three Dornier factories, including the one at Allmansweiler, the Maybach tank engine plant, the Zeppelin hangar and the *Zahnradfabrik* supplying panzer gearboxes, were heavily damaged. Also reported was the loss of a large Latécoère *631* seaplane which, named *Maréchal Pétain* and a symbol of the pro-Nazi Vichy faction in France, was worth its demise. '*Pétain*' was sunk at the Seemoos Dornier seaplane station, together with its sister boat, an *SE-200* which had also been impressed into Luftwaffe service.[7]

Furthermore, unknown to analysts in the UK, the April raids had achieved results commensurate with the efforts: destroyed were all the production tools for the fast twin-engined Dornier *Do.335*, an unorthodox push-pull fighter. Accordingly, only a handful of the mysterious fighters were built, none ever becoming operational. After the war, a captured example demonstrated how deadly the machine could have been against Allied bombers. In that same period, German officials were also to report the loss of the gearbox factory as the most damaging attack on panzer production, although output was soon made good under the efficient leadership of armament minister Albert Speer.

VAST ARMADAS

At this stage of the war, bomber attacks were quite elaborate affairs, much different from the puny early raids. The nights – and days – of 1944 were dense with bombers and raiders intent on destroying German war industries and undermining the morale of their manpower. Hundreds of heavy aircraft roamed the skies of the Reich and of the occupied countries, flying complicated strategic operations that were the aims of finely-planned air battles. These were battles in which the loss of life often reached staggering proportions – in the air as on the ground. This 'Friedrichshafen night', for instance, cost the German population 136 killed and 375 injured, most of them in the 656 houses that were destroyed with 421 others damaged. That was the price to pay for annihilating their cities' significant war factories.

It had been feared by the RAF planners that losses could dramatically emulate those of the Nuremberg raid a month previously.[8] Similar were the clear weather, the full moon and the distance involved. As it was, the route planning had carefully avoided known flak regions and the fighters, mislaid by diversions and radio countermeasures, arrived late; they were only able to engage the force over the target and on the return leg. Even so, the RAF lost eighteen *Lancasters* and ninety-three young fliers were thus to rest forever in European earth, twenty-eight others escaping with their life to become either Prisoners of War (seventeen), evaders[9] or Swiss internees (nine). Losses over and near the target were serious, including no less than three bombers falling in Swiss territory, the first one being W/O Bertram Noble's 101 Squadron machine, downed at 0123hr (CH).

NUISANCE SQUADRON

As seen by the surviving airmen, the F'hafen raid certainly seemed successful: heard at de-briefing were laudatory comments such as 'good concentrated attack' and 'best illumination ever seen'. Some attackers, for instance USAAF 2.Lt S.Hausnik[10] who bombed forty-five seconds after 0200hr (GB), thought 'the main raid a bit scattered [and] no big fire seen'. This was a surprising statement in view of the inferno observed, albeit later, by many crews and ground witnesses in or near 'Zeppelin city'. It was generally acknowledged by the former that the change of zero-hour had been given too late for many aircraft to arrive on time over the target. Even if some airmen such as W/O Joseph Kemp, had avoided an early arrival by orbiting for seven minutes near Strasbourg, close to the adversary's Haguenau nightfighter field, of which more later.

The RAF's 101 Squadron had its quarters between Lincoln and Grimsby, at Ludford Magna, derisively known as Mudford Magma by the Base tenants and loathed by pilots because of its main runway prone to crosswind conditions. The unit had been operating *Lancasters* since October 1942. They were not just ordinary *Lancasters* since the unit was the only one in Bomber Command – outside the specialist 100 Group – to operate radio countermeasures to jam Luftwaffe controls. Most of its aircraft were by now equipped with *Airborne Cigar* (ABC) jamming apparatus designed to play havoc with German nightfighters' radio frequencies. ABC had begun its operational life on 7/8 October 1943, in a raid on Stuttgart when the Squadron used the secret device to identify enemy voice frequencies and disrupt the fighters' control. The system comprised three transmitters, each sending a jamming 'wig-wog' note now deemed more efficient than broadcasting engine noises as had been done since December 1942. Speaking of deceptions, it is of interest to note that, by coincidence, the Germans' first use of their *Düppel* radar-jamming foils comparable to the Allied *Window* strips, also occurred on that same October night, when the Luftwaffe bombed Norwich.

Aboard ABC-equipped aircraft were German-speaking crewmembers, trained to operate the device and also to confuse enemy flyers and controllers by jabbering at them.[11] Their knowledge of the enemy language furthermore provided valuable information on nightfighter control, supplementing what radio-intercepts at Kingsdown in Kent provided to British intelligence.[12]

ALP GRAPPELEN

'One-0-One' Squadron was, on this night, to provide seventeen *Lancasters* to Bomber Command's main effort. Two of them would fail to return. One, that of F/Lt B. Dickenson, was to crash in Germany; the other, W/O Bertram Noble's, was destined to wreck itself in eastern Switzerland, 5,250ft (1,600m) above sea level, on the slopes of Alp Grappelen, below the Windenpass and north of Walenstadt.

Warrant Officer Noble had been born in Salisbury in 1912; his wife Dorothy lived at Awbridge, Hampshire. As a young man, he had entered the Service by joining the Halton Training School for Engineering Apprentices, and later volunteered for flying duties. His flying career began with an Air Observer's course in

November 1936. He thus flew on Hawker *Hinds* until May 1938, when he was accepted for pilot training. The RAF was then in full expansion in view of the prospects of war becoming more and more ineluctable.

Bert Noble gained his pilot's brevet in March 1939. He had by then flown 147 hours and the endorsement in his logbook graded him as an 'Average Pilot'. After a stint on the Flying Instructors' course, he became a staff pilot training observers. In June 1939, he started ferrying aircraft. This assignment lasted a year, during which he flew passengers and new aircraft to various locations in the UK and France, where the RAF's Advanced Air Striking Force and the British Expeditionary Forces' Air Component were poised to engage the Luftwaffe.

AFRICAN JAUNT

September 1940 found F/Sgt Noble among the twenty-five pilots ferrying new aircraft to Egypt from Takoradi in West Africa.[13] The long, mostly featureless route, was most exacting for pilots and machines alike. During this period, Noble had his first accident: ferrying a twin-engined *Blenheim* bomber, he encountered a tropical storm over Lagos and crashed upon trying to land. He fortunately came out unhurt. Bert Noble was promoted to Warrant Officer in March 1942, and had his flying range extended to India. Still under Middle East Command, he was, in June 1942, 'Mentioned in Despatches'. He would actually be 'Mentioned' a second time but this was seemingly an administrative error when his name was confused with that of a Sgt Noble.[14]

When Bertram Noble returned to England in early 1943, he had not flown since October 1942, having suffered from a severe bout of malaria contracted in West Africa. Fit for flying again and with his large experience of 1,335 flight hours,[15] he was assigned to Bomber Command. After converting on *Wellingtons* at No.18 OTU, Finningley, in the summer of 1943, he briefly became a test pilot on type at Helmswell. January 1944 saw him flying the four-engined *Halifaxes* belonging to No.1667. Heavy Conversion Unit.[16] This was when he picked up his crew; he remained there to go through the mill of a *Lancaster* Finishing School where, like many others, he felt the unfortunate omen hidden in the word 'finishing'! In any case, Bert came through the course, assessed as an 'Above Average' bomber pilot.

On 21 March 1944 Bert had been posted with his crew to 101 Squadron in the 'Real Air Force'. Here, his mid-upper gunner was soon replaced. At the same time he acquired an eighth man: an extra 'Wireless Operator, Special Duties', nineteen-year-old Sgt Maurice Smith. There remains a slight uncertainty about the identity of the Special Operator who could have been either Smith or Albrecht. Whoever he was, he must have trained not only at No.4 Radio School, Madley, but also at Fakenham to complete his trade, mastering the devilish T.1154 nuisance transmitter. If Smith was the extra operator trained for radio counter-measures and harassing German air controllers in their own language, one could

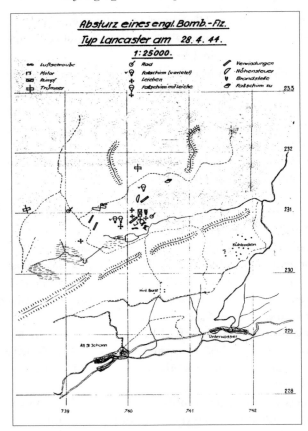

A Swiss Army drawing showing the location of the remains of Bertram Noble's Lancaster LL.750 (SR°P) on the snowy slopes of Alp Grappelen, south of Appenzell in eastern Switzerland. The twelve items listed at the top read: airscrew, motor, fuselage, wreckage, wheel, wounded in parachute, bodies, killed in parachute, ailerons, elevator, fire, unopened parachute. (Berne archives)

surmise that his quite common surname hid another of German origin which would have proved embarrassing in case of capture.[17]

At this stage, anyway, Noble was an experienced airman: his logbook bore witness of 285 hours spent in the air as an Observer, plus 1,550 more as a pilot. With all that experience, Noble still had to fly his first sortie in Bomber Command's time-honoured capacity of second pilot. This was on 9 April to the Villeneuve-St.Georges marshalling yards in France. His second sortie, the first as captain of his own crew, came the night after when he raided Aulnoye, again in the framework of the Transportation Plan devised to weaken Germany's capacity to oppose the forthcoming Normandy invasion. From then on, Noble flew his own regular machine, a Rolls-Royce-engined *Lancaster* Mk.I, serial LL.750, coded SR°P and known to air and ground crews alike as 'P-Peter'. His five subsequent sorties were to Rouen, Cologne, Brunswick, Munich and Essen. On average, crews were required to fly on operations one night out of two; however, Noble's was again slated for an operation on the very night after Essen, this time to F'hafen.

1 *Right*: The RAF plot at Vevey's St Martin cemetery, where thirty-four Second World War aircrew rest in the shadow of Swiss mountains. (Author)

2 *Below*: In 1940, defence of Swiss airspace rested mainly on two types of day fighter: one being the Morane *D-3801 (MS.406)*, and the other the Messerechmitt *Me.109 E* (the Swiss did not use the preix 'Bf'). This formation seen in the Swiss Alps in late 1944 includes J-377, belonging to the 21st Aviation Co. (G.G. Gorgerat)

3 In the Second World War, Switzerland lacked a nightfighter force and *C.3603*s such as this could not oppose nocturnal infringements of her neutrality. (Coll. Albert Violand)

4 Swiss fighter–control station in the Rugen hills near Berne in September 1942. (Aér.Mil.Suisse)

5 A civilianised Bucker, *Jungman* biplane, wearing an evocative Swiss registration soon after the Second World War. (Hugo Dübler)

6 *Whitleys* from 58 Squadron, such as this one, took part in the first RAF raid on Italy on 11/12 June 1940, overflying and bombing Switzerland in the process. (IWM)

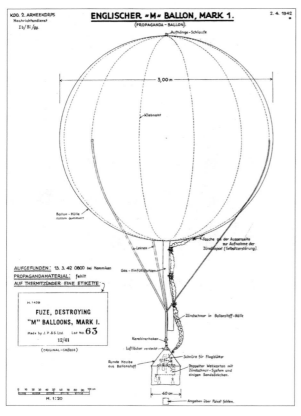

7 *Above*: Turin under attack on 11/12 June. Pointer 3 indicates a Fiat factory (now replaced by buildings, as the racetrack has been) adjacent to the Corso Mediterraneo and railroads. Pointers 1 and 2 refer to fires leaving a long trace on this long-exposure shot, as the aeroplane weaves out after bombing. (AIR MINISTRY)

8 *Left*: Swiss-drawn sketch of a British propaganda balloon, probably the first found in Switzerland, which landed near Hemmiken-Basle on 13 March 1942. (Gefr. Hans Gysin)

9 *Right*: F/Lt Gerald Wooll (right) and his navigator John Fielden, during their internment in Switzerland. (F. West)

10 *Below*: A poor quality, but rare, photograph of interned belligerent aircraft carefully hidden from public view at Dübendorf airbase, near Zürich. In the foreground, a Junkers *Ju.88.A4* that landed at Düb on 21 October 1943 shares the facility with the Berne-Belpmoos *Mosquito* (background). (Author's collection)

11 *Above*: *Mosquito* DK.310 under civilian guise when tested and operated by Swissair towards the end of the war as HB-IMO. White recognition bands around the front and rear fuselage have been added, as well as an extended Pitot tube. (Dübendorf Museum)

12 *Left*: Apart from smouldering craters and a small load of debris, nothing was left of the 431 Squadron (Iroquois) *Wellington* that was the first RAF bomber to crash in Switzerland. The aircraft fell vertically to bury itself in soft earth, leaving only the imprint of the front fuselage and two engines among small pieces of wreckage. The mark of a wing leading edge can be seen here, pointing to the crowd. Note the plume of smoke issuing from a buried engine. (Dübendorf Museum)

13 The rear end of a *Wellington*, showing the turret rotated to allow the gunner's escape. The crew is not the one who jumped over Switzerland; this aircraft was to be shot down at Averbode, Belgium, on 3/4 July 1943. (R. Williamson)

14 The crew of HE.374, the Birmenstorf *Wellington*, with their debonair captors, probably the day before their repatriation. Observer/navigator William Shields is third from left, back row, and pilot James Avery, second from right. Seated in the middle row are rear gunner Ronald McEwan and wireless operator Joseph Cash. Air bomber Wilfred Boddy is sitting on the ground on the right. (Coll. Ernst Killer via Max Rudolf)

15 *Above*: 'Wings for Victory' week (6–13 March 1943) featured this 207 Squadron *Lancaster*, on display in Trafalgar Square, London. This sister machine to Sgt Badge's, downed in Switzerland, was one of the earliest *Lancs* built. (via Raymond Charlier)

16 *Left*: Pilot Horace Badge had been promoted to Pilot Officer by the time of his death aboard *Lancaster* ED.412, close to the Swiss–French border. (Walter Badge)

17 *Right*: Demonstrating the cramped position of the *Lancaster* wireless operator, is Jack Hyde of 207 Squadron. (via Peter Kamber)

18 *Below*: In a *Lancaster*, pilot (left) and flight engineer shared the 'front office'. Note the throttle quadrant (right) with two master cock levers and the engineer's ready-for-use oxygen mask. (via Peter Kamber)

19 The scene of the *Lancaster* ED.412 crash on the steep, rocky slope of Mont Grammont, overlooking Lake Geneva. In the background is the Jura mountain range where Swiss flab batteries were positioned. (via Claude Grept)

20 This aerial view of Mont Grammont on Lake Geneva helps our understanding of the final moments of Horace Badge's *Lancaster* and crew. It looks north–west towards England and the Jura ridge where the *Lancaster* had probably been disabled by Swiss flab. The aircraft flew towards the mouth of the Rhône River (right), emptying into Lake Geneva, and Le Bouveret (centre). In the thunderstorm that prevailed on 12/13 July 1943, Badge flew over the mountains on the left, then descended into the Rhône valley (foreground), flying low from left to right, before veering to port and smashing into the mountain. (Author)

21 Officials arriving at Vevey's cemetery on Thursday 15 July 1943, to attend the burial of the fourteen victims in the two Lancasters downed in Switzerlaand on 12/13 July. Two unidentified survivors of previous crashes stand at attention as Sir Clifford Norton, British ambassador to Switzerland, walks past. Behind him, from left to right, are: Air Commodore Ferdinand 'Freddie' West, Air Attaché at the British legation, General Barnwell Legge, his American colleague and British Military Attaché, Col. Henry Cartwright. (Author's collection)

22 A Swiss soldier ponders over the river of molten metal that ran off the blazing front fuselage of the Sion-Thyon *Lancaster* ED.531. (Marc-André Pfefferlé)

23 Above Sion on 13 July 1943: this photograph shows the port side of the *Lancaster*. The rear turret guns point left, an indication that the turret might have been rotated by Sgt Bolger in his attempt to bail out. However, the mechanism may well have been deposited that way by rescuers freeing the body. (Marc-André Pfefferlé)

24 *Above left*: F/O G.D. Mitchell, pilot of the 467 Squadron (RAAF) *Lancaster* downed at Sion, Switzerland, on 12/13 July 1943. (via Jim Wright)

25 *Above right*: The left rudder of *Lancaster* ED.531, PO°T. The picture has been overprinted with measurements by the Swiss technical evaluation unit. (Dübendorf)

26 Dinghy drill near a Swiss airbase, using a round unit salvaged from one of the eight *Lancasters* that ended up in Switzerland, probably the Sion machine. With eleven men aboard, the device safely holds its own. The Swiss found it rather stable, with easy access, but less manoeuvrable than a German equivalent, eight minutes being needed to paddle across 150m (500ft). (Dübendorf)

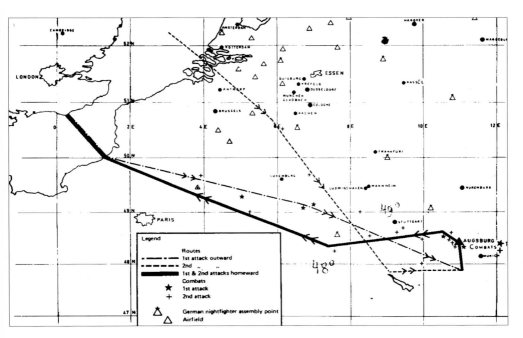

27 The complex routeing of the double-pronged raids on Augsburg, 25/26 February 1944. Bish Smith was part of the second raid, entering the continent over the Dutch isles and flying south-east to the tip of Lake Constance. (Air Ministry via A. Truscott)

28 Flak damage on a *Lancaster*. This one from 426 Squadron was peppered on 20/21 October 1943 over Leipzig, with shrapnel just missing the upper gunner. Note the open (or missing?) rear door. (Can. Joint Imagery Centre)

29 The six survivors of *Lancaster* ND.595 during their internment at Adelboden, spring 1944. From left to right: P/O Basil Medcalf (navigator), Sgt George Beevers (flight engineer), F/St Eric Hiley (wireless operator), Sgt Arthur Truscott (mid-upper gunner, in foreground), F/Sgt Ronald Carr (rear gunner) and P/O George 'Bish' Smith (pilot). (via Jim Wright)

30 Alice, Maria and Hedy Lienert, the three sisters who, at their Rössli restaurant, cared for the survivors from Smith's *Lancaster*. In the background is the causeway crossing Lake Sihl. (Hedy Lienert)

31 The scattered wreckage of Smith's *Lancaster* HM°V (ND.595) rests on the thick ice of Lake Sihl, Switzerland, on the morning of 26 February 1944. In the background is the eastern shore where a German *Dornier* crashed on 13 November 1940. (Dübendorf)

32 At dawn on their rain-soaked base, mixed *Lancaster* crewmembers return from operations. (IWM)

33 Sam Atcheson's original crew. From left to right, back row: Kenneth Reece, mid-upper gunner and only survivor; Sam Atcheson, the Irish pilot; and Scottish Anthony McCall, navigator. Sitting, are bomb aimer Jack Greenhalgh and Frank Weaver, wireless operator. Flight engineer Brian Thomas and rear gunner James Naylor were not present here – both added to the crew when passing through Heavy Conversion Unit. (Ken Reece)

BUCKINGHAM PALACE

The Queen and I offer you
our heartfelt sympathy in your
great sorrow.

We pray that your country's
gratitude for a life so nobly
given in its service may bring
you some measure of consolation.

George R.I

C. Atcheson, Esq.

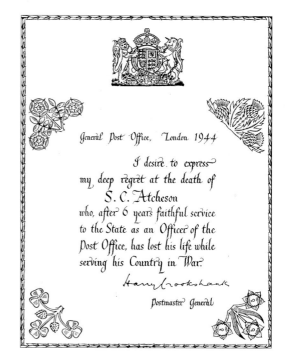

General Post Office, London 1944

I desire to express
my deep regret at the death of
S. C. Atcheson
who, after 6 years faithful service
to the State as an Officer of the
Post Office, has lost his life while
serving his Country in War.

Harry Crookshank

Postmaster General

34 *Above left*: Telegrams heralding the non-return from operations were often followed by such a message of condolences from Buckingham Palace. (Isobel Atcheson)

35 *Above right*: A note of appreciation from the Postmaster General to the family of Sam Atcheson, who had been a Post Office employee in peace time. (Isobel Atcheson)

36 The left wheel assembly of *Lancaster* W.4355 (LS°A) sheared off the wreck of the auto-landed aircraft. (W. Nydegger via E. Rieser)

37 *Above*: A *Merlin* engine torn from its mount ended in front of a wing (on the left, flat on the ground) and split fuselage sections near the Remund farm. (W. Nydegger via E. Rieser)

38 *Below*: Light snow dusting fields near Golaten show the path of *Lancaster* W.4355 as it pancaked all by itself before burning out at the centre. Note the proximity of dwellings. (Capt Loderer)

39 *Right*: A portrait of S/Ldr Michael Negus, who lost his life near the Swiss shore of Lake Constance on 6/7 April 1944. (via John Havers)

40 *Below*: The wooden structure of *Mosquito* NS.875 (UP°R) acted as a flotation device for an assortment of electrical components. (Dübendorf)

41 *Top*: No doubt such *SN-2* radar antennae (here on a *Bf.110* German nightfighter) were vastly responsible for the demise of the three *Lancasters* downed in Switzerland on 27/28 April 1944. (via van Kampen)

42 *Middle*: Of these seven men of the original Noble crew, two were destined to survive the Alp Grappelen crash: Sgt Ron Bridges (bottom centre) and F/O 'Hughie' Prowse (standing on the right). To his right are Sgt 'Frankie' Bathmaker, W/O 'Nobly' Noble and F/O Johnny Burton. Kneeling on the right is Andy Anderson, and on the left, Jack Gordon, who was replaced on the fateful night by Oscar Albrecht. (H. Prowse via Dorothy and Bernard Noble)

43 *Left*: Sgt Maurice Smith, eighth man and special radio operator with the Noble crew. (Dorothy Noble)

44 *Top*: The ground crew attached to Noble's *Lancaster* SR°P (LL.750). At top centre is Donald Bruce, who supplied this photograph.

45 *Middle*: Survivors of the Grappelen crash were interned at Adelboden. Here, internees sitting near the main street post office (left) watch a parade of firemen going past Hotel Bären. (Ron Bridges)

46 *Right*: The crew of *Lancaster* AS°X (ME.720) seen in happier times neat their Nissen hut at Kirmington. Pilot Robert Ridley stands on the left of the middle row, with bomb aimer Roy Philips on the right. Behind them are Allan Weir and Leslie Cotton. At the bottom in the centre is navigator Albert Piggott flanked by Roy Phillips (left) and Ross Clark (right). (via Jim Wright and Michael Clark)

47 *Left*: W/O Robert Ridley, RCAF, pilot of *Lancaster* AS°X (ME.720), killed at Hamikon, Switzerland, on 27/28 April 1944. (RCAF via Jim Wright)

48 *Below*: The crumpled starboard side of the fuselage rests where it fell, a couple of hundred yards from Otto Hochstrasser's barn (the arrow shows its position). (Dübendorf)

49 *Above*: Survivors of the Hamikon, Grappelen and Steckborn *Lancasters* carrying the coffin of one of their eleven comrades killed on 27/28 April 1944. Funerals with full military honours were held here at St Martin's cemetery, Vevey, on the afternoon of 3 May 1944. (via Robert Plante and Jim Wright)

50 *Below*: A *Lancaster* etching itself over searchlight-illuminated cloud or smoke. Flares leave haphazard tracks in this time exposure by the automatic camera of a bomber above. Straight horizontal streaks may well be tracer fire between aircraft. Oblique tracks at the top right are left by markers cascading on the target.

51 Robert Peter's initial crew at 21 OTU, Moreton-in-Marsh, August 1943. From left to right: Vin Graham (rear gunner); Bob Peter (pilot); Noel Davis (bomb aimer); Geoff Foulkes (navigator); Murray Bartle (wireless operator). Note the dark uniforms worn by all RAAF personnel. (Bartle's collection)

52 In June 1954, Peter's Lancaster rose out of Lake Constance. Intact fuselage emerges from its fifty-year stay underwater. ('*Weltwoche*' via J.P. Wilhelm)

53 Diver Siegfried Naumann being readied for underwater work during the salvage operation of *Lancaster* TL°R. Note the tail turret in rotated position. ('*Weltwoche*' via J.P. Wilhelm)

54 The tail turret of *Lancaster* TL°R, salvaged from the deeps in 1954, was part of a commemorative display arranged in August 2003 at Utzenstorf, Switzerland, by collector Rolf Zaugg. (Author)

55 *Above left*: Two *Mosquitoes* landed in Switzerland on 30 September 1944, courtesy of such 34mm flab anti-aircraft guns.

56 *Above right*: F/Sgt Reginald Fidler, navigator of *Mosquito* PZ.440, brought down near Dübendorf on 30 September 1944. (Reg Fidler)

57 *Left*: First page of the aeroplane logbook for NS.993, alias B-5, in Swiss military code. (via Andreas Lareida)

58 Swiss Morane *D-3801* fighters similar to this J–32 intercepted the two RAF *Mosquitoes* on 30 September 1944, over their rolling countryside. The 'J' is short for Jäger (fighter). J–32 was one of the earliest D–3800s on strength, part of a batch of thirty-two built under license in 1939-40. (George Gorgerat)

59 The sorry remains of *Mosquito* PZ.440 after its single-engine crash landing near Volketswil. Contrary to expectation, the engine on the right is the port unit! (Dübendorf)

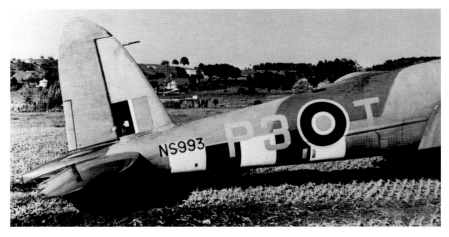

60 Tail section of *Mosquito* NS.993 with the correct code, P3, for 515 Squadron. Note the 'patch' on fin flash. (Dübendorf)

61 On a Jurassic backdrop, S/Lt Nicolas (right) explains the intricacies of W4°L, his reconnaissance *Lightning*, to an interested Swiss customs officer. (Berne archives)

62 Note the 37mm cannon protruding from the propeller shaft on this Bell *P-39*, with belly tank and further underwing armament. Two similar machines crashed simultaneously in Switzerland in the summer of 1945. (via Serge Blandin)

63 On strength with the Free French Air Force GC.2/9, this *P-39 Airacobra*, serialed 44-3914, was the one flown by Sgt Francois Laurens when it crashed at Teufen on 16 July 1945. (Coll. Jacques Mutin)

64 A typical five-man crew posing near a *Whitley* in 1940, possibly prior to an 'Italian sortie' taking them across Switzerland. Although neither their names or unit have been recorded, they are, from left to right: navigator, wireless operator, rear gunner, captain and second pilot. (Air Ministry)

65 This 'dud', a 1,000lb (454kg) unexploded British bomb, penetrated a cellar in Basle–Binningen on 11/12 December 1942 in the course of a raid on Italy.

66 *Left*: Hans Zeller's house and neighbouring dwellings in Basle–Binningen on the morning of 17 December 1940, after RAF raiders intent on attacking Italy unloaded by mistake over Switzerland.

67 *Below*: Justifiably proud soldiers have unearthed an RAF 'dud' that landed near the Restaurant Waldegg in Zurich–Rumlang on 17/18 May 1943. The weapon is possibly a 1,000lb (454kg) Medium Casing bomb.

68 Out of this assortment of RAF ordnance, several types and incendiary canisters found their way into Switzerland. The two armourers on the right work on a 12,000lb (5,450kg) 'Tallboy' weapon of the type used against the Kembs dam in October 1944.

69 *Right*: A 'Tallboy' exploding on the Rhine Kembs dam, north of Basle, on 7 October 1944. (Han. Christen)

70 *Below*: Seen near Vevey in 1944, this group of interned airmen arrived in wartime Switzerland either by foot or wing. RAF Arthur Truscott stands in the centre, with Ron Carr to his left. Standing in the second row are two Americans, Lts Jack Keefer and Homer Ford, as well as the tall RAF pilot, 'Bish' Smith, and the moustachioed Eric Hiley. (George Alistair Crowley-Smith)

71 *Left*: P/O Jan Zumbach was introduced to King George VI when he visited 303 (Polish) Squadron in September 1940. (Jan Zumbach)

72 *Middle*: Throngs of sightseers gaped at the 'captured' *Mosquito* NS.993, now under Swiss markings and coded B-5, when it was displayed at Dübendorf in October 1945. (Albert Violand)

73 *Below*: In 1949, *Mosquito* NS.993 served as test bed for the Hawker Siddeley *Mamba* jet engine, expected to propel a new Swiss fighter. (Dübendorf)

A THIRTY-FIVE HOURS *LANCASTER*

LL.750 was a new aircraft with only thirty-five hours of flying time, obtained from 32.Maintenance Unit where it had been fitted with its three tall ABC radio masts. Take-off time had been 2140hr (GB) and four hours later, Noble had left Dijon and Mulhouse behind him, had veered to port and was approaching the target. The hours had been long ones, filled with tension and the hardy business of night-flying. Now, the bomb aimer was taking over guidance, preparing for the bomb release. He was a twenty-year-old Flying Officer: Hubert Prowse, from Taber, Alberta. Once a medical student, he had joined the Royal Canadian Air Force, hoping to become a fighter pilot. In finale, he found himself poring over a Mk.XIV bombsight in the nose of heavy aircraft. This was his eighth sortie.

Five minutes after 0200hr, four hours and twenty-five minutes after take-off and flying on a 126° heading at some 160mph (250kmh),[18] bomb aimer Prowse uttered his relieving 'Bombs gone'. The load he thus dropped comprised one AN–M65 1,000lb (454kg) General Purpose bomb, one AN–M64 500lb (227kg) Medium Capacity and assorted incendiaries. The total amounted to 6,120lb. (2,779kg), a relatively low figure reflecting the presence of the ABC equipment, of an extra crew member and above all, the extra fuel tankage needed for the long range sortie.

Weather over the target area was fair, the moonlight clearly showing some ground features. With the Nuremberg disaster still in mind,[19] the crews feared another holocaust of bombers brightly etched in the clear sky. Fortunately, the diversions and 101 Squadron's radio intrigues[20] confused the enemy fighters: there were no casualties before the target. Once there, however, the first losses occurred and Noble became one of them.

The *Lancaster* had made its left turn, diving slightly away from the city to take a new heading towards England, when a nightfighter attacked from behind. Corkscrewing did not prevent the assailant from scoring hits, oblivious of the return fire from the rear gunner[21] Sgt Francis 'Frankie' Bathmaker and his upper turret mate, a Canadian Pilot Officer. This was Oscar Albrecht – a man married to Julia O'Connor in Toronto – who, at thirty-nine, was the oldest member of the party. Early in the war, on 11 November 1939, he had enlisted into the RCAF where he became a Military Policeman. He volunteered for aircrew duties on 18 May 1943, and it took four months to train him as a gunner. He had sailed to England from New York on 8 October, reporting in Bournemouth on the 14th. He then went through the pipeline of 30.OTU, 1662.HCU, 1.LFS before ending up in 101 Squadron on 31 March 1944, less than one month before being killed.

FRIEDRICH DEFENDS FRIEDRICHSHAFEN

A surprising and rare clerical error did crop up in connection with him in the Squadron's operations records. These fail to mention Albrecht, reporting a Sgt Frank Walter in his stead. In fact, Walter was supposed to replace Noble's regular mid-upper gunner, Sgt 'Jack' Gordon, who was ill, but eventually it was Albrecht who replaced Gordon at the last minute, in what was to be his ultimate flight.[22] A typical illustration of how in wartime, haphazard circumstances make the difference between life and death...

Their adversary was almost certainly Hauptmann Gerhard Friedrich, who with a name reminiscent of the night's target, would soon become *Gruppenkommandeur* of I/NJG.6. He was, for the moment, flying a Messerschmitt *Bf.110F-4*. Friedrich was to achieve thirty kills, all at night, before meeting his death in a combat accident.[23] On this night though, he succeeded in placing a five-second burst of cannon from below and starboard into Noble's *Lancaster*. A wing was damaged, an engine set ablaze and the bomber immediately began to lose altitude, descending from 19,000ft (5,800m) as it maintained its wide left turn.

Friedrich followed his prey to the south, firing as he went. His must have been one of the Luftwaffe fighters plotted by the Swiss in combat over their territory. As he crossed into Switzerland near Kreuzlingen, Noble was further tormented by Swiss searchlights, east of Frauenfeld. Soon, Swiss 75mm anti-aircraft flab opened up, firing 134 rounds against Noble and other unwanted outsiders. *Flab Detachement 104*, shooting south-east from its sites on the Thur River, reported an aircraft on fire.

The three *Detachements of Flab Gruppe 13* were not unanimous in claiming the downing of the *Lanc* but Oberstdivisionär Fritz Rihner, commandant of the Swiss air arm, was, nevertheless, still asserting such a probability in August 1944. It is indeed questionable that his flab hit Noble's *Lancaster* at all, but it must have been his machine that was seen plunging like a fiery meteor south of Appenzell, towards the high Santis mountain range, culminating at 2,501m (8,200ft). The time was 0123hr Swiss time (0223hr GB time at that period). Noble, and five of his comrades, had but a few seconds to live.

Their aircraft was then in a steep dive, throwing Prowse and Sgt Bridges together[24] and blocking the front escape hatch. Ronald 'Buck' Bridges, the twenty-two-year-old flight engineer, was from Bolton near Manchester. He heard his pilot order: 'Quick, chaps – get out!', clipped on his parachute, stowed away his seat to let Noble follow him, and slid down to the front of the aircraft, falling upon the bomb aimer.

THROWN OUT

Abruptly, the scream of the *Merlin* engines and the hissing of the wind on wings and fuselage were eclipsed by the apparent crumpling of a huge plastic bottle. The sudden, brutal explosion shattered the big aircraft. It also stunned the two men in the nose and, before they could reflect on the situation, they were hurtling through the icy void. Bridge's 'chute opened first; he drifted for what seemed to him a long time. As for Prowse, he hurt his head on the bombsight and passed out before being thrown out of the disintegrating *Lancaster*. He did not remember pulling the ripcord but came to as the inflated parachute was depositing him in snow. Debris was raining around him. It would spread over half a mile (800m), close to snowbound mountain barns on the secluded southern slope of Mount Lütispitz. They would not be recovered before mid-May from their lonely eastern Toggenburg hideout.

The site was rather deep, 50km (31mi.), inside alpine Switzerland, due south of where the *Lancaster* had entered the country, and no more than 20km (13mi.) away from Austria. That day, a few small items gleaned on the Vord Grappelen site can still be seen on display at the Dübendorf Aviation Museum near Zürich.

South across the Wildhuser Thur valley, residents of the sparsely populated and desolate slopes of the Churfisten, had been awakened by resounding engine noises, an unusual occurrence this deep into neutral Switzerland. In Iltios, M. Keller, the tenant of an isolated chalet, left his bed to investigate. Looking north, he suddenly saw the night sky turn into a reddish hell. The phenomenon did not last more than ten seconds before the cold night returned to its primeval serenity. Keller's watch showed about 0120hr (CH), and the man could telephone the local police in Unterwasser that in his opinion an aircraft had crashed nearby. Soon, a posse comprising a couple of locals and policeman Jäckli was on its way, their car clattering up by-roads and stony tracks towards the Oberlaui gap and Lake Grappelen.

An hour later, they were startled by the desolation. Three engines, a burning wing, smashed sections of fuselage, a wheel and four bodies were clustered just north of the little lake. The *Lanc*'s second main wheel had buried itself in snow 500 yards away. Another large chunk of wrecked wing attached to a *Merlin* engine lay nearby, complete with its paddle-blade propeller, and showing damage by a 20mm shell. Where it had not been melted by fire, the torn, blackened wing, with its stringers and what appeared to be bullet-proof skinning, gave ample evidence of the force of the exploding petrol fumes which had blown apart the four-engined bomber. Bits of chocolate, a crushed orange and other parts of the flying rations were strewn in the snow. No one bothered to record such finds. Official reports ignore them just as they do for the escape pouches with their clever gadgets and foreign currencies!

Much further north, at 101 Squadron's station, other personal effects would soon be sorted by a 'Committee of Adjustments'. Only a few hours before, they had belonged to the missing men; they were now to be forwarded to the RAF Central Depository at Colnbrook near Slough, for processing, and were eventually to be given to the next-of-kins, by now dismally distressed by the dreaded Priority Telegram.

TWO SURVIVORS

Spread among the remnants of a once proud *Lancaster*, were pathetic human remains. Six airmen had died suddenly of multiple massive traumatic injuries on the grim, dull slopes of Alp Grappelen. They had been on Squadron strength for just thirty-eight days, an indication of how dangerous it was to fly with Bomber Command! The victims included: Oscar Albrecht; William Anderson, a twenty-one-year-old Sgt wireless-operator from Murton, County Durham; Francis Bathmaker, also twenty-one, from London, who was found inside his rear turret amongst fir trees; John Burton from Hutton Rudby, Yorkshire, who at twenty-two was an experienced Flying Officer and navigator; veteran pilot Bertram Noble, thirty-two, whose body had been thrown fifty yards away from the wreckage; and nineteen-year-old Sgt Maurice Smith, the man listed in the crews battle order as an 'extra wireless operator'.[25] One of them had died of facial and internal injuries, even though his parachute had opened. Too late.

All were gently laid in rough coffins in Alt St Johann before laying in State in the village's Reformed Church until the 1 May. They were then taken for burial to Vevey cemetery's British plot, in a ritual that was, alas, becoming well established.

Prowse, one of the two fortunate survivors, was found by policeman Jäckli, sitting forlornly under a tree, next to the body with the opened parachute. He was to end his eighth sortie in St Gall hospital on 2 May 1944. He quickly recovered from partial amnesia, and indicated his wish to pursue medical studies in Switzerland. As for Bridges, who had been wounded in the eye and found refuge in a barn – his relief was immense, not only on account of his narrow escape from death, but also because he thought he was in Germany and, in his state of shock, was expecting to be shot!

Bridges' and Prowse's wounds[26] were taken care of by Dr Bernoulli from nearby Unterwasser, a remote village from where they were driven to the Wattwil and, later, St. Gall hospitals. Even though their fighting spirit remained high, according to the Swiss interrogators both men were quite disturbed by the death of their six comrades. They were repatriated after five months, in early October 1944.

Their six crewmates rest, never to be forgotten, in the picturesque and well-tended Vevey cemetery, at the eastern tip of Lake Geneva. Six casualties they are, forever silent witnesses of the tragic peculiarity of 101 Squadron, the specialist unit that lost some 1,100 of its men, more than any other RAF Squadron.

13

Claimed by Swiss Flab

AIRMEN AND AIRCRAFT:
Pilot: W/O Robert Ridley
Flight Engineer: Sgt John Eaton
Navigator: F/O Albert Piggott
Bomb Aimer: F/O Roy Phillips
Wireless Operatr: Sgt Leslie Cotton
Mid-upper Gunner: Sgt Ross Clark
Rear Gunner: Sgt Allan Weir
Lancaster Mk.I ME.720, code AS°X, 166 Squadron

White wine had been plentiful at the cheesemakers' reunion in the tiny village of Hamikon, deep into Switzerland, 20km (13mi.) north of Lucerne. Fresh air and a clear starry night were quite welcome to set Otto Hochstrasser on a straight course for home to the outskirts of the hamlet. Combining his farming skills with that of communal writer, the stocky forty-one-year-old man was returning from the Linden restaurant where he had acted as secretary for a gathering of local cheese producers.

At the Linden, the men had heard bombing in progress, way north in Southern Germany. The rumbling had, however, had little impact on the meeting, being just a mere incident irrelevant to life in the village. And now the serenity of the night was only vaguely disturbed by the hum of far-away motors.

DRAMA TOWARDS LUCERNE

For no reason at all, Hochstrasser looked over his shoulder. A faint reddish light could be seen, eerie in a sky dimly lit by the waning moon. At first the thing did not seem to move and he did not perceive the prime ingredient of a drama being played out. Over there, some miles south towards Lucerne at around 15,000ft (4,600m), cannon and machine-gun fire was ripping through air, metal and perhaps bodies. The incident involved the second RAF aircraft that came down in Switzerland during the raid on Friedrichshafen of 27/28 April 1944. Again it was a *Lancaster*. From 166 Squadron.

'One-six-six' was based at Kirmington, near Grimsby and the mouth of the Humber; it was under the command of an outstanding airman and experienced leader: W/Cdr Francis Powley, DFC, AFC.[1] To fulfil its part in the raid, the Squadron had mustered twenty-five aircraft, including one spare. One had to abandon the sortie owing to 'navigator unable to cope', and of the twenty-three others, three failed to return, a sample consistent with the losses suffered by the unit at that time.

One of the unfortunate machines was to spread itself practically in Hochstrasser's backyard, but for some time he remained unaware that his country's anti-aircraft artillery claimed to have shot down 'his' bomber.[2] Actually, it was later ascertained that the aircraft had fallen victim to a German nightfighter, again operating deep into neutral airspace. Whether or not the claim had been made in good faith, it came at the right moment to soothe German tempers ruffled by the apparent impotence of the Swiss to counter the RAF overflying their country. Still worse, these were the times of the Swiss refusal to hand back to the Reich the most secret radar-equipped Messerschmitt *Bf.110* nightfighter which they had unwillingly acquired that very night.

For half a minute, the light remained seemingly poised in the still of the night. Then, suddenly, the tempo accelerated. The object moved from east to west and veered north towards Hochstrasser. Its graceful but deadly descending curve abruptly ended in a tremendous detonation. The blinding flash lit the village in a fantastic orange aura. The air swooshed as heavy debris hurtled overhead. Within a few seconds, the night seemed to regain its hold over the village – not quite, for flames sprang up near Hochstrasser's own house. Quite sober by now, Otto ran home, towards the glow that started to etch trees and barns. Panic seized him at the thought of his wife Anna and the eight children. He should not have let the wretched cheese meeting drag on for so long. His door was locked and nobody answered his frantic shouts. Nearby he could see the roof of his own barn, grotesque against oily flames. After what seemed a century, Anna opened the door: the whole family was safe and sound in the cellar. Otto sent them away to the village.

THE TORN *LANCASTER*

Surveying the situation, Otto noticed that a ditch behind the barn was filled with blazing fuel. Like every able-bodied man in Switzerland, Otto was a member of the *Orstwehr*, the local guard trained for such emergencies. Before his colleagues arrived, complete with hose and German-looking steel helmets, he had found a broken fuselage lying near his cowshed. At least two human figures could be seen crouched and incinerated inside. A little further on, a huge wing smouldered, its spilled fuel aflame in the U-shaped ditch ending near the barn. Further east, another part of the fuselage rested against a half-burnt apple tree. Noticing that the other half was, bizarrely, still in bloom, Hochstrasser went on to discover another wing section detached from an engine and a large amount of thoroughly crumpled, shredded metal. A huge wheel protruded, partly buried in the soft ground.

Two more bodies were also located. In all probability, both had been thrown out when their aircraft had exploded, perhaps 400m (1,300ft) above ground; the poor souls had left a deep imprint in the earth. A cursory search failed to identify them but their names were soon ascertained when Cpl Walter Stössel, a military policeman from *Territorial Kommando 8*, arrived on the scene. Helped by a survivor, he found out that the two victims were a gunner, Ross Clark, and the pilot, Ridley. As was often the case when fuel tanks exploded, he must have been ejected through the perspex roof of his cockpit. Their machine, a British *Lancaster*, could be identified by its serial number, ME.720, stencilled near a large X^3 and a roundel visible on the broken fuselage.

Warrant Officer Robert Ridley (his promotion to P/O came through as his family in Port Credit, Ontario, was notified of his death) was, at twenty-one, an example of operational main force pilots. He had enlisted in Toronto on 6 November 1941 and received his pilot's brevet after some fifteen months. He docked in England on 17 March 1943, and it had taken eleven more months of operational training before he was at long last assigned to a combat unit: 166 Squadron, Bomber Command. Altogether, it had meant twenty-seven months of training and just eleven weeks of war service before he would be posted missing and killed! Such was the wastage of life and resources in the air war over Europe.

Ridley and his crew had been posted to the Squadron on 10 February and had since flown ten sorties, only one of which had been a relatively 'easy' one, a mining operation. He had been 'broken-in' by W/Cdr Powley himself, to Schweinfurt on 24/25 February.[4] In sixty-seven hours of operational flying, Berlin, Stuttgart, Frankfurt, Essen, Aachen and even Nuremberg on 30/31 March, had failed to stop him. In the meantime he had been granted two six-days leaves, returning from the last one on 24 April. Three days later, the young Canadian was dead in the gently rolling Swiss countryside, a victim of the combined efforts of a German nightfighter and the Swiss flab artillery. The time warp was again to be grimly apparent when diplomatic and administrative red tape interfered. It was not until 31 October that Canadian bureaucrats in London's Oxford Street were able to forward to Ridley's mother Abigail, in Ontario, a typically soothing letter complete with details about her son's funeral in early May.[5]

OUTWARD ROUTE (GB)

Bob Ridley had left Kirmington at 2135hr, GB time, for the long haul to F'hafen. A fortnight before, a new procedure had been implemented at 166 to prevent take-off swings. That was after the phenomenon had caused a *Lanc*'s undercarriage to collapse and sent the bomb-laden machine to explode and block the runway in use. On this night, Ridley had clamped wheel-brakes, given full throttle to the inboard engines and, once their rpm stabilised, gunned the outboarders and released the brakes. Then, as his sluggish machine rolled, the four throttles had been pushed through the gates.

Once airborne, Ridley's fifty-nine-hours-old *Lanc*, code letters AS°X, had circled to gain altitude over the airfield and the village with its renowned pub, grimly dubbed The Chopper. The machine was the one flown by the crew on their last three sorties. A comparatively new aircraft, taken on charge by the Squadron a month previously, it would never exceed sixty-three hours of fly-ing time, becoming representative of the high attrition rate suffered by Bomber Command's aircraft and crews alike.

Ridley's penetration route had been that of the whole bomber stream: south-east to avoid London, then over the English Channel to cross the enemy (French) coast west of Abbeville. A change of heading to Nevers was then given by the navigator, F/O Albert Piggott. This was in accordance with the briefing which had called for this southerly deception intended to have the defences believe the target was Northern Italy. Piggott, at the 'advanced' age of twenty-six, had been a farmer in Keppel, Saskatchewan, before joining the Royal Canadian Air Force in July 1941. Like the rest of the crew, this was his eleventh operation, somewhat more than the five which, until the turn of the year, had been the average expectancy for RAF bomber crews.

Reaching Nevers, the stream had turned east towards Dijon and Besançon. This new heading would eventually bring it over Switzerland unless a further course alteration was made to the north-east. Ridley and crew complied with this but many others did not, which explains the numerous violations of Swiss air-space occurring between 0018hr and 0158hr. Swiss time, as the attacking stream flowed towards Friedrichshafen.

Shortly after 0200hr, as the *Lancaster* neared the target, F/O Roy Phillips noticed that the area was a mass of fire-belching black smoke rising up to 12,000ft (3,660m). He had been a meteorologist in Toronto before volunteer-ing in the RAF in April 1942: he wanted to be a pilot but, like so many, had had to water down his hopes and had been trained as a bomb aimer juggling with the intricacies of an Mk.XIV bombsight. Below, the Pathfinders' red and green indicators were showing well in spite of the smoke. Prompted, like all main force air bombers, by the Master of Ceremonies,[6] who could be heard very clearly, Phillips released his load. It consisted of a single 1,000lb (454kg) bomb and a rain of 1,074 mixed incendiaries. That is minus two hang-ups, two phosphor contrap-tions which would end up near a blossoming apple tree in Switzerland.[7]

Over the target, ground opposition was termed moderate, but nightfighter activity could be observed to the north-west as the returning bombers met the late-coming fighters. Running the gauntlet, AS°X was singled out by an enemy aircraft. German nightfighters at this stage of the war were well equipped with *Lichtenstein BC* and *SN-2* radar allowing them to acquire flying targets in the darkest of nights; in clear conditions like tonight, however, most pilots relied only on 'eyeball radar'.

ENTERS OBERLEUTNANT KRAFT

In the past, Ridley's crew had met several of the breed, but this one they could not shake off. The enemy machine belonged to II/NJG.5, i.e. to the second *Gruppe* of *Nachtjagdgeschwader 5*; it was flown by Oberleutnant Josef Kraft, an *Experte* who would end the war with forty-nine kills. Some twenty minutes into the return leg, he intercepted Ridley. The *Lancaster* pilot attempted violent corkscrewing evasive manoeuvres when its foe was spotted, but an engine was hit.

At this stage, Ridley elected to head south towards the Swiss haven. Haven perhaps, but not quite as peaceful as expected, for within minutes he ran into range of the Frauenfeld 75mm batteries of the Swiss *Flab Gruppe 13*. A hit caused a small explosion inside the aircraft and this may have been the cause of the reddish light noticed from the ground.

The crew had been told at base to go and seek refuge at Zürich-Dübendorf airfield in case of emergency over or near Switzerland. Now, from his perch at around 18,000ft (5,500m), navigator Piggott, who had left his cosy cubicle, could clearly make out the town's outline at the tip of the banana-shaped Lake Zürich. Safety was in sight and, all being well, they would be secure on *terra firma* in ten minutes or so. Descending, the *Lanc* was ready to initiate a right turn when all hell broke loose again. The nightfighter had rejoined the fray. Deliberately or not, Kraft had crossed into Switzerland in hot pursuit of his *Kurier*, his victim, outlined against the crescent moon now low on the horizon.

According to Léon Bühlmann – a lieutenant in the Swiss Observer Corps, on leave at nearby Hitzkirch – the duel must have occurred over or near the small Baldegger Lake, which is deep inside Switzerland and 100km (62mi.) from the target. Evidently, on this night, the German defenders did not bother more than the RAF about Swiss neutrality!

Quite professionally, Bühlmann went on to report another explosion ten minutes after Ridley's demise. This happened at high altitude, far to the north-north-west, and it must have heralded the loss of one of a cluster of five bombers lost over the French Vosges mountains. They comprised the two other crews from 166 Squadron lost that night, at Heiteren near Colmar (P/O D.M. Bridges with LL.903) and at Granges-Vologne east of Epinal (P/O Alfred Cooper in ND.825). They were but two of the eighteen crews lost on the raid.

As for Ridley, the usual drama developed in all its deadly routine. Kraft had slid behind the *Lancaster*, undetected by either gunner. His fire added to previous damage to the right-wing root. Aboard the *Lancaster*, the terrific noise shocked all souls. It was as if great panes of glass were being smashed. The aircraft shuddered as if hit by a giant whip, the crack covering the roar of the engines. The weird noise ceased abruptly but the port wing was alight. The *Lancaster* banked to starboard, all hopes of reaching Zürich now nullified. Fearing the explosion of the petrol tanks, Ridley gave the word 'jump' on the intercom, ordering his crew to bail out. It was too late!

GROUND DISASTER AVOIDED

The bomber was now south-west of Hamikon and its descent developed into a right-hand diving turn. At this moment, Ridley was probably leaving his pilot's seat, trying to reach the front escape hatch that his bomb aimer had desperately wrenched open. He did not succeed. Within seconds the aircraft had disintegrated, torn apart in an horrifying detonation by the exploding petrol fumes in the half-empty wing tanks. The machine was by then above Hamikon: two seconds earlier and the debris would have rained on the village.[8] As it was, the momentum of the dive hurled the fragments 500m (1,600ft) forward to open fields, sparing the villagers a major disaster, also sparing Britain a major crisis with the Swiss government which was still smarting from the murderous bombing of Schaffhausen by the 8th USAAF on 1 April.

Swiss clocks showed 0138hr when the disaster occurred. The pilot was thrown clear from the main wreck, killed by either the conflagration, his cockpit frame, shards of metal or by striking the ground. Three others rode, trapped to their death. There was John Eaton, the flight engineer and another sergeant, Ross Clark, the mid-upper gunner from Fareham, Hampshire. Once a police constable in Portsmouth and as such dispensed from military duties, he had – as Walter Morgan in the Sion tragedy – forfeited that immunity and volunteered for aircrew service. Accepted as an under-training pilot/observer, he had washed out, but, keen on flying at all costs, had re-mustered as air gunner.

Clark and Eaton remained trapped in the aircraft, as did the twenty-one-year-old wireless operator Leslie Cotton, recently married Kathleen at Staple Hill, South Gloucestershire. A fifth man was Sgt Allan Weir, the rear gunner, who would never return to Thornliebank, Glasgow. It will never be known if he succeeded in opening the two armoured doorlets of his turret to crawl to the main exit door, or if he rotated the turret to let himself fall out backwards. In any case, it was too late for his 'chute to open and he fell to his death in trees at Altwis, near Lake Hallwill, one mile west of Hamikon.

By daylight, all were lying in state besides their pilot in the mortuary at Hitzkirch, their coffins resting under flowers brought by the local inhabitants. Fate proved kinder for the navigator and the bomb aimer, who were both Canadians, as was their unfortunate skipper. They had reached the front exit when the *Lancaster* began its final plunge. Roy Phillips, whose station was practically on

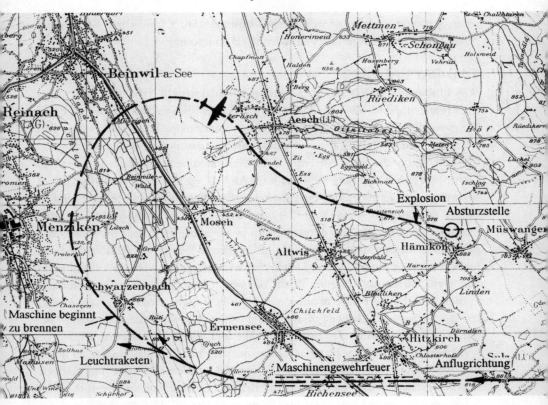

Reconstructed approximate final trajectory of Lancaster AS°X (ME.720), terminating at Hamikon, north of Lucerne, on 27/28 April 1944. Notes at the bottom say, from right to left: 'Arrival, Machinegun fire, Flares, Aircraft afire'. (Theo Wilhelm)

the hatch, was out first.[9] He had clipped his parachute on and proceeded to pull the small door open instead of releasing the latches and kicking it out. For some unexplained reason, the door reacted with a vengeance, hitting him on the head. Phillips passed out. The next thing he knew, he was floating down in mid-air with his parachute open!

Al Piggott had also clipped on his 'chute upon hearing his pilot's order. The explosion knocked him out and threw him clear of the same fractured fuselage that saved Phillips. What miracle opened his parachute he shall never know. He regained consciousness lying on the ground. His eyes were swollen, his clothes torn. He presumed his parachute had dragged him along the ground. At daylight, foresters discovered him fast asleep in a wood. Brought to the nearby village of Ermensee, he rested in the post office. Then, as nobody spoke English there, he was taken to the Elmiger family. They summoned Hitzkirch's Dr Fischer, who diagnosed and tended the navigator's minor injuries. That same day, Piggott was brought by Cpl Stössel to the scene of the crash where he had to help identify his unlucky friends. After interrogation, he remained in Lucerne's hospital until 1 June when he rejoined many of his colleagues in the Adelboden hotel compound.

TWO DAYS AT LARGE

Roy Phillips, the bomb aimer, had a more unusual story to tell. Still dazed under his white canopy, he misjudged his height and hurt his right ankle upon touching the ground. He later found out he was close to Menziken. This largish village had been the extreme western reach of the doomed *Lancaster*'s path. When interrogated by Lt Achard of the Swiss Air Force,[10] Phillips stated he believed himself to be in Germany. He had therefore removed his RAF 'AB' wing and other tell-tale pieces of uniform, and had started to bury them together with his parachute. This standard evader procedure was interrupted by the arrival of a man who must have seen him floating down. Phillips distracted him by throwing rocks into the bushes and made off in the opposite direction. He, too, reached Menziken[11] but as daylight was breaking, he hid in the undergrowth and went to sleep. He woke up around noon and stayed hidden until evening. Again, this was in accordance with the escape and evasion drill the RAF gave to aircrew: walk only at night, avoid towns, try to find civilian clothes and to contact underground helpers, knowing that, generally speaking, priests and working-class people were the most likely to give initial help.

A night owl, like all of Bomber Command's aircrews, Phillips walked all night, just twenty-four hours after his traumatic arrival on the Swiss scene. His aim was to reach Geneva where he thought the British Legation was, and from there be helped in crossing the border towards Spain and Gibraltar. His silk escape map, his button compass and the malted-milk tablets in his escape kit eased his journey.[12] On the evening of 29 April, he was near a large city, Aarau, actually just 20km (12.5mi.) almost due north of his landing place. Skirting the town, he went to Olten and started south-west to Langenthal. Here the railway station was full of troops, probably going on leave since this was Saturday night. Wary of being recognised, Phillips hid for a while in the cemetery. Then, making use of the escape money provided by his evasion pouch, he bought a rail ticket to Lausanne which he reached, without being bothered, at 0500 the following morning.

It was 30 April. When walking uptown he met an English woman who told him of the condition of British military personnel interned in Switzerland, and persuaded him to report to the British Consul. Faced with the quite unusual situation of having a British airman on his own in the host country, Vice-Consul Howell-Thomas reported to W/Cdr William Jones, the Deputy Air Attaché in Berne. After talking to Phillips, the decision was taken to abide by the rules and hand the airman over to the Swiss who would intern him.

As it was, Phillips had remained at large for two days, a rare occurrence in Switzerland, a country where incoming evaders were usually rounded up within hours or even minutes of their crossing the border. True, he was deep inland where patrols were non-existent. Also, clad in his grey-blue dress and trousers, he must have resembled any foreign civilian refugee to local residents, not very aware of how belligerent uniforms looked.

After reporting to the Swiss authorities, Phillips was allowed to stay with the Consul for four days until he could attend the burial of his crewmates in nearby Vevey. Later he spent three weeks in an hotel in Berne, and was then sent to the Adelboden 'camp' (see Chapter 10). For men freshly out of wartime England and its restrictions, men who furthermore had escaped with their life from the fearful madness of being shot down, life at 'Adel' was indeed quite comfortable. There were practically no restraints except reporting once a week to the local police, and securing passes from them if they wanted to travel from one Canton to another.[13]

ENFORCED VACATION

Phillips remained in the ski station deserted by all but Allied airmen, from 21 May to the end of July 1944. From then on he was allowed to attend French lessons in Lausanne, together with Sgt Reece, the survivor from the Saignelégier crash (see Chapter 9) and another RAF NCO, Sgt Mattock.

Apart from its educational interest, Lausanne proved productive in a less formal enterprise. Phillips made contact there with Swiss 'underground' workers who arranged for his escape with five others into nearby France, reaching Sancey-le-Grand on 10 October. By the 22nd, he was in liberated Paris and was given passage to England by air. There remained for him to be subjected to a thorough debriefing at MI.9,[14] meant as much to make sure the bomb aimer had not become an agent for the Germans, as to gather first-hand information about life on the Continent. Returning to base, Phillips was quite astonished to find out he had been beaten there by two weeks by his co-survivor, Albert Piggot. Phillips was returned to Canada, went back to civilian life and emigrated to the USA.

As for Piggot, he had been allowed back to England in the third exchange involving German and Allied men stranded in neutral territory – not in a regular exchange of airmen, however. Piggott had also been confined in the plush Adelboden camp from 1 June to 4 October 1944. On that date he managed to conceal himself among British troops who were officially leaving Switzerland. By train to Geneva and truck to Annecy, they were taken on charge by the Americans and their ACRU-2[15] processing returning aircrew internees. He was flown to Northolt, UK, on 8 October, and was back in Canada within a few weeks. He married twice and passed away in 1997. Today, his uniform, medals and other artefacts can be seen at the Saskatoon Military Museum in Saskatchewan.

Not too far from the fields where Ridley and crew took off from, a remembrance tree and plaque erected by Michael Clark, Ross' devoted cousin, perpetuate the memory of the gallant airmen who left Lincolnshire ground to meet their fate over Switzerland.

14

Border Ditching

AIRMEN AND AIRCRAFT:

Pilot: W/O Robert Peter
Flight Engineer: Sgt Alfred Brereton
Navigator: F/Sgt Geoffrey Foulkes
Bomb Aimer: F/Sgt Noel Davis
Wireless Operator: F/Sgt Murray Bartle
Mid-upper Gunner: F/Sgt David Balmer
Rear Gunner: Sgt Irvine Graham
Lancaster Mk.III, ND.759, code TL°R, 35 Squadron

*Struggling to bring his sluggish, burning four-engined bomber smoothly on the water,
Warrant Officer Robert Peter peered through the slight nocturnal haze. In front of his gliding Lancaster ND.759, the dark surface of Lake Constance lay forbidding. Suddenly, as
the wallowing aircraft hit, a cascade of water gushed through the open front hatch and the
numerous shell holes peppering the rear fuselage.*

Within seconds, the four men huddled behind the main spar were awash. Then,
as the machine settled in the freezing water, the dinghy sprang open, inflating out
of the starboard wing. The date was 27/28 April 1944 and the third *Lancaster* to
reach Switzerland on this night had almost made it.

R FOR... PETER

W/O Peter's flight had originated at 2221hr British time at Graveley, Huntingdonshire.
This was the home of 35 (Pathfinder) Squadron, where the *Lancaster*, a Mk III coded
TL°R, had been loaded with marking flares, four 2,000lb high-capacity bombs and
three of their lesser brethren of the 500lb medium-capacity variety (908 and 227kg
respectively). The crew was to act as a PFF (Pathfinder Force) supporter on the raid
to Friedrichshafen described in the two preceding Chapters.

Peter, a native of Geraldton, Western Australia, was not yet twenty-seven years old. He had been a schoolteacher in Victoria Park when the need for less sedate occupations had called on him. He had enlisted to fly in the Royal Australian Air Force and was inducted on 17 August 1941 to become one of the 12,300 aircrew Australia provided to help the British war effort in Europe. At the end of May 1942, Peter was complete with the coveted wings on his dark blue uniform and ready for posting overseas. He arrived in England on 17 November, but it was not until 19 March 1943 that he sat at the controls of an aircraft again! Ten months elapsed between his last flight in Australia and his first in England. The wartime training of aircrew did not proceed without serious hiccups entailing the loss of skills. Peter then went though a succession of new courses such as refresher, beam approach and 21.Operational Training Unit at Moreton-in-Marsh.

Meanwhile, Robert Peter had gathered most of his crew and, at OTU, flown one 'easy training' operation: a leaflet sortie to Compiègne in occupied France, on 15/16 August 1943, aboard an old 'clapped-out' *Wellington IC*. This, their first combat sortie, was also almost their last: the *Wimpy* suffered an engine failure which proved quasi-catastrophic. For having gallantly mastered the situation, Peter was awarded a 'Commendation', a distinction that was later to help him and his crew become part of the elite Pathfinder Force.

On 17 September 1943, the crew was posted to 1652. Heavy Conversion Unit, at Marston Moor, to familiarise themselves with relatively new *Halifax II* heavy bombers and smell again the distinctive odour of aircraft interiors mixing scents of petrol, heated oil and radio components, burnt gun powder, perspiration and human exhausts at the Elsan relief stool. The period was when Alfred Brereton replaced the original flight engineer who was the unfortunate victim of air sickness. Sgt Brereton was a fair, slim, witty Briton from Salisbury; this 'good-looking prototype of the understating Englishman' was twenty-eight years old[1] and had volunteered from ground staff to aircrew duties.

TO LIBYA

The crew was then assigned to ferry a big black *Halifax* to Benghazi in Libya, where they were supposed to become part of a local Squadron. The trip was not exempt from danger as witnessed when at night over the Bay of Biscay, they were attacked by a German fighter. An administrative hiccup then had them returned to the UK, hitch-hiking rides in American aircraft.

On 27 January 1944, Peter and crew became part of 51 Squadron, a *Halifax*-equipped outfit engaged, within Bomber Command, in the task of destroying the German war industry. Peter flew his initiation sortie to Berlin on 15/16 February 1944 with an experienced pilot, F/O Douglas Jackson.[2] From then on he was on his own, his decisions involving his own life and those of six friends.

Together they completed four attacks with 51 Squadron: to Schweinfurt (24/25 February when their 'career' again almost came to an end as a bomb load from an aircraft overhead barely missed them), to Stuttgart (1/2 March), Trappes (6/7 March) and Le Mans (7/8 March).

Soon afterwards, when a call again occurred for crews to be posted out to the elite Pathfinder Force, Peter and crew were selected for transfer.[3] One member of the crew did not stay long as Peter's first action in the Corps was to request replacement of his mid-upper gunner. The man had fallen asleep during the Schweinfurt raid in February, a breach of discipline that the captain could not accept since it jeopardised the life of the whole team! The culprit was replaced by F/Sgt David 'Paddy' Balmer, a stout, twenty-nine-year-old Irishman who once had been a salesman in Bangor; an experienced man in his thirty-fourth operation within a second tour,[4] he was the oldest member of the crew.

They were posted to 35 Squadron at the end of March, but before reaching their new base at Graveley, west of Cambridge, they had to proceed to nearby Warboys for a special PFF indoctrination course. This included a conversion to *Lancasters* and, for the bomb aimer Noel Davis, the mastering of the *H2S* navigation and bombing radar. The night before being shot down in the eventful F'hafen sortie, Peter's opening taste of PFF operation was an onslaught on Essen in the Ruhr. For this, his ninth operation,[4] his mount was *Lancaster* ND.759, which had spent only fifty-two hours in the air. The aircraft was one of fourteen heavies despatched by 35 Squadron among the force of 323 aircraft on their way to wreak havoc in the industrial city sitting on the shore of Lake Constance, just north of neutral Switzerland.

FIGHTER AHEAD!

Some 50 miles (80km) short of Friedrichshafen, the four *Merlins* were humming smoothly, their short blue exhausts generating a false sense of safety. In the clear grey night, the friendly silhouette of another bomber could be noticed. Then it happened. Peter spotted a twin-engined German fighter hurtling in for a low, almost head-on attack. An immediate corkscrew was only partly successful in evading the enemy fire which hit the starboard outer *Merlin* engine. Notwithstanding the emergency, Peter elected to press on to the target, but the relevant propeller had to be feathered. He activated the built-in fire extinguisher, ordered flight engineer Brereton, operating next to him, to turn off the engine's fuel cock, closed the throttle and hit the feathering button, holding it long enough to ensure it stayed in. Outside, the damaged engine's propeller gradually stopped rotating and the pilot cut the ignition. He then had time to check that the invalid engine was starved of fuel.[5] 'Killing' the engine had, however, entailed the loss of power to the *H2S* radar set and, worse, to the mid-upper turret hydraulic pump. Up there, gunner Paddy Balmer was thus practically reduced to the role of spectator in the action.

The *Lancaster* reached F'hafen at around 0200hr, a few minutes after the first PFF flare, a green, had gone down to mark the target. Searchlights were raking the night sky and the flak artillery was already going full swing. Its distinctive T-shaped puffs of brown-black smoke drifted lazily in the glare of searchlights, looking harmless though everyone knew how deadly they were – the more so since the smell of cordite sometimes penetrated the oxygen mask and the occasional shrapnel rattled pebble-like against the duralumin skin.

The town could be easily identified visually under its pall of smoke, allowing accurate bombing. The crew heard F/Sgt Noel Davis, the skilful bomb aimer,[6] chanting 'Bomb doors open' prior to taking control of the aircraft and directing his pilot to the centre of the target with small corrections of heading punctuated with the ritual 'Steady, steady now…'. The load was dropped from 16,000ft (4,880m), a little later than the briefed time on target; to the relief of everyone, they heard the pilot confirm 'Bombs away' and felt the *Lancaster* lurch as its burden was released. There remained to maintain heading for some thirty seconds – an eternity in the face of flak defences – until the automatic camera had portrayed the mute flicker of the bombs churning the target. A course for home could now be steered.

PROLONGED TRAINING

Davis' long, sometimes tedious and frequently dangerous itinerary from Australia to the ranks of 35 Squadron is an example of what young men from faraway countries faced to become freedom's air combatants. Sadly, and too often, they would become mere statistics, terminating their training in frightful accidents or ending up in the vast aircrew necropolis in the European countryside.

Noel Davis had fallen in love with flying in his boyhood when his father reluctantly offered him a ride with Kingsford-Smith, the aviator-hero who had just completed the 1930 flight from England to Australia. Noel of course wanted to become a pilot when, at nineteen, boyish and almost shy, he enlisted in the RAAF. This was in 1941, and by April 1942 he had accumulated sixty-four hours aloft. He then opted for multi-engine operations and was soon on his way to Canada for more training. Having crossed the Pacific and sailed through the Panama Canal, run the gauntlet of the *U-Boot*-infested Caribbean sea and turned twenty-one 'without any fanfare' at Key West, Florida, he disembarked in New York. A train trip followed, to Montreal and Saskatoon in central western Canada, where he progressed in flying two-engined Cessna *Cranes*.[7] He was lucky to have an excellent instructor but when the man was grounded for medical reasons and losing continuity with another, he understood he would never progress satisfactorily. Noel then re-mustered, at his own request, to embrace the new trade of Air Bomber (Bomb Aimer). Suitably trained and after a winter-crossing of the savage Atlantic with its *U-Boot* menace, he arrived in the UK in January 1943. More training ensued after 'crewing-up' with his pilot and other mates. It had taken him nearly two years to be able to crouch in the nose of a heavy bomber to help free Europe of German domination.

On the night of 27 April 1944, he was in the thick of the real thing. Soon after releasing his bombs, all hell broke loose: a second nightfighter was striking at the crippled *Lancaster*.[8] As the bomber turned left, slightly descending to gain speed and start the return journey, the wireless operator, F/Sgt Murray Bartle, spotted what looked like glow-worms overtaking them. They were tracer bullets arcing in from behind. The drill called for Bartle to act as observer from the astrodome while in the target area, and the young Australian immediately ordered a corkscrew evasive action – to no avail. The dive, again initiated too late, did not prevent ND.759 from sustaining hits between the two turrets in the rear fuselage, where some hydraulic fluid was set ablaze. A lot of smoke resulted, soon filling the cockpit to the extent that Peter could not see his instruments. By then, the *Lancaster* was furthermore engaged in a flat right-hand spin, slowly losing altitude.

BAIL-OUT ORDER

Unable to maintain control, the captain ordered the crew to bail out. The parachute exit procedure called for the bomb aimer to leave first through the escape hatch near his station at the bottom of the nose. He was to be followed by the flight engineer and the navigator who would have to, like the pilot later on, slip into the nose via the opening under the right-hand side of the control panel. As it happened, Davis the bomb aimer had gone aft at the pilot's request, to investigate the situation, and this may have saved his life. It turned out that tall, dark F/Sgt Geoffrey 'Lefty' Foulkes, the twenty-eight-year-old Australian navigator from Cremorne, New South Wales, jumped first. He was followed by Alfred Brereton, the flight engineer.

Davis then came back from the rear with the news that both gunners, Balmer and Sgt Irvine Graham, were badly burned. Furthermore, they were unable to jump, their parachutes having been damaged by flames in their stowage near the fuselage door. To top it all, Davis' own 'chute had opened near the front hatch as he picked it up. Now the pilot had no other choice than to attempt a hazardous ditching. It would be difficult, but no more than attempting, at night, a crash-landing in mountainous territory.

Opening the front hatch had provoked an interesting side-effect: this induced a rush of air which cleared the smoke obscuring the cockpit. Peter could now see his instruments and try to regain control of the doomed bomber. His single-engine training came back as second nature: he used the standard spin recovery procedure... only to discover that the trim control was out and that the control column itself seemed jammed in the full back position; even with Murray Bartle's assistance, he did not succeed in budging it.

Meanwhile, *Lancaster* ND.759 continued down in its flat spin and the time-honoured process of throttling back and forth on the three good engines proved of no avail in stopping the motion. Then, desperately experimenting with throttle positions, Peter put the inner starboard 'through the gate' and cut the two port engines. That was it! The marathon spin stopped miraculously, the control column freed itself and the aircraft became sluggishly flyable again. Now Peter could reflect in amazement on the feat of having regained control of a spinning four-engined aircraft! Never in his training had he been confronted with induced spins on multi-engined machines – nor of course had any of his instructors taught him how to correct the manoeuvre.

Altitude was now close to 3,000ft (914m), only about 1,700ft (518m) above the level of Lake Constance. The *Lancaster* headed south-west towards Switzerland, near Konstanz and over the tongue of land which splits in two the western part of the lake. Soon Peter was flying down the southern Untersee, and as he gradually lost height, mountains intervened between him and the fiery lights of F'hafen, by now well ablaze. The moonless night became pitch black, blotting out the surface of the water.

CRASH STATIONS

Heading on 270° to the western tip of the lake with a slight tail wind, the pilot switched on his landing light, coming in tail low while the remaining members of the crew huddled at crash stations against the rear spar,[9] just ahead of the still-burning fuselage oil fire. On three engines and with 30° of flaps selected, Peter maintained 110mph (176km/h). His aircraft sank slowly in the cool air, skimmed the water for a moment, then slammed abruptly on its nose, immediately shipping water through the openings and the smashed perspex up front.

The *Lancaster* stayed afloat for about five minutes. In the meantime, the crew, well acquainted with their dinghy drill, scrambled out of the top hatches. Wading on a wing already awash, or, for the gunners, gingerly making their way atop the fuselage, they reached the raft bobbing at its painter over the starboard wing. Getting away from the floundering machine proved to be a problem in view of the round shape of the dinghy which was still brushing the tailplane when the aircraft sank. The time was near 0215hr (CH) and the position must have been just within Swiss waters,[10] north-east of Steckborn. This was, and is, a picturesque, small red-roofed city in Canton Thurgau, facing the German shore no more than 500 yards away. Of the three *Lancs* that came down in Switzerland that night, Peter's was the one closest to the target, and its crash had been observed by local bystanders watching the fireworks on both shores.

Shivering, soaking wet in freezing water, the five airmen reached neutral territory after some seventy-five minutes of a gruelling ordeal. In the meantime, they had heard the all-clear sounding on the German shore, had alternately paddled away from the crash site, attended the burned gunners, bailed the shrapnel-holed dinghy and fought adverse currents. Here, indeed, the Untersee which is the westernmost part of Lake Constance, narrows into what becomes once more the Rhine River. The waters of Lake Constance funnel between Swiss hills and Germany's Schiener Berg, creating a current pushing the dinghy towards the enemy shore. It would have been quite a disappointment for the castaways to find themselves Prisoners of War instead of spending time as internees in neutral custody, endowed with a status of quasi-holidaymakers!

IN GERMANY

That very mishap befell Al Brereton: his parachute deposited him, slightly wounded, on German soil near Konstanz. He was to spend the rest of the war as PoW N°3825 in Stalag Luft VI at Heydekrug, near Memel on the Baltic.

For the tall, ever-smiling P/O Foulkes, fate proved much more tragic. Long afterwards, the Swiss recovered his body from the lake where he had drowned, either of exhaustion in the frigid water or snared in his parachute. He would never return to his young wife, Betty. And it was one of the innumerable poignant tragedies of the war that, as late as October 1945, there was in Morgan, New South Wales, a bereaved mother still hoping that her son was alive somewhere and merely suffering from amnesia. He now rests at Vevey, alongside comrades who also died on Swiss soil. Ill-fated F/Sgt Foulkes was about to receive a commission to Pilot Officer:[11] the notification reached his Squadron two days after his death, at the same time as that of Noel Davis and of their pilot's.[12]

Again, Geoffrey Foulkes' passage through the intricacies of training shows what an aviation enthusiast of the time had to go through before reaching operational status. A clerk in the large AMP insurance concern, he had enlisted in the Royal Australian Air Force in September 1941, aged twenty-six. A year later, after attending schools for Air Observers, Bombing and Gunnery and Air Navigation, he had been sent to Canada for more training, until January 1943 when he sailed to the UK. Here he went through 21.OTU where Peter had spotted him at the crewing-up session. Like his pilot, he was then assigned to 51 Squadron, navigating *Halifaxes*.

Back in the dinghy, the castaways had noticed, while paddling south, a lot of activity on both shores as bystanders searched for them with torches and lanterns. All this had died down by the time they reached land. Still unsure of which country they were in, the men decided to hide in nearby hills. They cast off their wet and bulky clothing, stripped off their insignia, sank the faithful dinghy and clambered in the dark onto the boulders lining the shore. They still had to climb over a high shore fence before crossing a road and rail tracks, and ascending a steep incline before settling down in a clump of trees. At first light they became aware of the full extent of the gunners' burns, and it was decided that medical attention had first priority.

FRIGHTENING SIGHT

Near the Hohrain farm, they startled a farmer digging his garden. No wonder the man was frightened at the sight of five muddy, damp men, two of whom had their face covered in violet burn ointment from their first-aid kits! The farmer confirmed they were in Switzerland, gave them refreshments and took them to the Steckborn police station, less than a mile to the west. Here, an English-speaking teacher attempted to interrogate the airmen. Later in the afternoon, military policemen arrived to take charge. They were the overworked Oblt Rittmeyer and Gefreiter Wyder, arriving straight from their investigation of the Grappelen disaster (see Chapter 12). Here in Steckborn, they met airmen reticent to proffer any useful information. The crew even refused to indicate what type of aircraft they flew and Wyder had to rely on the chance finding of a floating tail wheel to ascertain that it – and they – belonged to a *Lancaster*.

Both Irishman David Balmer and the short Irvine Graham, who had been a butcher in Bury, Lancashire, had suffered serious facial burns. This was quite an anticlimax for moustachioed Vin Graham: it so happened that he had married just one week previously, only to be recalled to duty while on his honeymoon! By evening, the two men had been taken by ambulance to the Munsterlingen hospital. This, ironically, sat on the lakeshore almost opposite F'hafen where their action had created havoc. Robert Peter and his two unhurt friends were taken to Hotel Stadthof in St-Gall and, the next day, 29 April, to the central Swiss military air facility at Zurich-Dübendorf, where they were again interrogated.

For practically the duration of the war, the Swiss wondered whether or not airspace violations by the Allies stemmed from a deliberate policy. Their interrogators were therefore always on the lookout for indications that would justify their government in lodging formal complaints with Britain or the United States. To a direct question to that effect, W/O Peter stated that the attack route brought the stream on target from the north-west, with a left turn away from Switzerland after bombing. However, he said, it was not impossible that wind drift could have blown some aircraft into overflying Switzerland, the probability being increased by a stronger than expected rear wind. The pilot very much impressed his interrogator – again Lt Achard – by his strong-willed attitude and by stating that he hoped to return to combat against Japan after his release from internment. He also apologised for not being able to tell more about the Luftwaffe's ways of operating, which could help the Swiss in eventually fighting that possible opponent.[13] Peter's attitude was indeed in line with his state of mind when he said after the war, 'We were a great crew… all inspired by the prospect of a long and glorious career in operations'. It is of interest to notice that after his leaving as an exchangee, Peter was the subject of a commendation letter from his surviving friends striving to obtain for him a well-deserved decoration. Forwarded on 18 September 1944 to the Air Ministry by Air Commodore Ferdinand West, the Air Attaché in Berne, the move succeeded and Peter became a recipient of the much-coveted DFC.

FOUR AUSTRALIANS

As seen, Peter was not the only Aussie amongst the crew. Besides Foulkes, there was Davis who had been a bank clerk in Sydney, a job to which he returned after the war. Another who had come from 'down under' was short, stocky Murray Bartle with his enormous sense of fun. An interior decorator from Perth, he enlisted in the RAAF in July 1941 and arrived in England via America in February 1943 as a trained gunner/wireless operator. Like many Australia-trained aircrew who had spent too many months idling, he had to go through refresher courses before meeting his crew mates at 21.0TU. In Switzerland, he somewhat frayed his interrogators' nerves by sticking to the 'name-rank-serial number' litany and answering all other questions by the standard 'I don't know'. Again, a perfect case of observing regulations to the letter.

From Dübendorf, W/O Robert Peter went on to live at the small Schweizer Hof Hotel in Berne until he was lucky enough to be included at the last moment in a batch of nine exchangees leaving Switzerland on 13 May already. Like two other RAF pilots, Walter Blott and Bish Smith (see Chapters 8 and 10), he transited through Paris with his German chaperons, was at Gibraltar on 23 May and in England the day after. He returned to faraway, hot Australia in July 1944 but did not succeed in being posted to the Pacific zone of operations. Peter flew as an instructor at the RAAF College, Point Cook, Victoria, then instructed on *Oxfords* at Mallala, South Australia, no doubt passing on his knowledge of how to recover from spins in multi-engined aircraft. His next task continued until his discharge in March 1947: it was to help Australian veterans to readjust to civilian life.

In 1967 while in England, Peter retraced his fateful last operation, motoring down to Steckborn and Switzerland. He has kept in touch with Murray Bartle who lives like him in Western Australia, and he saw Noel Davis, now in New South Wales, a couple of times. On 25 April 2001, on Anzac Day[14] and two days before the 57th anniversary of their ultimate ordeal, Bartle, Davis and Peter were again re-united, marching in the military parade in Perth. As for Paddy Balmer and Vin Graham who returned to their respective European islands, he never saw them again after the Swiss took them to hospital in Münsterlingen.

WHAT STATUS?

Rightly or not, Peter's crew had been given by the Swiss a status of winged internees, meaning foreign refugees arriving by air. As such, they had to wait like their fellow evaders (airmen shot down, never captured and walking into Switzerland) until the end of hostilities would allow them to return to the UK and home. Many grew restless, however, electing to go illegally over the border into recently liberated France to be channelled back to Britain or North Africa.

Such was the case for the four remaining survivors of *Lancaster* ND.759. On 22 May they had been sent to Adelboden, an internment camp for Americans (!)

nestling in an isolated Swiss alpine area where they lived a safe but rather boring life. Early in October 1944, after France adjacent to Switzerland had been liberated, they elected to masquerade as ground troops and merge in a large party of such 'brown jobs' who were escaped prisoners being officially repatriated. There was of course the risk of being caught and punished by the Swiss.

Two, Noel Davis and Vin Graham, managed to squeeze themselves out of their internment domain and into the convoy of such former Army escapees, leaving by train on 4 October 1944. Davis teamed with the Canadian Albert Piggott (see Chapter 13) to slip through the Swiss border controls in Geneva into nearby France, and was soon back in England. After a spell at Patriotic School in London to ascertain that he was not a German agent, he registered with RAAF Headquarters in Kodak House near the Strand to obtain new uniforms, and then went on leave awaiting posting to Australia. He sailed back, arriving – again through the Panama Canal – in Sydney in February 1945 to be reunited with his family.[15] Noel Davis did not fly again: he became an RAAF paymaster and resumed duties with the Bank of New South Wales in September.

Vin Graham's escaping experience was peacefully eventful. While spending Christmas with British friends in Berne he met, by chance, an American sergeant. The airman asked him if he wanted to go home without delay. The answer was obvious and so, after midnight and a few hours at an American address, Vin and twelve US airmen embarked in a large van. They were driven to the French border, again near Geneva. Graham was in Paris for the New Year and was flown back to Britain by *Dakota*. Vera, his wife for a week before he was shot down, had the surprise of her life when her olive-complexioned Vin arrived home just a few hours after the telegram announcing that, after all, he was not in a Swiss hospital any more!

TOURING WAUWILLERMOOS

Bartle and Balmer were not so lucky. Swiss guards almost literally flushed them out of the lavatory they were hiding in at the Geneva rail station and they had to wait until the very end of the year to return to the UK. Indeed, after their trial they served time in the infamous Wauwilermoos punishment camp.[16] Representations by the British Legation in Berne came to no avail, the Swiss refusing to accept the notion that they had landed in German waters and escaped from German custody.[17] It was not before 14 November that Paddy Balmer was released on a thirty-day parole. This time he was sent to the Arosa camp, from which he escaped again on 16 December, with four other inmates. Helped by a British-sponsored 'escape line', he crossed into liberated France near Geneva and was taken to a US unit gathering 'Swiss re-evaders'.[18] From here the men were channelled back to England where Balmer arrived on 31 December 1944.

Murray Bartle's escapade – actually his second attempt, the first having failed in the Alps – also terminated in Geneva's Cornavin station lavatory! He, too, became another guest at Wauwillermoos and Arosa until 16 December 1944. With Balmer and the others out of Arosa, he went once more to Geneva, reached France and was taken by the Americans to Lyons and Marseilles. There he had, again, a brush with authority: in this case the US Military Police who questioned his identity. When cleared, he was flown to England, landing there on New Year's Eve.

SALVAGING A *LANC*

Lancaster ND.759 had sunk in about 30m (100ft) of water just off the hamlet of Nächsthorn, about 3km (2mi.) north east of Steckborn. At the time, only two items were recovered by Oblt Rittmeyer's team: the crew's dinghy and a wheel. Much later, in June 1954, the wreck was raised from the deep by Martin 'Bomber' Schaffner, a scrap dealer turned salvage operator.[19] The aircraft was exhibited in situ for a couple of years and the remains were scrapped at the end of 1955. Several items seem, however, to have survived and one could be a rear turret now exhibited in the Reuenthal museum near Leibstadt and the German border.

Further west, Rolf Zaugg proudly displays in his well-appointed museum at Utzenstorf,[20] a mid-upper turret and a tail wheel which once belonged to *Lancaster* ND.759. Another piece of equipment could also have survived: a Mk.IXA bombsight, No.8792/41. That intricate apparatus found its way to the Dübendorf air museum near Zürich. Doubts linger, however, as one wonders why an ordinary Mk.IX would have been aboard a PFF aircraft, the corps having by the time of the crash switched from the more sophisticated Mk.XIV to the excellent Mk.II Stabilised Automatic model, the SABS. The theory expounded by the Dübendorf Museum is that the Mk.XIV belonged to a *Mosquito*, three examples of which did arrive in Switzerland during the war. Two were to land at Dübendorf in September 1944 (see Chapter 15) but both were fighter-bombers with 'solid' noses devoid of bombsight. The Mk.XIV did indeed equip glass-nosed *Mossies*. Such a configuration can be seen on the machine flown into Berne in August 1942 (see Chapter 4) but it is difficult to understand why a bombsight would be aboard a photo-reconnaissance machine. That is unless the aircraft was a converted bomber version, but then why keep the device during its conversion ?

15

The Last of the Few

AIRMEN AND AIRCRAFT:
Pilot: S/Ldr Henry Morley
Navigator: F/Sgt Reginald Fidler
Passenger: LAC Gordon. 'Ted' Harper
Mosquito FB.Mk.VI, PZ.440, code P3°-, 515 Squadron

Pilot: F/Lt Arthur Callard
Navigator: F/Sgt E.Dixon Townsley
Mosquito FB.Mk.VI, NS.993, code P3°T, 515 Squadron

Two Mosquitoes *set off from England on the last day of September 1944. Both belonged to 515 Squadron, Fighter Command. Both were bound for a Day Ranger patrol over Southern Germany. Both were intent on landing on the Continent. Little did their crews suspect that they were flying themselves into history as being soon the last RAF airmen to end up in Switzerland in the Second World War.*

30 September 1944 was perhaps typical of air operations over North-Western Europe at this stage of the war. Bomber Command had resumed daylight raids against oil targets and today, it was sending 139 heavies to Sterkrade and 136 more to Bottrop. The American 8th Air Force had 765 *Fortresses* and *Liberators* roaming the skies over the Continent in search of transportation targets, and 673 fighters on escort and sweep duties. Their colleagues of the 9th Air Force were dispatched on fighter sweeps all over Europe. *B-26 Marauder* medium bombers operated against the ill-fated Arnhem bridge in Holland, where the RAF's 2nd Tactical Air Force was also busy. Fighter Command's aircraft were shepherding their bomber compatriots on daylight raids. Also, a host of so-called minor operations was taking place: British radio-counter-measures flights, petrol-carrying sorties to the Continent by both American *Liberators* and British *Halifaxes*, weather-reporting missions, Resistance supply operations... [1]

DAY RANGERS

There were several Day Ranger patrols: freelance flights by *Mosquito*es roving under reasonable cloud cover. In this autumn of 1944, some sorties used forward bases such as St-Dizier in Eastern France. No.515 Squadron[2] had a long experience of positioning aircraft and groundcrews at advanced bases: it had inaugurated the process early in 1943 when flying *Defiants* for 'Moonshine' radio-counter-measures operations from the south coast of England.

St-Dizier was a busy spot. On 28 September for instance, a couple of *Mossies* from 605 Squadron[3] had used it as jumping-off point to Munich and, a month from them, on 29 October, two more from 515 Squadron would land there on their way to Prague, deep in Czechoslovakia. The lucky pair would have a double escape: first from 'friendly' American anti-aircraft fire and then from bad weather rolling in on the way back and forcing them to divert to Reims-Juvincourt and Amiens-Glisy.[4]

No.515 Squadron had been in business since March 1944 with *Mosquito* FB.Mk.VI[5] armed with four 20mm Hispano cannon and as many 0.303in (7.7mm) machine-guns. It could carry bombs under the wings but extra fuel tanks usually took their place for long-range sorties. At the time, 515 shared with 23 Squadron its base at Little Snoring near King's Lynn and Sandringham in Norfolk. This is rather far north, near the Wash and whenever sorties were scheduled towards Southern Germany, extra fuel tanks and an intermediate landing were the order of the day.

The previous day, two crews had been alerted to conduct the Day Ranger of 30 September to Munich and beyond. They were S/Ldr Henry Morley with F/Sgt Reginald Fidler as navigator, and F/Lt Arthur Callard with F/Sgt E. Dixon Townsley. Morley had joined the expanding RAF Volunteer Reserve way back in 1934, flying light aircraft and had been called up the very day the war started: 3 September 1939. He was then twenty-six and a draughtsman, living in Bognor Regis. His career had included target-towing duties but after training for operations at 51.OTU, Cranfield, Morley had been posted to 515 Squadron in early July 1944. He had flown his first offensive sortie on the night of 5/6 July to the Zuider Zee in Holland. In September he had been on six operations.[6] On 26/27 September he and Fidler had destroyed a twin-engined aircraft, probably an *He.111* landing at Zellhausen, Germany. Their next and most recent sortie had been a five-hour affair to Wunstorf and Langenhagen airfields near Hanover. They had brought their bombs back, finding no suitable target.

WRONG CODE

Early on Saturday 30 September, Morley walked 'with his crew' to *Mosquito* PZ.440, an Mk.VI fighter-bomber. The machine had reached the Squadron on 23 September and was so new that although the Squadron's red code had been hastily painted on the rear fuselage, the lettering had been inverted, showing P3 instead of the official 3P. Furthermore, no individual aircraft letter had yet been allocated. The aircraft was thus to fly with a code showing it incorrectly as belonging to 692 Squadron, another *Mosquito* outfit. Only its serial was to permit a correct identification.

With pilot Morley was the unusual complement of *two* other flyers: his regular navigator and a mechanic-passenger. Lance Corporal Gordon 'Ted' Harper, MiD, the extra man, was needed at St-Dizier[7] to check the aircraft and help in fitting the extra-long-range tanks. He was supposed to fly back to England the same evening, again sitting on the floor, squeezed between the navigator's legs.

Reg Fidler, the navigator, had always had one passion: aviation. Born in Acton in 1924, he had worked with the engine manufacturer Napier & Sons Ltd in their engine test section. Although exempted from military service he had volunteered for aircrew duties in 1941, 'massaging' his age to eighteen. He succeeded in reaching pilot's Elementary Flying Training but 'because of (his) novel way of landing *Tiger Moths* or of (his) experience with figures', he was earmarked for navigator training. Returning from South Africa in 1943 the RAF had acquainted him with airborne radar. In June 1944 he had crewed up with his pilot at 51.OTU Cranfield. Now, following a premonition, Fidlerhad packed all his kit after briefing the night before.

The mission had been in the offing for several days but the crew had had to be updated on routes, defended areas, airfields and weather. The flight left Little Snoring at 0715hr;[8] they flew south across the Channel and France to St-Diz where they landed after one hour and forty minutes of uneventful cross-country in moderate weather.

The other machine had flown the same route a few minutes earlier. This was F/Lt Callard's *Mosquito* NS.993 which, again, bore the same wrong code P3. This second lapse could indicate that a clerical error was made by some 'wingless wonder' somewhere high up at Air Ministry. In any case, NS.993 had acquired during its Squadron life the individual letter T, making it 515/T in official RAF rhetoric. Callard had, within his operational experience, flown this *Mossie* several times since a first trip to Grove near Hamburg on the night of 8/9 August, visiting amongst other distant destinations Dijon, Bordeaux, Handorf, Lübeck and, on 6/7 September, Flensburg where NS.933 had been holed by intense flak.

EN ROUTE REFUELLING

In the morning at St-Dizier, both aircraft refuelled. They carried extra-large 200gal (909 litres) drop-tanks instead of the usual 100gal ones. Then Harper, the 'flying mechanic', checked his machines again and went off to town, 'armed' with pounds of coffee and a revolver lent to him by F/Lt Callard. His quite unofficial secondary assignment was to try to barter the coffee the trio had brought out of

England. This was a scarce commodity on the Continent and its exchange rate in lipsticks and other trinkets was quite high. When, in the event, Harper had to return home alone, he shared the spoils honestly: personal effects sent to the missing airmen's families included amazing items he had acquired 'over there'.

The combat sortie took off at 1150hr Heading south-east at nearly 290mph (385km/h) the machines avoided the cloud-shrouded Vosges mountains. Weather there and over the Black Forest precluded a direct route to destination where their assignment was to attack airfields and other military targets south of Munich and east of Vienna, 530 miles (850km) away from their advanced base. Preparing for the flight, they had chosen a more southerly route, into Switzerland near the German border.

Swiss intelligence Captain Gottfried von Meiss was later to study with understandable interest a pencilled map found aboard one of the *Mosquitoes*: its intended track ran 137° magnetic, straight from St-Dizier to the Swiss border in the Jura mountains, exactly where poor Sam Atcheson had crashed with his *Lancaster*, near Saignelégier, six months earlier (see Chapter 9). Here the river Doubs flowing in narrow ravines could be pinpointed by the *Mossie*'s crews. They would then proceed north-east, following the Swiss-German border, safely tucked inside Switzerland, via Laufen, Frick and Frauenfeld and then exit neutral territory over Lake Constance, near Altnau.[9]

The map indicated that the navigators had planned to reach Switzerland at 1229hr. As it was the *Mosquitoes* were spotted five minutes late by Swiss observers of *Flab Detachment 66* at Reconvilier, thundering over the hills en route to Soleure. They were a little south of plan and remained so all the way. The pair of low-level prowlers with F/Lt Callard leading arrived in sight of Lake Constance and Kreuzlingen at 1308hr. Ack-ack had sporadically fired at them along the way, light and fortunately inaccurate. Heavy flab from *Flab Detachments 3 and 8* also went in action, lobbing 186 of their 7.5cm shells (2.95in) at the intruders, claiming hits and smoke issuing from one machine.[10]

THEY WOULD MEET AGAIN

One battery was at Märwil, 8/9 miles (15km) inland from the lake. It fired 20mm and 7.5cm rounds at 'many unidentified aircraft flying at 30-200m above ground' (100-600ft). It missed the *Mosquitoes* but they would meet again!

Callard's windscreen became covered with dead flies, a usual occurrence for aircraft hugging the ground in mild weather. Furthermore, his navigator, F/Sgt 'Dickie' Townsley, had become sick and Callard asked Morley to take over the lead. The *Mosquitoes* reached Holzkirchen airfield, due south of Munich at about 1320hr Skimming low at 200ft (60m), they spotted a Messerschmitt *Bf.109* stationary near two fat twin-engined Siebel *Si.204* trainers. Morley was able to fire a four-seconds cannon burst at them, observing strikes on all three and smoke pouring from the Siebels.

Smoke, however, was not the only thing emitted from the ground: Morley's *Mosquito* was hit by light flak in its starboard drop-tank. Fidler could see petrol streaming out of it and Morley had to jettison both tanks to maintain trim. By now the two aircraft had almost reached Austria but fuel was becoming a problem for Morley who thus had no alternative but to turn for 'home'. On his *TR.1143A* radio he informed Callard of his predicament, suggesting that he, Callard, could continue alone. He did. With no drop-tanks and with his four outer tanks now dry, Morley ideally now needed to fly the most direct route back. This would, however, entail passing through the strong defences of Munich and Augsburg. Fidler thus computed a southerly course, again to Lake Constance, the largest landmark on the border between Germany and Switzerland. This was the reverse of the morning's route. It would be a somewhat longer but less hazardous.

When *Mosquito* PZ.440 (Callard's) reached a point south of Munich slightly after 1400hr, the crew searched for enemy aircraft reported to be dispersed near the autobahn leading to the Bavarian Alps. Passing Neubiberg aerodrome, six miles south of the city, Morley was able to fire their 20mm cannon at a twin-engined machine parked on the southern boundary. It was one of a number of Junkers *Ju.86s*. The crew later claimed it as damaged after strikes from their explosive and armoured shells were observed on the starboard wing root.

Half an hour later, at 200ft (60m), Morley buzzed the Austrian tip of Lake Constance, roaring out of enemy territory between Bregenz and Lindau. Flying in haze against the sun was impairing visibility. Now heading due west, he penetrated Switzerland within sight of Uttwil where his unknown comrade, S/Ldr Negushad perished in April (see Chapter 11).

LIMPING HOME

Morley was reported over Amriswil at 1426hr in what the Swiss recorded as the thirty-fifth of the day's forty-four border violations! One minute later *Flab Detachment 111* (the one at Märwil) spotted the *Mosquito* flying at 500m above ground (1,600ft): the gunners did not know it but this was the same aircraft that had been past them before, on its way out. Anyway, this time they and other units opened up with all they had, including 20mm and 34mm weapons. They had time to lob twenty-two rounds of 20mm and just two shots of 7.5cm.[11] Why they again hurled such heavy-calibre ammunition at low-flying aircraft remains a question. Seconds later the four 20mm guns of *Detachment 116* at Bürglen let go twenty of its shells.

Two spectacular events resulted from their action. First the gunners observed a trail of dark smoke issuing from the *Mosquito*. 'Flugzeug brennt!' was their shout down the telephone to their headquarters. Morley's port *Merlin 25* had indeed been hit: it was later ascertained that 20mm splinters had cut a coolant line and disabled the supercharger. Two hits were also scored in the starboard wing. The second outcome of the flab *Mosquito*-repellent activity was the setting alight of another 'target': Walter Bischof's barn in Hard, just east of Weinfelden! Neither Morley nor Fidler noticed the burning barn although they flew low over it, en route west to Affeltrangen. They were busy controlling the now single-engined machine with Morley only too well aware of the *Mosquito's* unfriendly behaviour below its rather high safety speed of some 160mph (260 km/h) recommended by the Pilot's Notes.[12] The useless powerplant was feathered and Fidler kept on map-reading, trying to retrace his earlier route.

In the meantime Swiss interception patrols had been scrambled from Dübendorf and Payerne airfields. '*Emil*', their reporting station had indicated a double *Mosquito* violation as early as 1302hr, apparently when the two machines flew east. Now, the crippled *Mosquito* was overtaken at 1435hr by four Swiss fighters. They belonged to *Flieger Kompanie 14* out of Dübendorf and flew Morane-Saulnier *406*s, Hispano-Suiza-powered French interceptors built under licence in Switzerland. They were known there as *D-3800* or *D-3801*; 188 of them were on hand at the end of 1944. By waggling their wings, losing height and firing flares, their pilots motioned to Morley to follow them. He had little choice other than to comply as by then he was also discovering another pre-dicament: his inability to climb since his good engine was also showing signs of weakness. As a landing was becoming imminent, Fidler tore up maps and papers, throwing out the fragments.

Within a few minutes, the formation reached the Dübendorf military airfield, a few miles east of Zürich, and prepared for a left-hand circuit. Then, suddenly, the remaining engine decided to pack up. Gliding at 150ft or so (46m), Morley had insufficient height to contemplate a dead-stick circuit even with the drag-inducing undercarriage up. He turned into the easterly wind, endeavouring to reach an open field, south-east of the aerodrome. Rapidly losing height, the pilot shut off all switches, nursing the *Mosquito* past a row of trees… where the machine stalled! It cut a telephone pole as if it were matchstick and still doing a good 100mph (160km/h) slammed into the soft ground, fortunately without nosing in. The starboard wing had dropped first, the engine digging in at the edge of a meadow and getting stuck in a ditch, pulling the eight-ton machine to the right. Then, as the aeroplane scraped sideways across a harvested cornfield, the propeller broke, hurtling away crazily. The left wing now dipped, striking the ground sideways, engine first. The *Merlin* snapped from its mount and dug itself into the wooden fuselage which cracked open like a broken cigar near the wing trailing edge.

FROM NEW TO WRECK

The once pristine PZ.440 had turned into several heaps of torn wood and hot metal some 500m (1,500ft) from the point of impact. The solid nose had separated, lying with its weapons near the port engine, on the right of the main wreckage. For a few seconds, Morley and Fidler lay were dazed. A small electrical fire sputtered quietly in the wiring on top of the instrument panel. It soon went out by itself and no other fire broke out that could have been fed by leaking petrol. This was particularly fortunate for Morley who had his right foot trapped between the ground and the now floorless crumpled *Mossie*.

Fidler, whose straps had surprisingly been undone, went over the instrument panel, suffering a cracked collar bone and acquiring 'a beautiful black eye'. Within a minute he was crawling back to the wrecked cockpit now lying practically at ground level. Morley's exit 'took a little longer'. The *Mosquito* had crashed at 1437hr, south-west of Volketswil, a tiny farm village near Dübendorf.[13] Most of the locals quickly arrived and started to free Morley. However, as fuses began to blow and with petrol fumes all around, they made a hasty retreat, dragging Fidler clear. Poor Morley got out all by himself 'by a massive heave, badly lacerating his legs'.

The military eventually reached the scene and awaiting whatever development they would decree, the crew witnessed a most extraordinary scene. What they saw was a second *Mosquito* – their own colleague bearing the code P3-T – re-enacting their own arrival at Dübendorf, complete with one propeller feathered and a Swiss fighter escort!

This machine had, meanwhile, carried on F/Lt Callard's solitary assignment. This tall, moustachioed, twenty-five-year-old aviator had been, pre-war, a police constable also, in London. After joining the RAF in December 1940 he became an instructor in Canada before returning to the UK. He had passed through 58.OTU's course No.16 in February 1944. His navigator, frizzy-haired, small and smiling F/Sgt Townsley, was twenty-two, from Leeds and in the RAF since February 1942. Both had been in 515 Squadron for three months during which their sorties had taken them, as seen above, to Northern and Central Germany but also to Denmark, Belgium, Bordeaux and Dijon. This was their first foray to Southern Germany.

Their mount, also a *Mosquito* FB.VI, Callard knew well for he had flown this NS.993 on seven occasions during his 11 combat sorties since early May. The aircraft's nose was adorned with three black crosses, showing the number of German aircraft destroyed. The incorrect squadron code letters were painted in red over the grey-green camouflage and invasion stripes on the rear fuselage.

SINKING A DORNIER

Callard and Townsley had reached Lake Chiem,[14] south-east of Munich, at 1328hr: a juicy target awaited them on the picturesque island in the lake's western part. Several aircraft were there, including a pair of elegant Dornier *Do.24* flying-boats moored quite near the shore. Diving from 500ft (152m) Callard hosed them with short bursts, zooming over his preys so fast that no result could be observed.

Townsley then directed his pilot to Salzburg, 20mi. (32km) north-east of which the crew located Friedburg airfield. On this small grass surface, a forlorn *Bf.109* waited near the single hangar. A two-second burst of fire subtracted it from the Luftwaffe inventory. The fighter blew up as the *Mosquito* roared over, pieces of the victim hitting it. The time was 1342hr, according to Townsley's log.

The crew flew on to Atter Lake and at 1400hr, over the railway maze of Vocklaburg, decided to turn back, their opaque windscreen definitely hampering useful observation. Back over Lake Chiem at 1420hr and 200ft (60m), Callard saw the sunken wreckage of the *Do.24* he had strafed.[15] A quick turn and its mate was again in his reflector sight. It too disintegrated, settling in shallow water. Callard was indeed getting into the habit of destroying floatplanes. With Townsley and their faithful NS.993, he had already claimed one Arado *Ar.196* and damaged another during an Intruder sortie on 6 September.

At 1433hr, as Morley was nearing Switzerland, Callard was speeding south of Munich at the incredible height of 7ft (2m)! Suddenly he spotted four *Bf.109* fighters closing fast at 500ft (152m). The *Mosquito* turned into them, flew underneath unseen, scurrying at full boost of 18lb/in² (36.65 in.Hg or 1.27 kg/cm²) for thirty seconds. The Rolls-Royce *Merlin 25* could in principle sustain full emergency boost for five minutes. However, was it the extra power abruptly demanded or was it a consequence of debris from the *109* at Friedburg hitting a radiator? In any case the starboard engine temperature then rose swiftly off the clock.[16]

The *Merlin* had to be feathered as the crew flew towards the south of Lake Constance at zero feet. They too found it difficult to cross the hills near Bregenz. North of Zürich, Morley's experience repeated itself for Callard's benefit. Four Morane fighters stamped with white crosses on red background, slowly overtook the ailing *Mosquito*. One pair took position to port, the other to starboard. None showed any belligerent intention. Townsley fired a single red flare, to which the Swiss answered with a white. Nobody really knew what it all meant and the international formation flew on as the *Mosquito* tried to ignore its neighbours!

SINGLE-ENGINE LANDING

South-east of Basle, the Swiss lost patience: all four aircraft closed in, signalling the British machine to land. So, everybody turned back towards Dübendorf. There, maintaining a touch above 160mph knots (260km/h), Callard executed a perfect single-engine landing. Aware of the *Mossie*'s shortcomings in single-engine landings and of the high drag of the lowered landing gear, Callard had endeavoured not to undershoot. This may explain why he slightly overshot the boundary and came to rest in a vegetable patch. The watches showed 1523hr and the last wartime RAF aircraft had touched down in Switzerland.

True to form, the crew succeeded in destroying the logbook and the flimsies bearing radio frequencies and other data relevant to the raid. Immediately however, armed guards appeared, taking over the aircraft and overpowering the flyers.

The Swiss thus acquired their second, practically intact *Mosquito*, complete with its VHF transceiver and eight frequency crystals, its type *ABK-1* IFF identifier, a fully-fledged *TR. 1355* unit for *Gee*-navigation and a *C.45* cine-gun-camera, albeit without film. The aircraft itself was to lead a protracted if rather unruffled second life, sitting sedately in a Dübendorf hangar prior to being turned in a test bed for Swiss jet engines (see Chapter 19).

What became of the four RAF airmen of 30 September 1944 once they were safely on the ground? From Volketswil, the wounded Morley and Fidler were taken to Zürich hospital, 'examined and dumped in beds in a large ward'. Then the Swiss realised Morley was a high-ranking officer and moved him to a private room. There, a pleasant surprise awaited the pilot: a bottle of VAT 69 'tonic' with compliments from Col. Brandli, the man whose unit had downed his aircraft. After a couple of weeks he and Fidler were deemed fit for transfer to Davos and internment.

Reginald Fidler ran away before that and waited in hiding with a Czech couple in Zürich until Henry Morley could do the same on 18 October. With an American captain, they travelled to Perly near Geneva, at the western tip of Switzerland which by then was surrounded by liberated French territory. Whilst attempting to cross the fenced frontier by night, they were fired at by a Swiss border patrol. They ran in opposite directions. Morley returned to Geneva and succeeded in crossing into France the next day. Through the Jura mountains, he eventually reached Lyon-Bron airfield on 28 October. That same day he was back in England, landing at Hartington. Three days later he was welcomed at 515 Squadron's base by all and sundry, including their successful CO, W/Cdr Frederick Lambert, DSO, DFC.[17] Post-war, he returned to architect's work and made a point in the seventies to re-visit Switzerland where he was fêted by Gottfried von Meiss, the Swiss intelligence officer he had met in the war.

INMATES IN WAUWILERMOOS

Meanwhile, Fidler had been brought back to Geneva and had again been picked up after one more attempt to reach France. He was put in a school used as a holding camp from where he almost escaped once more. This time the Swiss were not amused: they jailed him first in St-Antoine prison in Geneva, then on for an unpleasant month at Wauwilermoos. After this he was sent to Arosa in Central Switzerland on a month's parole. Soon getting fed up of skiing he toyed again with the idea of escaping with his colleague navigator Townsley and three other RAF aircrew, all former inmates at Wauwil. The latter were apparently John Millard from the Golaten *Lancaster* (see Chapter 10) and David Balmer with Murray Bartle from the Steckborn *Lanc* (see Chapter 14). After their time on parole had lapsed, they again departed Geneva, this time managing to leave the country: in the case of Fidler in a train of returning French refugees. In civilian clothes he managed to hitchhike a ride to Lyons, to wangle his way into an

American aircraft to Marseilles and then to Paris and finally to England. He was back in 'Old Blighty' by the end of 1944. Fidler was then assigned as instructor; he wanted to return to operations but administrative snags and the end of the war put a stop to such wishes.

Arthur Callard was the first to reach the UK. He and Townsley had at first been interned in the officers' barracks in Dübendorf. Then, on 2 October, he was sent to Adelboden from where he escaped to France; he reached England on 21 October. The following day he lectured his Squadron on his and Morley's Swiss experiences. Callard flew one more operation, on 5 January 1945. Morley also resumed flying with 515 and 23 Squadrons[18] until January 1945.

16

Misleading Cockades

PILOTS AND AIRCRAFT:

20 April 1945	*Spitfire* IX MH.366	Lt V. Koechlin
25 May 1945	*P-47D* n°44.33681	S/Lt Carrere
25 May 1945	*P-47D* n°44-33686	Lt Toulouse
2 July 1945	*F-5G* n°44-26121	S/Lt Nicolas
16 July 1945	*P-39Q* n°44- 3044	S/Lt Devolvé
16 July 1945	*P-39* n°44- 3914	Sgt Laurens

National markings of Second World War Allied aircraft changed with the passage of time, and RAF roundels – or cockades – were not immune to the phenomenon. The RAF's standard fuselage cockade displayed a yellow circle outlining what was the real national round insignia – from outside to centre, a blue circular band, a white one and a red disc.

On some occasions after 1942, the yellow disappeared and what remained was bound to be confused with French markings which showed a red outside circle, a white one and a central blue 'dot'. The same applied to the fin flashes, which for the RAF consisted of a red band leading (towards the front of the aircraft), followed by a narrow white strip and a blue band aft.

The possibility of confusing the RAF and FAF (French Air Force) markings disappeared with the fall of France in June 1940. However, the chances of mistaking one nationality for the other returned with the arrival of rejuvenated French Air Force units and, more particularly, of French fighters, fighter-bombers and medium bombers from the Autumn of 1944 onwards.[1] A typical example of the confusion induced by French roundels is apparent in a Swiss report in July 1945 referring to 'British markings' (on a French reconnaissance *P-38* alias *F-5G*) described as a cockade with red-white-blue concentric circles.

Roundel-sporting French machines operating near the northern borders of Switzerland in the last phase of the war were bound to appear in the country.

They did, albeit in limited numbers: seven are on record in Swiss archives for 1945, just a few weeks before and after VE-Day.[2] The six that arrived after the end of the war in Europe cannot be labelled as operational machines of war. They did not seek asylum in neutral country because of enemy action: they were either lost in bad weather and/or short of fuel over unknown territory. For the sake of completeness in the coverage of this trilogy[3] of Allied aircraft flying into Switzerland during the war years, it seems appropriate to include here a short description of the French-Swiss connection.

FIRST (AND LAST) *SPITFIRE*

Thirty-year-old Lieutenant de Vaisseau Henri Koechlin was a naval aviator.[4] On 20 April 1945, he was on loan to a French fighter unit: Groupe de Chasse GC.1/7 '*Provence*'.[5] With nineteen other *Spitfires*, he had lifted off Strasbourg-Entzheim at 0635hr for an early sweep over Southern Germany. He flew a sleek, grey Mark IX, serialed MH.366 with a simple 'Y' as code letter. By 0755hr the posse was returning from the Reutlingen-Donaueschingen-Offenburg area. It had been a disappointing sortie because, apart from a light personnel car and a couple of steam engines, they had not spotted anything worthwhile strafing.

The returning formation had climbed to some 18,000ft (6,000m), hoping against all odds for an encounter with German aircraft. What the *Spits* met were icy conditions, but it is not clear if this was the source of Koechlin's engine conking out nor if the conditions rendered his pitot speed indicator useless. Luckily, the formation was flying just north of the Schaffhausen bulge, in sight of Swiss territory. Still, the almost three-ton *Spitfire*, nose-heavy with its large Rolls-Royce *Merlin 66* engine, glided like a brick.

In this region, the Swiss-German border follows a quite tormented line, winding back and forth without apparent purpose across hills and rivers. The frontier was actually marked with several large white crosses on red backgrounds but its tortuous path made it difficult to ascertain, even in the most sedate conditions of flight. So it was more by chance than by design that Koechlin avoided a good tract of hospitable-looking ground on his left: this was Germany, south of Talheim, where he would probably have been captured. A mile or two further on, in crossing a brook and rail tracks, the pilot barely cleared the border. Avoiding sunken ground, he was now faced with forested land and aimed at a clearing on a hilltop.

With the sliding hood locked open, gear retracted, electrical switches off to prevent sparks and maintaining an estimated safe gliding speed well above the recommended 105mph (170km/h), he brushed a large pine tree. The silent machine slammed on the ground. Coming in too fast, the *Spit* bounced on the rocky ground and hit again some 50m (150ft) further on. The strain was too much for the airframe: the wings buckled and the fuselage broke in two, the *Merlin* engine separating at the firewall. The main fuel tank between engine and pilot was punctured and it lost most of its contents[6] but, fortunately, no fire broke out.

It was just a few minutes before 0800hr Koechlin was not seriously hurt but for a sore neck, a bump on his head and bruises where the restraining harness had eroded his shoulders. He was discovered by a woman near the round Osterberg hill, north of Merishausen and Schaffhausen. The Good Samaritan helped him out of the wreckage and covered him under his parachute. This was barely inside neutral territory but Koechlin had made it into the peaceful safety of Switzerland, where he would remain interned until the armistice. Meanwhile, his colleagues had wanted to make sure he was all right. A pair of *Spitfires* returned to the spot a little later, overflying the wreck, noticing the pilot was alive among a throng of soldiers and sightseers.

TWIN THUNDERBOLTS...

During the mid-afternoon of Friday 25 May 1945, thunder echoed among the narrow streets of the border city of Basle. Across the Rhine to the north-east, Germany was at long last relieved of the heavenly damnation that had destroyed her might. To the west, France, now one of the victorious nations, was basking in a peace that would allow her to rebuild her shattered ego and economy. Aircraft of her reconstructed fledgling air force, now part of the Allied occupation forces in Southern Germany, flew back and forth between their metropolitan bases and the Baden-Würtemberg area.

However, it was a ferry flight from Paris to Strasbourg that almost proved fatal to a pair of stubby, brand-new, unarmed[7] *P-47D-30-RA* fighters. Short of fuel in marginal weather, their pilots – Lt. Toulouse and S/Lt. Carrère – elected to make a precautionary landing in Basle-Birsfelden. They explained to their Swiss hosts that their uncamouflaged Republic *Thunderbolts* – serials 4433681 and 4433686 – had fuel-feed failures. It is not known whether or not the Swiss did cure the deficiency; anyway, they pumped 500 litres of petrol into each aircraft. The pair was thus able to fly off the morning after towards their initial destination. They had spent just nineteen hours in the comparative cosiness of Switzerland.

TWIN BOOMS...

Monday 2 July 1945 turned out grey with low ceilings over western Switzerland and Charles Bratschi, Geneva airport's manager prepared for a week during which a couple of civilian airliners were expected to land on his domain. Much sooner than expected, the hum of powerful engines reverberated between Lake Geneva and the Jura mountains.

Startled observers then spotted a surprising contraption approaching the airfield. They had heard of the twin-boomed heavy fighter operated by the US Army Air Forces but this was the first of those Lockheed *P-38s* that ever visited

Swiss skies. The *Lightning* did not actually display US insignia as did so many air-craft stranded in the country.[8] This one turned out to be a French reconnaissance machine similar to the one lost the preceding summer with the great Antoine de St-Exupery, the French pilot–writer. It was 1140hr when the peculiar aircraft touched down on Geneva's short concrete runway.

Out of the gondola that acted as cockpit between the two powerful Allison V-1710 engines stepped a mature-looking pilot. S/Lt Edouard Nicolas was a Frenchman, born in April 1917: he claimed to belong to a Colmar-based French photo reconnaissance unit: GR 1/33[9] and the yellow lettering W4°L on his aircraft indeed indicated a machine belonging to the unit. The *P-38*, or more precisely the blunt-nosed *F-5G* as it turned out to be, bore the US serial 426121 indicative of a batch of about 100 machines lend-leased to France outside the USAAF inventory. The aeroplane's fuselage was devoid of armament and housed two vertical and two oblique cameras, a frontal example not being fitted in the nose.

Nicolas' training mission had been a meteorological flight over the Bavarian Alps: he had lifted off from Colmar at 0820hr and, returning over Basle had met a solid undercast that prompted him to seek better conditions further south, namely in Geneva where the pilot knew he could find the concrete runway that he favoured because of his relative inexperience on the *P-38*. This sortie was indeed only his fifth on type even if his fighter pilot training Stateside had been quite thorough. A pre-war student in survey engineering, Nicolas had been an observer in the post-1940 French Air Force. After the fall of North Africa he had, in November 1943, been sent to the United States for pilot training. He returned in May 1945 with some 180 hours under his belt on such aircraft as the Vultee *BT-13 Valiant*, North American *AT-6 Texan*, Curtiss *P-40 Kittyhawk* and Republic *P-47 Thunderbolt*.

Geneva and the Swiss authorities – namely Lt Charles Bratschi – looked after Nicolas with extreme courtesy – after all, the war was over and he flew a harmless machine, they spoke the same language and he had arrived with the rare treat of a quite unorthodox aircraft hitherto never seen in Switzerland. Contrary to regulations, Nicolas was allowed in town to acquire such unfamil-iar delicacies as Swiss chocolate and tobacco. This, with enough petrol to reach his home base, loaded up his aircraft when it took off the day after towards eastern France.

Take-off time was 0935hr and Nicolas would have been well-advised to post-pone his departure by a few hours, letting the morning strato-cumuli dissipate over the high ground. Indeed, one hour later Bratschi was summoned on the phone. Was he, asked the commandant of Payerne military airbase, aware of a *Lightning* pilot flying from Geneva to France in an aircraft most nooks of which were stuffed with contraband goods such as Laurens cigarettes and chocolate bars? Yes? Then be advised that the said pilot is now in Payerne, just 100km (62mi.)

to the north-west, stranded again due to bad weather! Duly cleared and with the weather of the same vein, Nicolas was able to leave Payerne. He took off at 1457hr, this time chaperoned by a pair of Swiss fighters, up to make sure the visitor would find his way out of the country.

... AND TWIN 'COBRAS

Weather over north-central Switzerland on 16 July 1945 was not conducive of festive moods, all the less so at Teufen north of Zurich.[10] Here, in the afternoon, a Swiss *Bergungskompanie* was at work on the grim remains of a crashed aircraft. Low stratus cloud hung over the steep hills overlooking the Rhine half a mile (800m) north of the tiny village. This is where a placid Rhine draws the border between Switzerland and Germany. On the Swiss shore the wartime strong points were now deserted and silent. Then, around 1545hr, the noise of aeroplane engines reverberated against forested cliffs and crags. The sound was reminiscent of the dozens of occasions when in the past months the villagers had watched in awe as gaggles of fighter-bombers plied their neighbourhood, shooting up whatever moved on the German shore. This time, however, the deep-throated hum came to an abrupt end, giving way to the screech and squeak of tortured metal.

It seemed to all that an aircraft had found an untimely end in the low clouds concealing the treacherous Irebei ridges. Within minutes a search party was on the spot but all the rescuers could find were heaps of twisted metal and the pathetic remains of a once proud airman. When the police arrived they identified him as S/Lt François Devolvé,[11] a fighter pilot flying a not too popular Bell *P-39-Q Airacobra*. The machine was a small, low-wing, low-altitude interceptor, peculiar for its time in that it sported a tricycle landing gear. The slim fuselage housed the 1,325hp Allison engine mounted behind the pilot. Driving a 10ft (3m) shaft, it terminated in a reduction gear box whose secondary propeller shaft also acted as a 37mm cannon. This, the Swiss noted, was loaded as were the two fifty-calibre (0.5in/12.7mm) machine-guns.

The day after, as the Swiss army began man-handling the wreckage downslope, a second body was discovered: that of Sgt François Laurens. Further investigation thus revealed that not one but two *P-39s*[12] had crashed together near Teufen! In all probability, the two aircraft had been flying along the Swiss border, from eastern France towards Germany. At the time, a triangle of Southern German land between the Rhine and a line cutting across Baden-Wurtemberg was part of the French Occupation Zone.[13] It can be surmised that the team was on a training-patrol assignment to a French airfield in Germany, possibly Neuhausen, Mengen or even Friedrichshafen although the limited range of the *Airacobra* seems to preclude this destination. Caught in bad weather with low clouds prevailing, the leader must have elected to press on, following the excellent Rhine River landmark.

CROOKED RHINE

All went well as long as the stream meandered along its alluvial valley. Then, speeding to the east at a good 250mph (400km/h)[14] the pair inadvertently entered Swiss ground with the river, near Eglisau. Just about 3 miles (5km) further the Rhine abruptly turns to the north, flowing between the steep Rinsberg and Irebrei hills. These must have been shrouded in low cloud, a typical case of rock-stuffed clouds. Losing sight of the guiding river, the pilots – or at least the leader – made the split-second decision to enter cloud. Perhaps did he intend, taking advantage of his machine's high rate of climb to go 'upstairs' on instruments in order to come out of the murk. Perhaps also did he elect to turn left in so doing. One can even speculate that his wingman reacted too late and collided with him. In any case both aircraft smacked straight into high ground just 1km (about half a mile) after the river bend. In a couple of days the two ill-fated pilots made their last flight when their bodies were repatriated by air to their nearby French base (see Chapter 19).

17

Bombing Switzerland

Just thirteen British aircraft ended up in Switzerland. Encounters with the Royal Air Force were, however, more numerous, mainly through accidental bombings. Out of a total of seventy-seven bombings of Switzerland during the war, twenty-two have been traced to British operations.[1] As seen in 'Why the RAF?', it was in June 1940 that Swiss civilians began to pay the price for RAF navigational errors. At the war's end the tally amounted to 84 Swiss citizens killed and 260 more maimed by the blunders of foreign aircraft.

The Swiss had thus ample excuse for resentment and for eventually claiming compensation for events other than crashes of belligerent aircraft. On a single night, that of 12/13 July 1943 for instance, when north Italian targets were raided by the RAF, five large high-explosive bombs (including 4,000lb (1,816kg) *Cookies* or 'block-busters' as they were known) and more than 250 incendiaries peppered their countryside. Two women were wounded and barns, a house and crops were damaged or set afire in the Cantons of Berne, Fribourg, Neuchâtel and Vaud.

ON THIRTEEN OCCASIONS

All in all this study has recorded thirteen dates when British bombs were strewn over Swiss territory, not counting three attacks against Swiss naval merchantmen, one against a neighbouring dam and one case of night strafing. In view of the number of attacks mounted to destroy German or Italian targets adjacent to Switzerland, the tally is indeed relatively minor. Considering, for instance, the forty-one assaults against Italy which took place in 1940 through 1943, considering also that all of them theoretically entailed skirting Swiss territory but that such orders could come to no avail in view of operational requirements, it is surprising that only three 'Italian raids' resulted in drops over Switzerland. What follows shall be a chronological tabulation of 'RAF events' that resulted in Swiss casualties or material damage.[2] Prior to that, some remarks should help understanding the contingencies of the times.

1940

Geneva, Lausanne	11/12 June
South of Zürich	29/30 June
Canton St.Gall	1/2 September
Basle	16/17 December
Zürich	22/23 December

Ever since May 1940 when German bombs had hit them, the Swiss had been wary of aerial border violations that could result in the warring powers dropping more unwanted cargoes of explosives.

The Swiss reported an initial infringement of their borders by a British aircraft on 2 March 1940. The intruder must have been a photographic reconnaissance *Spitfire* or *Hudson* surveying south-western Germany.[3] If so, the pilot was in all likelihood F/O S.D.'Slogger' Slocum who, on the morrow, was to lose his life when his *Hudson* was shot down by RAF *Hurricanes* over Gravesend, England. In any case, no harm resulted except to the ego of Swiss defences who saw yet another nation violating their sacrosanct neutrality.

Things however turned sour as soon as Italy entered the war. On 11/12 June 1940, as related in Chapter 2, British bombs fell on or near Geneva and Lausanne. And, sorry as the British were after this, their first accidental bombing of Switzerland, it did not prevent such an incident to happen again soon afterwards. On 29/30 June the RAF despatched eighty-three aircraft to various German targets on 'pinprick' nuisance incursions.

On those nights crews could still individually plan their own routes and means of attack, a far cry from the 'stream' policy to be adopted in 1942. Their aids to navigation were few and often not easy to use in operations: astro-nav and wireless telegraphy. The latter could also prove dangerous in betraying the aircraft's position to the enemy. There remained dead reckoning, almost always unreliable because of wind force uncertainty.

Required to find precise distant targets at night, in all sorts of weather and with skeletal navigation aids, crews very often failed to damage significantly the German war economy. On this occasion, some raiders strayed too far south and, once more, harried placid Swiss communities. In the central parts of the country, near Oberägeri which is 30km (19mi.) south of Zürich, eight 25lb (11.35kg) incendiaries were released in the fog banks covering the area; half of them did not ignite, allowing to clearly ascertain their origin. The region is some 60km (38mi.) south of the German border and indeed dead reckoning navigation was quite off the mark for the culprit crew. Just after this another stick of ten more incendiaries – with again six duds[4] – hit Altmatt-Rothenthurm, a few miles to the south-east, obviously released by the same aircraft. Five minutes later it was another RAF machine that let go more incendiaries on rocky shrubs near Biaufont in western Switzerland, 6km (4mi.) north of Chaux-de-Fonds and smack on the French border.

CUTTING CORNERS – OFTEN

More violations occurred on 13/14 and 15/16 August when British bombers going to and returning from Italy, shamelessly cut corners over Switzerland. No bombs were dropped, fortunately, but complaints lodged with the Foreign Office had yet to be answered when other incidents occurred. RAF night bombers missing objectives in either Augsburg or Iena on 16/17 August, strayed over Switzerland. One will perhaps wonder how aircrew and particularly navigators could miss their targets, let alone large towns, by as much as tens of miles. The answer would be, as previously indicated but as ought to be stressed again and again, the lack of high performance radio navigation aids that are nowadays taken for granted. As S/Ldr A.G. Goulding[5] who flew in 1943 with 51 Squadron rightfully relates, 'even on moonlit nights, clouds could blanket a target, leaving crews with two alternatives: to descend recklessly low through cloud to identify (their position), or bomb on ETA, the Estimated Time of Arrival, a solution prone to entail errors in view of, amongst other factors, the lack of precise wind data.

These events heralded things to come when attacks on targets in Southern Germany would often result in border violations and occasional bombings. Indeed the following night, 17/18 August 1940, bombers were once more at work attacking targets in Germany; again the '*Fliegeralarm*' sounded in Zürich and Bern. The month of August 1940 saw two more RAF incursions: on the nights of 24/25 and on 26/27 when navigation to Augsburg, Stuttgart, Milan and Turin caused Swiss flab to intervene against British intruders.

September started with violations on two consecutive nights when RAF *Wellingtons* and *Whitleys* intent to damage northern Italy reappeared conspicuously in Swiss skies. A few incendiary sticks burned harmlessly in open country, not far from Austria, in Canton St Gall. By this time the Swiss had had enough. Their flab anti-aircraft artillery was proving inefficient by lack of numbers and of training. Their diplomatic action seemed of no avail as Walter Thurnheer, the anglophile Swiss ambassador to the Court of St-James, lodged incessant complaints which invariably resulted in British regrets for 'accidental incursions due to weather conditions'. No wonder then that Anglo-Swiss relations became so strained in the autumn of 1940 that Marcel Pilet-Golaz, at the time head of the Swiss 'Foreign Office', thought of recalling Thurnheer. Furthermore, Germany considered taking over the Swiss defences, i.e. invading Switzerland, if RAF night bombers kept roaming freely in a Swiss airspace practically devoid of opposition.

NEUTRALITY – SPAIN AND GREECE

In such a context, the British answer formulated on 18 September 1940 to Switzerland's repeated protests is worth noticing. It stated that one could not, for the sake of neutrality, ask everything from the RAF in its Italian campaign. After all, Germany had overrun five neutral countries in order to strike England. Italy had also violated Spanish neutrality to attack Gibraltar and was daily violating

Greek neutrality in reconnoitring the Aegean Sea. The note continued with an indication that His Majesty's government did not consider cancelling operations implying overflying a neutral country but whose nature was not intended as a violation of that country's neutrality. Also, the RAF showed willingness to avoid Swiss airspace in the course of operations to Germany and Austria and even to Italy against Turin and Genoa. This left out Milan, further east, actually implying that flights towards that city could involve Switzerland's airspace.[6]

The release of bombs over Swiss territory would also be avoided, the Foreign Office promised: the RAF would not repeat its mistakes of 11/12 June over Western Switzerland. Meanwhile and as a measure to soothe Germany, Switzerland enforced its blackout, starting 7 November 1940. A month later British bombs once more came down: on Basle and Zürich, two Swiss cities on or close to the German border. This was on 16/17 December 1940. A full moon shone on snow-covered ground around Basle, a fact that should have eased navigation said the Swiss in another of their protests. In fact the target for that night was Mannheim, 220km (135mi.) north of the Swiss border. Knowing the difficulties and inaccuracies in dead reckoning navigation at the time, it can be surmised that a desperate crew, lost in cloud and getting short of fuel, spotted a large city on a large river conveniently looking like the target shown at briefing. Indeed both Basle and Mannheim/Ludwigshafen sit across a meandering Rhine – albeit on a slightly different heading; both regions feature dozens of tall chimneys with their associated chemical industries. For tense airmen it is only too easy, even in peacetime, to 'see what one wants to see' as far as identifying landmarks is concerned.

MANNHEIM, NOT BASLE

This date of 16/17 December is peculiar in RAF operations in that it was the first large assault not trying to hit a specific industrial target[7] but reaching for the centre of a city: Mannheim as it happened. Mounted as a retaliation for Luftwaffe attacks on British towns, the raid did in fact prelude the beginning of 'area bombing' through which Bomber Command sought to disrupt the life of workers engaged in the German war effort. Code-named 'Operation Abigail',[8] the task involved 134 aircraft, the largest force despatched to date to a single target; it also included an embryo of what would years later become the pathfinder component of a bombing mission. All this did not make the attack a success: although about a hundred returning crews declared to have bombed the objective, their bombs were widely scattered, as Basle could witness the morning after. The undertaking cost the RAF seventeen men in the nine aircraft lost, including six that crashed in bad weather upon their return in England.

Witness of the damage at Mannheim was F/O J.H. Blount of 3.PRU. On 21 December he took his photo *Spitfire* in the freezing rarefied air, 30,000ft (9,150m) over the city. The pictures he brought back showed the target practically intact. Again, all the blame should not be heaped upon the suffering bomber crews for missing an intended objective, 265mi. (420km) inside the enemy coast. Again, one must admit their navigational means were minimal, consisting of a large magnetic compass, a difficult to manipulate sextant and scant meteorological data.

The irony in relation with the accidental bombing of Basle, was that a similar mishap occurred that very night in Norwich, Norfolk. One of the *Blenheim* light bombers[9] taking off for Mannheim from a nearby base experienced engine trouble and jettisoned its load, hitting Bond Street in the process. As a further coincidence, one contemporary official report states: 'The rail congestion caused by the breakdown (of switchyards in Mannheim) blocked the yards in Basle, 160mi. [sic] away'. The statement went on to say 'Coal in transit from the Ruhr to Italy had to be diverted, a (longish) process that deprived Italy of 100,000 tons of coal during that winter'. At the time, Switzerland permitted German coal to transit to Italy via her rail system in compensation for the Reich allowing other transits vital to the neutral country; a stretch of imagination could connect this fact with the bombing of Basle but, besides the counterproductive diplomatic effects such an enterprise could have had, there exist no record available supporting such a theory.

BOMBS ON BASLE-BINNINGEN

On a more serious note it was the suburb of Basle-Binningen that took the brunt of British explosives and incendiaries. Around 2300hr local time on this clear and cold night of 16/17 December 1940, they killed Frieda Zorn on the Winkelriedplatz. Three women also lost their lives in the destroyed Zeller dwelling: the owner Valérie, her widowed mother Maria Boltz and her daughter Elisabeth. Nearby on the Hohenweg, another house was damaged: the sole occupants were the family's two children, Jean-Pierre and Lucette Merz, who escaped scared but unscathed. As on previous occasions an unexploded bomb revealed the provenance of the missiles when a 1,000lb (454kg) dud landed in a cellar at 67 Gutterstrasse.

* * * * * * * * *

As the second wartime Christmas neared, on 22 December 1940, still another bombing occurred, this time on Zürich. This was a day after a PRU reconnaissance *Spitfire* had assessed damage at Mannheim whilst Rüdolf Hess was making his first attempt to fly to England in a self-appointed peace mission.[10] This night of 22/23 December, forty-three RAF bombers were roaming European skies against several German targets, including Mannheim and Saarbrücken. One of them, again, 'dead reckoned' too far, too south, ending up over the Basle-Zürich area, orbiting for half an hour to identify a suitable target and finally dropping in two 'servings' on Zürich. Five HE bombs and about 160 Novobax incendiaries[11] impacted the town's industrial suburb. The viaduct over the Josefstrasse, close to the main rail sidings, was hit as were adjacent working-class dwellings in Hönggs where the sixty-five-year-old Rosa Nagel lost her life. General Henri Guisan, commander of Swiss armed forces, paid a compassionate visit there on the 24th, but another would-be visitor, Freddie West, the British Air Attaché, was denied permission to inspect the damage in Zurich and Basle. Why the snubbing is unclear but the action, like the bombing of course, did nothing to improve Anglo-Swiss relations.

1941

Central Switzerland	12/13 October
South of Konstanz	7/8 November

In 1941 it was the RAF, and the RAF only, that was answerable for accidental bombings of Switzerland. After a ten-month pause, British bombs were once more scattered over the central parts of the country on 12/13 October 1941. The wrongdoer was once more a single aircraft which spent fifteen minutes over Switzerland in fair weather with visibility deemed good on the ground. The machine had crossed into the country at 2212hr over the western tip of Lake Constance, flying inside the southern shore, descending from about 4,000m (13,000ft) towards Amriswil where it turned about towards Baden and homed for England. Meanwhile and probably in desperation of finding itself lost so far south, it had released three HE and ten incendiaries. Most of them harmlessly churned dirt and trees near Buhwil south of Konstanz but a bomb smashed the Bötschi's residence, killing – in a repetition of what had happened a year earlier in Binningen – the woman of the house, her mother and her child.

That night, the intended target for 152 bombers had been Nuremberg, the route briefed passing through the region of Charleroi, Belgium and then direct to the target. Actually the Bavarian town suffered only slight damage[12] as most of the bombs fell on distant cities and villages such as Sulgen. This small Swiss community is on a compass heading some 30° apart from that to the intended target, 70km further down track and 250km (156mi.) south-west of Nuremberg. Weather and haphazard navigation had cost dearly the poor souls remote from the affairs of war.

* * * * * * * * *

Around 2100hr on 7/8 November 1941 the customary incendiaries and a sprinkle of high explosives fell on Lausen and Asp, a few miles south of the Rhine in the vicinity of Basle, and in distant locations, at Jonschwil and nearby Schwarzenbach way in eastern Switzerland near St Gall. Swiss radio listening stations allowed Col. Rüedi from intelligence headquarters to ascertain the deeds to a single aircraft 'responding to a 9WSN or -R call sign'. It is, however, more likely that two or more machines were responsible amongst the six located by the Swiss.

MANNHEIM ONCE MORE

That night 392 aircraft operated over Germany in very bad weather.[13] One of their destinations was once more Mannheim and once more very distant from Switzerland. Out of the fifty-five bomber crews assigned there, forty-three stated they had bombed the target area even though Mannheim's records do not show a single bomb on the city! There were no Swiss casualties and as, a departure from the routine stray loads, French-language leaflets were strewn near Jonschwil although they quite possibly had been released by a propaganda balloon (see Chapter 3). Also, an intact 'bomb' was picked-up at the Alpine hamlet of Schwarzenbach: an unlit 23lb (10kg) parachute flare. Another dud, at Jonschwil bore the same markings as one found in Buhwil a month previously, showing it as a 50lb missile manufactured in England at the end of August.

1942

Raron, Sins	11/12 December

A long lull followed the year 1942, proving almost bomb-free west and south of the Rhine. The single exception took place on 11/12 December in the course of a mission targeting Turin. That night eighty-two aircraft were dispatched but less than half crossed the Alps due to severe icing in bad weather, a situation reminiscent of that in June 1940. Amongst those who abandoned the task, several strayed too far east over Switzerland, releasing their lethal loads over either the countryside or targets of opportunities wishfully 'identified'.[14]

Raron in Canton Valais, at the northern foot of the Alps, thus became the destination for the cargo of a single machine, part of the third wave of foreign aircraft heard between 2130hr and 2200hr on their way to Italy. The transgressor crossed into Swiss airspace over Porrentruy near Montbéliard, flew on to Lucerne and Altdorf, then south to wander near the Dammastock peaks menacingly pointing upwards at 3,630m (12,000ft). Apparently discouraged by the weather, the crew turned to the south-west and flew on to Brig. Here they may have spotted Raron's grass airfield[15] and tired of groping about hopelessly, elected to drop their load there and then.

What must have been a *Cookie* missed the main highway to the Simplon Pass and Italy, digging a large and futile crater in the Goller woods. At the same time (2158hr local time) many of some 200-odd incendiaries burned harmlessly on desolated slopes overlooking the Rhône valley and a refugee camp; here also, some turned duds and gave away their British origin. Meanwhile more incendiaries had landed on the aerodrome. Within an hour, firemen and men of

Capt Perret's *Company 3* of reservists had put out brush and phosphorus fires. At daybreak mayor Anthamatten was able to report 'about a hundred incendiaries on the airfield', one of them, again a brown-coloured dud, having gone through the roof of an empty hangar. All in all, it turned out that at least one RAF sortie had been quite a waste of means and effort 750km (470mi.) away from home base!

About 60mi. (100km) further north, beyond Lucerne, another aircraft dropped over Sins on this same night of 11/12 December 1941. The aircraft had entered Switzerland near Basle, heading too far south-east to hope to reach Turin. Thwarted by the threatening weather and probably realising how lost they were, the crew abandoned the sortie in sight of Lake Zug, releasing the load before turning back on a reciprocal course.

STRAFLAGER HÜNENBERG MISSED

Their *Cookie* produced a huge crater 40ft (12.5m) in diameter and 4m. deep, uprooting enormous trees close to what would later become *Straflager* Hünenberg, a concentration camp of sorts for unruly interned airmen. The accompanying incendiaries set fire to Jacob Suter's barn which young Anton Amrein and helpers failed to save; nearby a dud phosphorus missile came to rest on an empty bed at the Eigensatz building firm!

That only one release of British bombs was recorded that year on Switzerland, did not mean that numerous airspace violations went unnoticed. They once more produced a flurry of communications between Anthony Eden at the Foreign Office, the Swiss Minister in London and Clifford Norton, His Majesty's Minister in Berne. This was the period when Walter Thurnheer reiterated to Eden the Swiss government's concern about possible German reactions. He feared that Germany would one day announce that, 'since Switzerland permitted RAF aircraft to fly over her territory with impunity, the Germans and Italians would consider themselves free to disregard neutrality of Swiss air'.

An ancillary incident involving a 78 Squadron *Halifax* flown by F/Sgt Spraggs occurred over the country. 'We bombed the target and were returning over Switzerland when one of the motors cut', stated the rear gunner later. He, Canadian F/O Thomas Wiley, bailed out following this incident, breaking a leg upon landing near Marboz, no more than 60km (37mi.) outside Switzerland. Denounced to the French police by the doctor summoned by local helpers, Wiley later escaped from the Bourg-en-Bresse hospital and managed to reach Gibraltar and England the following May.

1943

Zürich	17/18 May
Basle	27/28 May
Frauenfeld, Staubikon	20/21 June
Throughout Switzerland	12/13 July

Oerlikon is a suburb of Zürich. It was also well-known for its armament industries and became another Swiss 'target-of-expediency'[16] in an incident occurring on '17 May' 1943 according to Swiss reports. The actual date should however be the night of 17/18 May, and the attack itself has brought many interrogation marks.

DID *MOSQUITOES* MISS MUNICH?

Bomber Command did not conduct operations against either Southern Germany or Italy on 16/17 May, busy as it was with 'Operation Chastise', now better known as 'The Dams Raid'. This was in the Ruhr region, much further north and did not generate any route deviation. True, there were nine *Mosquito* nuisance sorties that night but they were flown towards very remote northern German towns and it is most unlikely that any navigator could be blamed for straying at least 400km (250mi.) off-course. Likewise, the only sorties performed by Bomber Command on Monday 17 May proper were those of 13 *Ventura* medium bombers attacking Caen-Carpiquet airfield in Normandy.

On the following night, 17/18 May 1943, two 105 Squadron[17] *Mosquito*es were, however, detailed to attack Munich with another machine going to Mannheim. Munich is 'only' 230km (145mi.) to the north-east of Zürich and Mannheim the same distance due north. If the Zürich bombing was not a German ploy intended to worsen Swiss-British relations, then the culprit could very well be one or more of the *Mosquito*es whose navigation would then have left much to be desired.

Weather forecasts for the route to Munich[18] predicted ground haze and clear skies down to Stuttgart and then broken overcast with cloud tops around 15,000ft (4,600m), i.e. below the *Mosquitoes*' cruising altitude. More important for this analysis, upper winds were foreseen as moderate, from the north-north-west at up to 25mph (some 37km/h). With such information available to trained navigators, how could at least one of them blunder to the point of missing Munich or Mannheim by some 145mi. (230km)? An explanation could be that northerly winds were much stronger than expected.[19] Another theory could be a southerly penetration route via eastern France and the northern Swiss borders.

Such a southern route is, however, dismissed by continental observations that night. The Swiss defences only reported, 'RAF aircraft between 2344hr and 0005hr over Lake Constance', while the Germans kept track of the intruders plotting them, '… from Füssen [i.e. south of Munich] to Lake Constance to Mulheim [obviously near Tuttlingen] to Nancy' – all this without any mention of bombs being dropped on German territory.

AND NOW ZÜRICH

The answer to the enigma shall remain open to conjecture, at least until one ever unearths the navigators' logs for that night. In any case, seven minutes before midnight on 17/18 May 1943 several high explosives bombs fell on the northern suburbs of Zürich. A dud just missed the restaurant Waldegg in Rumlang and a bit further south, another bounced harmlessly on rail tracks in the Hürstholz woods. Another missile churned gardens at 43, Rumlangstrasse in Seebach, 2km (1.25mi.) to the north. There were no casualties but six houses and power lines were damaged.

The bombs could be consistent with the load carried by a long-range *Mosquito*. Two of the projectiles hit Zürich on a south-west to north-east line and about one mile (1.6km) to the left of a path running north-eastwards from the Zürich-Oerlikon rail station and the adjacent Oerlikon armament works. One needs only a mild stretch of imagination to theorise on navigator(s) misidentifying Zürich and its Limmatt River with the Mannheim-Rhine or Munich-Isar landmarks and releasing his/their lethal load upon factories and rail tracks before speeding home.

In all likelihood, one or several of the *Mosquito*es detailed that night ought to be held responsible for the Zürich bombing. One fable should however be disclaimed: the one suggesting the RAF would have bombed the Oerlikon factory on purpose because of its involvement with Germany.[20] The same fiction applies to stray bombs that landed on 12 October 1941 a few miles from a silk factory said to make parachutes for the Luftwaffe.

At the time, the 'Oerlikon bombs' were interpreted by the Swiss population as a sign that the country ought to discontinue delivering war goods to Germany.[21] With hindsight, one can, however, entertain intense doubts about Britain perpetrating an act of war against Switzerland and thus jeopardising its relations with a country whose neutral presence in central Europe offered unquestionable advantages. Had wilful bombing been intended, it further remains questionable that such nightly pinpricks would have been thrust at the plant.[22]

★ ★ ★ ★ ★ ★ ★ ★ ★

A similar mishap again occurred two weeks later, in the early hours of 28 May 1943, when the port on the Rhine at Basle received RAF bombs. Here the navigational blunder is still more apparent since the only Bomber Command raids in the period was by 518 aircraft sent to Essen in the Ruhr, i.e. 425km (265mi.) to the north!

STRAFING THE FLAB

At Friedrichshafen on the northern shore of Lake Constance, the Zeppelin works were building in mid-1943 the large light alloy dishes for *Würzburg* radar sets.[23] Since 1942 the apparatus had been a kingpin of the *Himmelbett* belt protecting

Germany from RAF night operations. Bomber Command therefore elected to curtail production. On 20/21 June 1943 a 'small' force of 60 *Lancasters* arrived in bright moonlight, bombed under the direction of a Master Bomber-Controller and departed towards temporary bases in North Africa, thus confusing the German defences deployed on the expected return route to England.

The tactic once more entailed entering Swiss neutral airspace and one could fear that stray bombs would be released over it. It was not to be, even if near-misses did occur, as witnessed by the schoals of dead fish floating off Romanshorn. Another incident recorded on that Sunday night involved a bright red indicator bomb deposited at 0128hr, near Frauenfeld. Obviously an RAF pathfinder thus marked the bombers' exit route to Africa. Perhaps it was the same *Lancaster* which, near Staubikon, strafed the Siemens searchlight of *Flab Detachment 110* that had had the arrogance to cone it.

No aircraft went missing in spite of the very dense flak encountered over F'hafen. However, anti-aircraft batteries followed the *Lancasters* on their south-erly course and inland from the Swiss shore, German (or Swiss?) shells meant for the RAF killed three men of the Wellauer family in Kummertshausen. On a less tragic scale, similar events were to occur during the more powerful assault of 27/28 April 1944 on the same target (see Chapter 14). Dozens of windows were then broken by concussion in Romanshorn whilst the Swiss shore was peppered with official papers, including ration coupons, blown in from F'hafen, 12km across the lake.

THE NIGHT OF MANY BOMBS

The night of 12/13 July 1943 was to remain in Swiss memories as the one when two four-engined bombers crashed in the not so peaceful oases called Switzerland (see Chapters 6 and 7). Less known are the 244 incendiaries and four HE bombs that spared Italy to dot the Swiss countryside in the Cantons of Berne, Fribourg, Neuchâtel and Vaud. A possibly fragmentary list of the incidents follows, where all hours are local Swiss times:

* Around 0100hr in the Val de Ruz, at Geneveys s/Coffrane near Neuchâtel, a large bomb explodes in woods 50m (150ft) outside Albert Nydegger's farm. Roof tiles are shuffled, doors and windows pushed in and hundreds of fir trees are uprooted. In nearby Crottets, two cows are wounded. More reports of bombs are also issued in Henniez, Surpierre and Gstaad.

* At Praratoud near Lucens and 30km (19mi.) south of the above, four HE bombs miss the hamlet. They are duds but anyway they give local policeman Ganther his hour of fame when he discovers they have been dropped safe with their securing pins attached. It is later rumoured that the bombs have been jettisoned by one of the *Lancasters* downed this night above Sion and Le Bouveret.

★ Open fields near Savigny and Forel, east of Lausanne on Lake Geneva, collect a share of explosives and incendiaries wasted by an aircraft flying 'lower than usual'. Here also, the machine might be Badge's *Lancaster* bound for a tragic end at Le Bouveret.

★ At Riggisberg, an opulent village 16km (10mi.) south of Berne, bombs follow parachute flares. An incendiary guts a house near Restaurant 'Adler' and four elderly persons escape with their lives including a man who passes out from fright. Another incendiary fizzles on the floor at the local hairdresser's, M. Kaspar; his wife Bertha puts the fire out with buckets of sand and suffers arm burns. Nearby, Rodolphe Bohlen's wife is not as successful: she fails to extinguish yet another stick with clothes and burlap bags. The damage results from a bomb load – including a *Cookie*, another HE and 200 incendiaries – which at about 0040hr straddle the village. The locals escape with their lives, thankful that more serious ravage is averted. Still another middle-aged women, Frieda Stautermann, endures a head-wound from splinters.

★ Bombs are also reported in the desolate expanses of the Schynige Platte and the Männlichen range, south of Interlaken; a barn is set afire in Gsteigwiler.

★ West of Berne at Flamatt's Bergli hill, what appears to be a *Cookie* ravages a wheat field, severs a high tension power line and blows off several roofs.

Although those jettisons cannot be ascribed to particular crews, one can nevertheless point out one of them: P/O K. McIver's. This Australian in 467 Squadron, reported at debriefing that he was forced to turn back after failing to master his port outer engine's airscrew running away. He stated that about three hours after leaving base, he had jettisoned his load before reaching the Alps. Considering that an average of three hours had elapsed between Squadron take-offs and bombings, it can be resolved that McIver's expediency occurred over Switzerland.

Later in the year, on 2/3 October 1943, the RAF attack on Munich severely hit the Bavarian town and suburbs. Having drifted far too south, one of the raiders succeeded in scattering some 150 incendiaries in open fields at Buch-am-Irchel near Bülach. This hamlet, north-west of Winterthur is also just about a mile (1.6km) east of Teufen where a pair of Allied *P-39*s would crash later (see Chapter 16).

1944

At sea	22 March, 6 May, 8 September
Rhine, Basle	7 October

Bombs dropped in emergency on 15/16 March 1944 by the doomed Saignelégier *Lancaster* have been documented in Chapter 9. A few days later, on 22 March 1944, a quite unusual bombing of Swiss 'territory' occurred. This was in the Mediterranean Sea, when RAF missiles pounced upon a Swiss-registered merchant vessel, the

Chasseral. Six 39 Squadron *Beaufighters* out of Alghero in Corsica, were then on an anti-shipping strike; their rockets scored on the vessel, causing a fire and serious damage. Likewise, on 6 May, a Swiss Red Cross representative was wounded aboard the *Cristina*, a Spanish merchantman chartered by the British Red Cross and carrying a relief cargo intended for British Prisoners of War. The twelve *Beaus* participating in the foray left the ship beached near Sète harbour in Southern France. Later in the year yet another similar incident happened in the vicinity of Marseilles, the *Maloja* being lost on 8 September.[24]

Another oddity regarding a 1943 bombing of Helvetic possessions by the RAF relates to the Swiss embassy in Berlin. The German capital was bombed on 26/27 November 1943 in one of the twenty-four large RAF attacks on the city.[25] The 450 aircraft dispatched wrecked 8,701 dwellings including, to the dismay of Hans Frölicher the Swiss Minister in Berlin, his legation on Bismarckstrasse.

THE KEMBS DAM

An important 'Swiss side-effect' of a bombing operation against Germany took place in the early evening of 7 October 1944. On that gloomy autumn Saturday the front lines separating the Allied and German forces ran north from Montbéliard, west of Basle. It would be a couple of months before French units would cross the Rhine in the area but SHAEF Headquarters wanted right away a tactical mission by Bomber Command. The rationale was to prevent the Germans from controlling the water level and to anticipate them in destroying the dam. When the Allied offensive started, unforeseen flooding of the lowlands further north would thus not stall the ground forces' progress.[26]

A specialist precision bombing unit of the RAF was therefore instructed to destroy the Rhine dam at Kembs, linking the German and French banks of the river just 13km (8mi) north of Basle. At No.54 Base, Woodhall Spa, 617 Squadron of the 'Dams Raid' fame was chosen for the raid. Under W/Cdr J.B. 'Willie' Tait's command, its *Lancasters* carried to-day the huge *Tallboy* bomb, a weapon well-suited to destroy dams, canals, dikes, tunnels and viaducts.[27] Six bombers were accordingly loaded with 12,000lb (5,400kg) *Tallboys* to be dropped at low level from around 500/800ft (150/250m) and fused to explode some time after release. Seven more aircraft made up a 'high-level' force attacking more conventionally from 5,000ft to 8,000ft (1,500 to 2,500m). Escort and antiflak cover were to be provided by three Squadrons of long-range RAF *Mustangs III* belonging to 133 (Polish) Wing. At this time the unit comprised two Polish Squadrons: 306 and 315 and one RAF Squadron, 129; all were almost exclusively engaged in providing distant escorts and occasional anti-flak duty.

The assailants came in from the south-west, speeding over the blur of Swiss neutrality markings – large white crosses on red background. They had been routed over recently liberated Eastern France and had been steadily losing altitude since Besançon. Very low over what is now Basle-Mulhouse airport, the flak-suppression *Mustangs* came in first,[28] followed by the low-flying *Lancasters*, their high-level colleagues closing the procession.

Some aircraft briefly crossed into Germany but here all except one carefully avoided Swiss airspace prior to proceeding down the Rhine towards the target, half a mile (0.8km) away. The single intruder became subject to the attention of the Swiss light flab. Soon after this, intense German flak took over with both 88mm and light anti-aircraft guns. From their perch on top of Basle chemical works, Swiss observers clearly saw tracers flying up in the gloom. Then a drama unfolded.

One of the low-level attackers – *Lancaster* LM.482 coded KC°Q – failed to release its *Tallboy*. With press-on determination, the pilot veered to starboard in order to go around and come in for a second run. It was 1658hr local time when the *Lanc* was seen to be hit and set afire in its rear fuselage. The stricken machine plunged towards Efringenkirchen, Germany, where twenty-two-year-old F/Lt Christopher Howard struggled to bring it in for a safe belly landing. The manoeuvre failed: the aircraft exploded with black smoke and dark-red flames hissing over the tree tops. There were no survivors: all eight men aboard perished, including an extra gunner. They now lie in Munich-Dürnbach cemetery.

TIME-BOMB

Twenty-five minutes later a hefty detonation shook the countryside: Howard's time-fused *Tallboy* had gone off. In Basle, numerous windows showered glass splinters and soldiers in the port area were blown over by the blast! They were some 5km away from the explosion, a fact that led the Swiss to rightly evaluate the bomb's mass at some four to six tons.

Another *Lancaster* must also have experienced a bomb hang-up: at 1735hr, more than half an hour after the initial attack, the Swiss observed a single machine returning from the German hills to drop on and miss the dam. According to the Swiss, a *Mosquito* also followed suit at 1746hr, 'whose bombs also failed to hit their target'. This twin-engined machine was actually a 627 Squadron aircraft: KB.215, coded AZ°H, used by the RAF Film Production Unit to record the proceedings. It was circling nearby when one more of the time-delayed bombs went off, damaging the left side of the dam. The *Mosquito* then came back for another look before flying off to the west.[29]

It was 1757hr, just one hour after the initial attack when a 'water alert' rang in Basle. The port there had been subject to an accidental bombing on 27/28 May 1943 but today the damage would be of a different nature. It was noticed that part of the dam-retained Rhine water was flowing away, threatening to beach ships and barges in docking basin No.2. Tugs and the fire-fighting boat *St. Florian* hurried to tow them to deeper soundings. By 1930hr, the Rhine level has sunk by 2.2m (7.2ft). This was one of the consequences on Switzerland of 617 Squadron's deeds in the neighbourhood. Furthermore there were once again flak shells showering on Swiss territory, threatening the numerous onlookers[30] with spent splinters while incendiary ammo set chemicals afire in the Ciba industrial compound.

For the RAF, there was to be another *Lancaster* casualty: the brand new NG.180. In this pristine mount that had just seven hours flying time, S/Ldr Drew Wyness was approaching the dam at 600ft (182m) when he was hit by light flak. With a wing afire and two engines disabled on his S–Sugar, he flew straight on downstream. Wyness elected to ditch in the Rhine near Bad Bellingen and the heavily defended Chalampé Rhine Bridge, some 17km (10mi.) north of the dam. He succeeded and as the hulk began to sink, the whole crew of seven came out unscathed and clambered in the dinghy.

Why they were to lose their lives that same afternoon remained unexplained. Speculations had it that French *Spitfire* and *Thunderbolt* fighter-bombers had accidentally killed their allies while strafing the general area. It was surmised that the captured Wyness' crew was killed in one or several of the staff cars and trucks claimed destroyed. Another hypothesis proved partly correct: that German troops on adjacent shores machine-gunned the hapless men. Thus the tail gunner, F/O George Cansell and two F/Sgts, mid-upper gunner Thomas Horrocks and flight engineer Thomas Hurdiss, must have fallen victims of such a crime. Their bodies were not recovered; their names are now commemorated on the walls of the missing in Runnymede, near Windsor.

The four survivors were jailed on the German shore, probably at Rheinweiler and practically in sight of the dam. Bad luck had it that the region was administered by *Kreisleiter* Hugo Grüner and his henchmen. Interrogated a year later by the Allied War Crimes Commission, Grüner claimed he had been under orders to execute captured Allied airmen in retaliation for their 'terrorist behaviour over Germany'. He confessed to having taken the survivors to the Rhine bank and assassinating them individually in cold blood by sub-machine gun. Grüner later escaped from an internment camp and his death sentence was never carried out.

The obliterated Wyness crew was further split when the bodies of the pilot and of his New Zealander radio operator, F/O Bruce Hosie, were found on the French shore; they now rest in France, at Choloy. As for F/Lt navigator Ronald Williams and the air bomber F/O Herbert Honig, they lie forever in the Durnbach British Cemetery, in Germany.

1945
Near Schaffhausen	28/29 February

The year that saw the long-awaited end of the conflict brought in Switzerland at least one event invalidating the principle that the RAF Bomber Command solely operated at night and the USAAF in daylight.[31] Indeed, the American heavy bomber arm had since 15/16 September 1943 sent on night forays the occasional *Fortresses* or *Liberators* mixed in the RAF streams,[32] or on lonely leaflet drops and occasional pathfinder training sorties.

One night-bombing of Switzerland can perhaps be traced to such representatives of the USAAF. The incident took place in the late evening of 28 February 1945 near Schaffhausen; it shall be dealt with in the third volume of this trilogy: *The USAAF and Switzerland in WWII.*

* * * * * * * * *

Another unusual occurrence that cannot be attributed with certainty to either the RAF or the USAAF, happened on 5/6 May 1944. It did not involve explosives but the drop by an Allied aircraft of a couple of men and packages. What is solid evidence is that they were the object of a clandestine sortie performed by a four-engined aircraft belonging to either the RAF or the USAAF.

On that night a so-called 'Sacristan' team of saboteurs was dropped 'into the Doubs area'. The two men – Ernest ('Alfred') Floege, who was an OSS American and André ('Narcisse') Bouchardon, his French radio operator – came down just inside Switzerland at Valbert-Ocourt. The spot is just a mile east of the karst cliffs outlining the sinuous French-Swiss border.[33] There, soon after midnight, their aircraft awakened the sparse population of these remote grounds.

Farmer Lehmann was one who gaped in the bright full moon at a large aeroplane flying low and slow. He thought it intended to land until it started dropping unidentified objects prior to veering west. In the morning Lehmann noticed a box and its parachute at the edge of the woods; he had also spotted two khaki-clad men hiding in the forest. He duly notified the Ste-Ursanne police station which sent out gendarme Wenger to investigate. They teamed to search the area and discovered another case wrapped in a parachute and camouflaged under boughs and moss. As for the 'chutists, they were never seen again: they probably had reached their intended destination in France.[34] As for the packages with their food and sundry supplies, they found their way to the Military Police in Porrentruy whence they disappeared from official records. What remains of their contents is a cryptic message typewritten in French, from a mysterious 'Totor', apparently a 'Chef du VIIIème', to his friends Marcel and Pierre in France. It underlined the presence in the package of code-books and the need to perform other drops further afield.

VIOLATIONS AGAIN

As for the RAF, no accidental release of bombs can be traced to that corps in the remaining 19 weeks of war in Europe. This should by no means be construed as proof that British bombers carefully avoiding neutral airspace. For example on the night of 7/8 January 1945, *Lancaster* PO-X of the Australian 467 Squadron flown by F/Lt John Blair was part of a stream attacking Munich.[35] The rear gunner, Gordon Coates, remembers that, 'on this occasion the (route) was reversed: we went there first and came back by way of neutral Switzerland, instead of going in that way as previously'.

TABLE 2

RAF BOMBINGS ON SWITZERLAND

1940

11/12 June (★)	= Geneva and in Lausanne area.
29/30 June	= South of Zürich in Zug (ZG) Canton.
1–2 September	= St Gall Canton.
16/17 December	= Basle.
22/23 December	= Zürich.

1941

12/13 October	= Buhwil (TG, Central Switzerland).
7/8 November	= Basle and St Gall regions.

1942

11/12 December (★)	= Raron (VS), Sins (AG).

1943

17/18 May	= Zürich.
27/28 May	= Basle.
20/21 June	= Frauenfeld area (TG).
12/13 July (★)	= all over Switzerland.
2/3 October	= near Buch-am-Irchel.

1944

22 March, 6 May, 8 September	= at sea.
7 October	= Rhine dam near Basle.

1945

28/29 February (?)	= near Schaffhausen (SH).

(★) indicates in the course of a raid on Italy.
AG–TG–VS–ZG indicate Cantons of Aargau, Thurgau, Valais and Zug.
(?) indicates not ascertained to RAF or USAAF.

18

The Men Who Did (or did not) Make It

Manning the nineteen roundel-bearing aircraft which made it into the Swiss peaceful haven in, or immediately after, the Second World War were seventy-five pilots and crewmembers.[1] Of those, thirty-eight, one out of two arrivals, lived to enjoy a comparative tranquil life for the duration. That was unless they had drawn the relative good fortune of being repatriated within one of the rare early exchange schemes that occurred with the approval of the warring powers. This was the case for seventeen of them who, mainly because of a fluke of fate in being at the right place at the right time, became exchangees.

As hinted at above, thirty-seven were not so lucky. Their young lives came to an abrupt end in the idyllic confines of a country paradoxically living in the midst of a continent at war whilst enjoying the relative tranquillity bestowed by a fragile neutrality. They amount to but a tiny fraction of the appalling fatalities suffered by the RAF, mostly by its Bomber Command arm (see note 5, Chapter 7).

DOOM

For those thirty-seven unfortunate airmen, their flight to Switzerland proved final. Except for the two aviators in the *Mosquito* lost in Lake Constance whose bodies were never found, all were given military funerals by the Swiss armed forces, many having their luckier comrades as pall bearers. All of them rest nowadays in the picturesque St Martin's cemetery at Vevey, overlooking Lake Geneva from its northern shore and close to its eastern end. By coincidence the cemetery faces the Bouveret mountains where Horace Badge's crew found their demise (see Chapter 6).

Vevey's British plots were initiated in 1923, after the First World War: eighty-eight British and Dominions graves of the 1914-1918 war can be counted there. The period 1941-1947 has seen the burial of a further forty-eight British and Commonwealth military personnel who were either escaped Prisoners of War or airmen who crashed or died in Switzerland. The tombs commemorate ten soldiers, one sailor, and thirty-seven airmen: twenty-seven from the RAF (including Sid Bradley, the evader who died swimming the river Doubs to enter Switzerland), seven of the Royal Australian Air Force (RAAF), two Canadians (RCAF) and one from New Zealand (RNZAF) who died after the war.

The site of the war graves has been granted to the Imperial War Graves Commission as a concession from the municipality of Vevey. The agreement expired in 2000, but was extended for a further term of ninety-nine years. Like all British Commonwealth and Empire military cemeteries over the world, Vevey is cared for by the town's municipality, on repayment by the Commission.

Numerous continentals and many relatives of the deceased come yearly to visit and pay their respects to their RAF heroes. There are also annual remembrance ceremonies such as on 11 November (Armistice Day) and the first Sunday after the Battle of Britain Day, 15 September.

SAFETY

Apart from civilians, two categories of refugees entered Switzerland during the war. One was made up of military internees who once belonged to belligerent ground forces. Disarmed, they were prevented from rejoining the hostilities. One source refers to about 12,000 of them arriving between September 1939 and May 1940. In June 1940 they were rejoined by some 28,000 troops of the French 45th Army Corps squeezed into Switzerland by the German push across the Rhine.[2] About 40,000 more crossed from Italy after the country's capitulation in September 1943[3]. The final batch of internees came with the influx of (mostly) American airmen flying into the country: 1,604 of them, counting forty-one casualties.

The second category comprised the escapees (prisoners of war having succeeded in leaving their PoW cages) and the evaders who were airmen from the RAF, the USAAF or the Allied forces who walked into Switzerland in order not to become prisoners. That category was covered in our first volume *Aviateurs-Piétons vers la Suisse*. Sub-groups such as disabled personnel, deserters and unwanted German SS troops also overloaded Swiss humanitarian facilities; they remain outside this study. The escapers were usually allowed to move around almost freely and to get in touch with their military attachés; the evaders were not unless – and the habit caught rapidly- they claimed to have escaped from Axis custody.

FEW EXCHANGEES

For RAF aircrew, reaching either Switzerland or England did not prove much different as far as difficulties in handling disabled aircraft was concerned. The ordeal asked for stamina of the highest degree and in such struggles was recognised the Royal Air Force's 'press on' attitude. Again and again in Second World War, this writer witnessed how RAF aircrew endeavoured to bring their aircraft home in the face of adversity, where others would have given up and resorted to the simple – and safest – expedient of parachuting into probable enemy custody. Such a statement is furthermore driven home when one is reminded that only 50 per cent of the RAF aircrew who succeeded in reaching the Swiss haven made it alive: just thirty-four of them.[4] All had been subjected to the throes of aerial warfare. Of course the air warriors seldom saw their enemy face to face, nor their dead friends for that matter. Unlike the ground combatants, hunger and discomfort were rarely their lot and however appalling, Bomber Command losses only translated into empty bunks soon refilled by incoming replacements.

In Switzerland the survivors subsequent destiny seems to have depended more on period and circumstances than on rigid policy. True, the Swiss view on how to handle the thorny problem brought by refugees dropping out of the sky stemmed in principle from international agreements, particularly the Hague Convention. There, however, remained much leeway to cope with circumstances. Just after the Allied debacle of 1940, the Swiss had, under pressure from the Reich, released the seventeen members of the Luftwaffe (and their aircraft) they detained. Later on and until the beginning of 1944, Swiss policy favoured the exchange of incoming RAF aircrew against equal numbers of stranded airmen from the Luftwaffe or the *Italian Regia Aeronautica*.[5] This was the case for seventeen men ranging from the two who brought the PRU *Mosquito* into Berne airfield in August 1942, to the dazed French *Spitfire* pilot crashlanding a fortnight before V-E Day. In between were the five aviators manning the Birmenstorf *Wellington* in April 1943 and the six survivors of the Silhlsee crash in February 1944.[6] After them, exchanges were limited to specialist aircrew such as pilots and wireless operators. The switch was perhaps due to a dearth of German counterparts or even, but this seems less probable, to a policy enforced by British officialdom in Berne and London. In any case, after the Sihlsee exchange three airmen only were repatriated: two from the Golaten *Lancaster* (15/16 March 1944) and the pilot who mastered the Steckborn ditching on 27/28 April (see Table 3).

FRUSTRATION

The other survivors, nineteen men, had to while away the time in the comparatively easy-going status of internees (see above and Chapter 1). Exchanges or not, the airmen were at first subjected to an interrogation more or less thorough depending upon their trade. Pilots and flight engineers were good material to investigate the performances of aircraft and – also aided by careful analysis of what survived of the machines – the Swiss were able to gather quite a lot of data on RAF aeroplanes. A typical instance is the large technical book accurately describing the *Lancaster*, eight examples of which spread themselves over the Swiss landscape. Wireless operators and navigators constituted another useful population; some were even questioned again, months after their initial interrogation.

In the summer of 1943, Switzerland had to refute renewed German claims that the RAF used Swiss high-powered radio stations at Beromunster and

Schwarzenburg to improve long-range navigation.[7] In August, Swiss interrogators thus re-grilled a number of internees such as F/O George Lamus[8] on this specific subject; his affirmations led them to conclude that the transmitters could be helpful but for German jamming.

Internees lived (see Table 4) in uniform in isolated resorts such as Arosa, Adelboden, Wengen and others set up to cope with the incoming tide of USAAF personnel . In September 1943, some internees were issued with 'red cards' allowing them to enter inns; a year later, aviators working outside internment camps were given 'yellow cards' as permits to wear civilian clothes in order to go and work in their respective legations or to attend university or special studies such as the IBM courses on automated computing.[9]

RAF men drew a daily pay that varied according to rank. For instance, a F/Sgt received 3.46 Sw.Frcs, a F/Lt 6.92 and a W/Cdr 10.36 (at the time one British pound was about 17.35 Sw.Frcs). For the Americans the rate was, irrespective of ranks, 3.- Sw.Frcs/day for officers and half that amount for enlisted men and noncoms. The Americans were however able to buy goods with vouchers, later reimbursed to the shopkeepers by the US legation.

GOING HOME

For such enforced tourists, going home was not allowed until, from September 1944 onwards, Allied forces began to skirt the Swiss borders. First out, through Geneva, were seventy-five interned PoW escapees (sixty-six on 13 September 1944 and nine on 4 October). Those men had been, according to the Hague Convention, entitled to leave the country as they chose but were prevented to do so since Switzerland had been surrounded by Axis forces – even though a number amongst the most enterprising had already run the gauntlet of re-evasion to Gibraltar.

Later on, the stranded RAF airmen were included in a vast exchange scheme whereupon 747 USAAF men were swapped against twice that number of German internees. Those 'late returnees' were, by the way, the rear guard of a much larger contingent. Almost 1,000 (947) US internees had indeed already fled illegally; amongst those re-evaders, 184 were caught in the act and sentenced to spend time in punishment camps such as the infamous Wauwilermoos compound. As for RAF men, initially walking evaders, at least sixty-nine of them had left their internment area well before legal repatriation, most of them making it successfully to Gibraltar. Sixty-one others crossed into liberated France after the US 36th and 45th Infantry Divisions overran the territory.

As for the initial exchangees, they lived through another surprising experience: that of travelling safely across enemy-occupied Europe under German protection. Alistair Smith's memorable trip is probably the consummate example of such an amazing voyage (see also Chapter 8).

SAFE PASSAGE TO SPAIN

'Our repatriation journey', said Smith upon returning in England:

> began at Adelboden where we had met F/Lt Walter Blott [Chapter 10] [who became] the senior officer in our party. On 6 May 1944 we were summoned to Berne and given a passport and civilian clothes. At 0300hr on 12 May our group of nine (sic) [actually the six Smith's crew survivors and two of Blott's] was escorted to Basle by a Swiss courier Lt. Col. Chauvet and a Swiss military policeman, Sgt Kuhn. We travelled second class and while crossing the frontier we were asked to pull the blinds down. At the first station after the border, a German officer accompanied by an interpreter came into the carriage. He told us that we were given a safe passage and we were expected to behave well. We then pulled the blinds up and went through Freiburg im Breisgau and Baden Baden. There we walked through the town to a hotel and then came back to a station before Baden Baden. [Actually the station must have been at Rastatt, after Baden Baden, on the rail line Karlsruhe-Paris.]

Blott continued:

> We left for Paris at about 2300hr, still on 12 May, travelling first class on the Vienna-Paris express. During this journey the blinds were again drawn. In Paris we were met on the platform by a German officer and a German civilian who spoke English and were taken to the Gare d'Austerlitz in a bus. At this station there was an air raid warning so we were sent down to a shelter for about ten minutes [USAAF *P-47*s were carrying out dive-bombing raids on various rail targets that day]. The German civilian whose Christian name was Wolfgang, was about twenty-eight, dark-haired, 6ft tall (1m 80cm), good looking and spoke fluent English with a slight American accent.

The German said he had attended Cambridge university and seemed aware that Blott was the senior RAF officer. He added he had lunched the day before with P.G. Wodehouse, an American reporter interned in Paris. He also told his charges – probably to see how this would affect them – that they would not be returning to the UK but would be sent to Japan. He furthermore asserted that no one on his side of the Channel feared the Second Front and that the British should of course be fighting with the Germans against the Russians. He then asked Blott if he would like to see Paris to which the pilot replied he did not want to go out.

TOURING PARIS, COURTESY GERMANY

'After an excellent lunch with five courses and a different wine with each course', continued Blott, 'the interpreter again asked me if I would like to drive through the Champs-Elysées. I again refused but Alistair Smith said he would like to go.'

When interrogated upon his return in England, Smith gave a vivid account of that experience:

The German officer in plain clothes who had met us at the station in Paris – he was a 'wolfgang' and had been educated at Cambridge offered to show one of us the sights. He said he had only one seat in his car and only two hours to spare. After consultation with F/Lt Blott I decided to avail myself of the opportunity and the German, who had a chauffeur, drove me off. We went first to a flat where he wanted to apologise to a girlfriend with whom he had missed an appointment because of us. This was in a side street near the Arc de Triomphe where the girl, called Gisèle, met us with a bottle of brandy. This I refused to partake but I was not unduly pressed; no attempt was made to interrogate me and conversation was on general lines. Later during the drive, the German brought the usual propaganda along the line 'What a pity that we and the British are fighting one another (instead of) fighting together against the Russians'.

'I felt', pursues Smith, 'that the drive and the encounter with Gisèle was because the German probably wanted to show off with a British pilot, to impress me with the amiability of the German race and to pick up any information I might have been willing to divulge.'

Both Germans had friends in England, to whom Smith was asked to pass the information that they were well. This Smith later did with permission from the MI9 intelligence people. The sightseeing ended in the late afternoon when Smith and his guides returned to the rail station where the other repatriated airmen had spent a much more sedate day. In the late evening the whole party boarded another first-class carriage. With the Swiss courier, the German captain and the interpreter, they travelled south to Bordeaux and Hendaye, entering Spain at Irun. Here the Germans left, the group continuing to San Sebastian. They reached Madrid the day after, remaining at the British Legation and attending a bull-fight before leaving the Spanish capital – this time in a lurching lorry – on 19 May. They reached Gibraltar via Xeres and more entertainment at its 'Bodega'. By 24 May 1944 they had all been whisked by air to Bristol-Whitchurch. They were home into a war-waging England where they would resume duty, albeit non-operationally, over Western Europe.

GRILLING

There remained for the men to be investigated, as were all arrivals from Europe, by Section 9(w) of the Intelligence Service, eager to extract from them any bit of information on life on the Continent, and to make sure the airmen had not become enemy agents.

A final interview was conducted by Bomber Command's operational research section keen to gather details about the demise of their aircraft. This would eventually find its way into the famed RAF 'K Reports' useful for Squadrons -and statistics. After a three-weeks 'survivor's leave' the Swiss internees of late went back their separate ways into service. For instance Smith's mid-upper gunner, Arthur Truscott had as next assignment, flying with 206 Squadron, Coastal Command, in big *Liberators* on anti-submarine patrols out of Cornwall and Scotland. He then became gunnery leader, was commissioned, got married in 1945 and left the Service in April 1946. He 'never flew since and do not intend to any more.'

Not surprisingly, it has proved well nigh impossible to trace all survivors-exchangees and hence to reconstruct their experience after they returned to England. As does Truscott's story above, the fortunes of the five men crewing 'The Birmenstorf *Wellington*' (see Chapter 5) gives, however, a typical cross-section of the destinies that awaited such returnees.

THE ALMOST

For many others, a much different lot was in store as they left by day or by night the misty skies of England. Disabled by enemy action, their mounts proved unable to take them back to England nor even to Swiss safety. There were many such failures and their number shall forever remain unknown. They are the 'Almost' whose ordeals often proved more taxing than the adventures of the winners at the lottery of Swiss luck. Three representative cases follow.

★ ★ ★ ★ ★ ★ ★ ★ ★

Essen, the *bête noire* of Bomber Command's chief, Air Marshal Arthur Harris, sustained 28 Main Force raids during the war. One of them occurred on 26/27 March 1944 when the Command despatched 705 aircraft for a successful attack which cost 'only' nine (1.3 per cent) four-engined bombers to the RAF.[10]

Such encouraging figures were however never of comfort for P/O Ronald Simmons' crew: five of them perished when their 10 Squadron *Halifax* crashed near Hastières-Lavaux in Belgium, north of Givet. Their demise was undoubtedly due to one of Major Wilhelm Herget's nightfighters, up from nearby Florennes airbase and operating in *Raum 7B*, an area belonging to the fighter belt erected to protect Germany from Allied raiders out of England. Returning from the target the *Hali* had its starboard wing shot off and so the skipper ordered the crew to bail out. One of the two survivors was the rear gunner, F/Sgt Ross Corby who landed in a wood. The morning after, he was given food and shelter by a man who also contacted an escape line. He was then hidden for three weeks in the nearby village of Doische where his helpers had ample time to tell him how they had witnessed the demise of another RAF machine.[11] They also reunited Corby with the other survivor: the mid-upper gunner, Sgt W. Formile. There followed several moves back and forth across the French border, staying in Hargnies and Vireux-Molhain.[12]

On 6 June, the maquis redoubt where they lived was attacked by the Germans and they had to scatter in the woods. They eventually joined two parachuted British underground officers and five evading American aircrew. These decided on or about 20 June to make it to Switzerland. Corby, Formile and a Sgt Beckwith waited until 21 July to follow suit. They reached Delouze, a village not too distant from Coussey where Thomas Harvell was to be downed in a week's time (see below). They were about halfway to Switzerland but did not go any further, electing not to run the gauntlet of another 160km (100mi.) of German-infested France. They rested and even fought with the underground until they were overrun by the advancing US Army. On 5 September they were safely back in England.

JOAN OF ARC

Several RAF airmen tried individually – and failed – to make it to Switzerland after being shot down and evading from German-occupied countries. An example was Thomas Harvell, a Sergeant flight engineer aboard *Lancaster* LM.206 coded JI°C by 514 Squadron. On its way to bomb Stuttgart on 28/29 July 1944, the aircraft was set afire and exploded in the air 0030hr, after being attacked by a *Ju.88* flown by Hauptmann Heinz Roekker of *Nachtjagdgeschwader 2*. Two men were thrown out and survived: Harvell and the navigator, Sgt G. Robinson who was captured. All the others, including the pilot F/O Robert Jones and his namesake Frank, the wireless operator, were killed and now rest in Neufchateau, Vosges. His parachute deposited twenty-year-old Harvell in a field where he injured his left knee and ankle; he was nevertheless able to walk and after hiding his parachute in the woods, he concealed himself in a tree for a few hours. From his perch he could see the burning wreck of his aircraft and hear the exploding ammunition. He did not know it but he was very close to the villages of Coussey and Domrémy where once lived an early opponent to the English invaders: Joan of Arc.

The man who later helped him was fortunately in a better mood: he took Harvell to his home 8km (5mi.) away where he cared for his injuries and gave him civilian clothes. The Good Samaritan was probably Charles Nang, a medical orderly in Neufchateau. On 1 August Harvell was loaned a bicycle and guided to Neufchateau to meet an English-speaking woman who told him the Germans had found his parachute and were after him. She also arranged that he meet the cemetery's caretaker who said he had had to bury the two Jones and three others whose identity discs had disappeared.

From there, Harvell was shown to a store to meet an underground worker, then to a safe house, a further 14km (9mi.) south, where another evader was already in hiding: F/Sgt Andrea Bell, a Canadian from Montreal.

Bell had been the rear gunner of *Stirling* LJ.882 from 190 Squadron detailed on 22/23 July 1944 to drop supplies and nine SAS commandos south of Epinal, in the mountainous region of Remiremont. 60km (38mi.) short of destination, the aeroplane had crashed in fog on high ground overlooking Graffigny, near Soulaucourt. Thirteen men had been killed: eight SAS and four crew including the pilot, New Zealander F/O Leonard Kilgour. An airman (F/Ovenet(?) who was captured), an SAS man and Bell survived,[13] albeit seriously bruised or injured. Bell found himself lying on the ground next to the burning aircraft; he crawled away and rested awhile, some hundreds of yards from the inferno. He then went down the mountain into the village were the locals fed him and provided civilian garb. Next afternoon he was spirited away from the village and that evening the French-speaking Bell was escorted by the FFI to a house in the woods at Soulaucourt. He met Harvell there, remaining in bed for a week whilst recovering from his wounds.

As their hideout was only 75mi.(120km) away from Switzerland, their helpers asserted that they ought to try to seek refuge there. The pair made it to Bains-les-Bains where another helper, Mr Beaurepaire, tried to arrange a route to Switzerland. Bell and Harvell eventually ended up on or about 20 August in the Landresse maquis, on a lonely mountain plateau east of Besançon, just 26km (16mi.) north of the Swiss border. They never made it across, becoming instead embroiled at Pierrefontaine in a brawl between maquisards and hundreds of Vlassov Russians, deserters of the German Wehrmacht. On 5 September the village was overrun by French troops and on the same evening they were trucked to Lons-le-Saunier. From here American forces took them to Bourg-en-Bresse to be evacuated by air to Italy. They were interrogated there on 11 September, six weeks after being downed.

UNDERGROUND DELIVERY

On the night of 20/21 September 1944, a big Handley-Page *Halifax*, coded 8A°M for 298 Squadron and serialed LL.333, took off from Tarant Rushton near Bournemouth. Its pilot, F/Sgt K. Goldsmith, knew of the dangers involved in low-level night precision flights over enemy territory but as for everyone in war-time operations, the nagging thought of possible injury or death was pushed back by the general feeling that 'it can only happen to others'.

Goldsmith's *Hali* was one of four despatched by the Squadron – with four more from 644 Squadron – to drop supplies to the French resistance fighters in eastern France. His own assignment, 'Stockbroker 26', was for the benefit of the ring of saboteurs who had been operating steadily since April 1943 along the Swiss border, under the leadership of Harry Ree, a British captain in SOE.[14] Stockbroker was marshalling units of liberated maquisards still supplied by SOE and currently partaking in the harsh autumn fighting endeavouring to push German forces back to the Rhine.

Reaching his drop zone, Goldsmith's crew was unable to find the recognition lights due to low fog blanketing the area. This was just 13km (8m.) west of La-Chaux-de-Fonds in Switzerland and only 5km (3m.) from the border river Doubs. Flying lower and lower in trying to ascertain its position, the *Halifax* met disaster, hitting high ground near a forlorn hamlet, Les Coires. Goldsmith's crew comprised six men only, the mid-upper turret being deleted on late production *Halifaxes*. Three men perished: the navigator, F/O Albert Sheffield, the flight engineer Sgt Hardy Day and the wireless operator F/O Gerald Borkett.

Goldsmith, F/Sgt F. Barnes his bombardier, and the rear gunner Sgt R. Titman, survived the crash which missed Switzerland by a few miles. Hidden and cared for in safe houses, they awaited liberation by the advancing US ground forces.

★ ★ ★ ★ ★ ★ ★ ★ ★

SWISS RAF PILOTS

This chapter would not be complete without giving credit to a couple of Swiss-born RAF pilots. One was Edgar 'Billy' Wicht whose birth is recorded in 1920 in Corminboeuf-Fribourg. While completing his education in England, he became a British national in 1936 and a private pilot the year after. He then joined the RAF on a short-service commission and by July 1939 was flying 233 Squadron's *Ansons*. This led him to be operational on 3 September, the first day of the war. On 17/18 May 1940 he was flying a *Hudson*, attacking Hamburg's oil refineries, when flak killed two of his crew. Himself seriously wounded in the chest, Wicht succeeded in bringing the aircraft back in the UK for a crash landing on the east coast. He then had to spend a year in or near hospitals, scrounging in the process some flying from Tangmere on various aircraft such as *Spitfires* and *Beaufighters*. Passed A-1G (fit for operational flying) in June 1942, he was posted to RAF Thornaby where, after a mandatory refreshing course, he instructed on *Hudsons*. Like many training and conversion units, his had to provide aircraft and scratch crews for the Millennium raid on Cologne on 30/31 May 1942.

In the spring of 1943 Wicht was posted as a F/Lt to 224 Squadron on long-range anti-submarine *Liberators* flying out of Beaulieu and St-Eval. He was later awarded the DFC for his part on anti-sub strikes in the Bay of Biscay and on Atlantic convoy protection. Wicht's chequered career also saw him on Transport Command *Dakotas* dropping paratroops over Normandy on D-Day and flying the last aircraft to re-supply airborne troops in Arnhem. He was then sent to Bari in Italy as adviser on airborne supplies to Yugoslavia and Greece. After the 1944 disturbances there, he flew the RAF aircraft bringing in Athens the AOC, Air HQ Greece. That same year, as a Flight Commander, he flew long-range *York* transports to the Far East and to Crimea for the February 1945 Yalta Conference.

VE Day saw Wicht the recipient of both the DSO and DFC. Post-war, W/Cdr Edgar Wicht occupied several staff posts at HQ Far East Command. Returning to the UK in 1950, he was chosen to command 207 Squadron, a remarkable coincidence since the unit had been the one losing P/O Badge's *Lancaster* (see Chapter 6) at Le Bouveret, a mere 50km (31mi.) from Wicht's birthplace. Wicht retired from the RAF in 1960, joining a tobacco company in Geneva. He died there, in his country of origin, in 1979.

WING LEADER

Jean Zumbach was another Swiss national for the RAF. Born in Poland in 1915, he flew for the Polish Air Force (PAF) in 1939 and for France soon after. Defeated but not beaten in June 1940, he escaped to the UK where he was posted as a P/O to the Polish 303 Squadron flying *Hurricanes*.

Language difficulties were but one of several hindrances restricting quick operational readiness of refugee-pilots eager to enter RAF service. The issue of radio-telephone understanding between ground control, formation leaders and individual Polish pilots has been well rendered in films such as the Fitz-Saltzman *Battle of Britain* in the 1960s. Other inconveniences were in units: miles per hour instead of kilometres, feet for metres, gallons instead of litres, but the most serious obstacle to mastering British fighters laid with the throttle. The RAF engines were logically unleashed by pushing it forward whereas the men trained in Poland and France had acquired the habit of retarding the (British) throttle!

With all those snags ironed out, 303 Squadron became operational early in September 1940 i.e. in the third phase of the Battle. When it was over, Zumbach had altogether and true to the Polish press-on attitude, downed seven enemy aircraft, been shot down once and been awarded his first DFC.

In 1941, as his Squadron took to the offensive over the Channel, Zumbach flew *Circus, Rhubarb and Sphere* operations, downing at least three more opponents. Such actions were however not without opposition, as witnessed by Zumbach being once more downed on 9 May 1941, fortunately again surviving the ordeal. He also survived a stint as instructor and returned to his Squadron in March 1942 as a Flight Commander. He shot down an *FW-190* on 26 April during a foray over Hazebrouck and St-Omer in northern France, as HM Commandos operated near Boulogne.

By now Zumbach's abilities as an aerial leader were being recognised and, mid-May, he was promoted Squadron Leader and CO of his 303 'Warsaw-Kosciuszko' Fighter Squadron. In that capacity the 'remotely Swiss' Zumbach subtracted at least one more *FW-190* from the Luftwaffe's inventory during the Dieppe affair, on 19 August. He was awarded a bar to his DFC a month later. Zumbach's irresistible climb up the promotion ladder brought him on 15 February 1944 to the largely rest-position of Wing Leader, 3d Polish Fighter Wing (PFW). Six months later he transferred to the less sedate leadership of No.133 PFW, comprising three Squadrons: one RAF (129) and two Polish (315 and 306). Incidentally, the latter happened to be the one escorting the Kembs dam-busting *Lancasters* of Chapter 17.

At the war's end, Zumbach's tally amounted to 12+⅓ victories, plus five probables and three damaged, but his thirst for adventure was by no means quenched. Like many of his contemporaries who had known war's hazardous excitement, Zumbach endeavoured to keep on flying. This he did on more or less covert operations between Switzerland, France, Britain, Poland and Israel. In 1961-

62, Zumbach was in Africa, leading the Katanga Air Force for the benefit of Mr Tschombé, the secessionist from Congo. In 1967 'Mister Brown' – as Zumbach had become known in Africa – was No.1 of Biafra's Air Force. In this capacity, he flew its single aircraft, a black, shark-nosed *A-26* used to bomb Nigeria on behalf of Biafra's Colonel Ojukwu.

TABLE 3

FATE OF RAF/FAF AIRCREW FLYING INTO SWITZERLAND IN THE SECOND WORLD WAR

(★)Canadian(RCAF)/(★★)Australian (RAAF)/(# French (FAF)/All others = RAF

WHERE/ WHEN	KILLED	EXCHANGED	INTERNED
Berne **24 August 1942**	F/Lt G.Wooll (★) Sgt J. Fielden		
Birmenstorf **14/15 April** **1943**		Sgt J. Avery Sgt W. Shields Sgt W. Boddy Sgt J. Cash Sgt R. McEwan (★)	
Bouveret **12/13 July 1943**	P/O H. Badge Sgt R. Wood F/Lt A. Jepps Sgt A. Wright Sgt E. Higgins F/Sgt R. Brett (★★) Sgt J. Spence		
Thyon/Sion **12/13 July 1943**	F/O G. Mitchell (★★) Sgt B. Evans P/O H. St George(★★) F/O W. Morgan F/Sgt J. Maher (★★) F/Sgt H. Bolger (★★) F/Sgt A. Terry (★★)		

WHERE/ WHEN	KILLED	EXCHANGED	INTERNED
Sihlsee **25/26 February** **1944**	P/O H. Benson	P/O G. Smith Sgt G. Beevers P/O B. Metcalf Sgt E. Hiley Sgt A. Truscott F/Sgt R. Carr	
Saignelégier **15/16 March** **1944**P	P/O S. Atcheson Sgt B. Thomas P/O A. McCall F/Sgt J. Greenhalgh Sgt F. Weaver Sgt J. Naylor		F/Sgt K. Reece
Golaten **15/16 March** **1944**		F/Lt W. Blott Sgt G. Gill	Sgt G. Mattock F/O C. Nabarro W/O R. Millard(★) Sgt T. Forster Sgt D. Murphy
Uttwil **6/7 April 1944**	S/Ldr M. Negus F/O A. Gapper		
Grappelen **27/28 April** **1944**	W/O B. Noble F/Sgt J. Burton Sgt W. Anderson Sgt M. Smith W/O2 O. Albrecht (★) Sgt F. Bathmaker		Sgt R. Bridges F/O H. Prowse (★)
Hamikon **27/28 April** **1944**	P/O R. Ridley (★) Sgt J. Eaton Sgt L. Cotton Sgt R. Clark Sgt A. Weir		F/O A. Piggott(★) F/O R. Phillips

WHERE/ WHEN	KILLED	EXCHANGED	INTERNED
Steckborn **27/28 April** **1944**	F/Sgt G. Foulkes (★★)	W/O R. Peter (★★)	F/Sgt N. Davis(★★) F/S M. Bartle(★★) Sgt I. Graham F/Sgt D. Balmer
	PoW (Germany) A. Brereton		
Volketswil **30 September** **1944**			S/Ldr H. Morley F/Sgt R. Fidler
Dübendorf **30 September** **1944**			F/Lt A. Callard F/Sgt E. Townsley

FROM THE FAF

Six French Air Force pilots appearing in this book landed in Switzerland just before or after VE Day (see Chapter 16): two were killed, one spent two weeks recovering from his injuries and the three others returned within hours of their arrival:

KILLED (#)	RETURNED (#)	INTERNED (#)
20 April 1945 **Merishausen**		Lt H. Koechlin
25 May 1945 **Birsfelden**	S/Lt Carrere Lt Toulouse	
2 July 1945 **Geneva**	S/Lt Nicolas	
16 July 1945 **Teufen**	S/Lt Devolvé Sgt Laurens	

THE TALLY

Killed: 37 including: 26 RAF, 2 RCAF (★ in table), 7 RAAF(★★) and 2 FAF (#)
(Not included is Sidney Bradley, RAF, an evader who drowned entering Switzerland (see Introduction).

Survived: 38 including:
Exchanged: 16 [13 RAF, 2 RCAF, 1 RAAF]
Interned: 19 [13 RAF, 3 RCAF, 2 RAAF, 1 FAF]
Returned: 3 FAF

★TOTALS
75 – 52 RAF, 7 RCAF, 10 RAAF, 6 FAF

Not included in the tally:
2 RAF – Alfred Brereton, prisoner in Germany Sidney; Bradley, evader drowned entering Switzerland.

TABLE 4

INTERNEES AND EVADERS
HOW THEY FARED

INTERNEES	EVADERS
Quarantine	Quarantine (not in theory, yes in practice)
Live in camps	Hotel accommodation
In uniform	Civilian clothes
Under guard, Swiss Army	Freedom of movements (in principle)
Report to Swiss EKIH (Federal Commission for Internmt. & Hospitalisation)	Report to own Legations
Repatriation after end of war or belligerents' agreement for exchange	Free to leave (depending on possibilities)

19

Aftermath

As hinted at previously, the carelessness — alleged or not — of the British air arm over Switzerland ushered waves of complaints from Swiss officialdom to His Majesty's Government. Four major topics were aired…

The first subject obviously related to the subsequent fate of the aircrew involved in the course of dramatic arrivals. This has been covered in Chapter 18 and thus shall only be cursorily touched upon here.

A second point at issue was more technical: what future laid in store for the aircraft which, complete or not, ended down on Swiss soil.

The third theme and perhaps the most outstanding in a country deeply involved in financial matters, touched economics – the coverage of expenses arising from crashes, bombings or simply maintenance and hangarage of equipment.

Fourth, and last but not least, were the exercises in diplomacy. Stirring starched routines, the often tragic arrivals of British aircraft or missiles generated sudden animation in the gold-lined offices of embassies and legations. Much guarded talks produced flurries of messages flowing back and forth via ciphered notes forwarded by radio or diplomatic bags between Berne and London's Foreign Office. Several instances that occurred in 1943 appear in the section below.

DIPLOMATIC BARTER
Tensions between His Majesty's and Swiss Governments further to RAF deeds on or over the Swiss island of neutrality consistently resulted in diplomatic turmoil. Often remote from the realities of war such parlour games sometimes proved quite sore for all parties. And the more so for individuals involved when the slow and starchy diplomatic channels linking wartime Berne and London did not come up to expectations.

Harsh as it may sound such a judgement is exemplified by one sad occurrence. On 13 July 1943, two complete Royal Air Force crews were lost over

Switzerland, fourteen young men in all. As indicated in Chapter 7, the Swiss queried British authorities in September 1943 in order to identify the badly burned or mangled victims. Their telegram laid dormant at the Foreign Office in London for six weeks! After this, London's Air Ministry took over in the slow down process: doling out its answer in January 1944 so that the information could again creep back through diplomatic channels towards Switzerland.

On less sensitive areas devoid of personal involvement, three main fields of contention kept straining wartime Anglo-Swiss association. One was the rigorous economic blockade imposed by Britain, on sea lanes mostly. On this matter Swiss relations with the warring countries had to steer carefully between preserving the nation's interests and avoiding antagonising the neighbouring Axis countries or those – Britain and the United States – upon whose goodwill Switzerland relied upon to obtain vital supplies. RAF operations had little impact on the matter, except, as related in 'Bombings', with the occasional attack on Swiss supply vessels.

It was, however, the controversy over Swiss supplies to Germany in the form of food products and war material, and the transit of German goods going to the Reich's Italian ally through Switzerland via the Gothard rail link, that stood as the major sore point in Swiss/Allied relations. Britain was quick to think that Swiss recriminations against aerial violations contrasted with the positive aid given to her Axis opponents in allowing the transit of war material over Swiss railways.

The subject came to a head again in mid-1943 when the passage of limited quantities of oil products was raised in discussions between Anthony Eden, UK's Minister for Foreign Affairs, and the Swiss Minister in London, Walter Thurnheer. The topic of airspace violations conveniently came up as a diversion allowing Thurnheer to skip the matter of the alleged German-controlled use of Swiss rail facilities.

The earliest wartime diplomatic point of dissent between the two countries rests on the ever recurrent RAF infringement of the Swiss neutral airspace. Actually, airspace violations – British, American and to some extend German – remained troublesome right until the end of the conflict.

AIRSPACE VIOLATIONS HELP

Looking up the transcript of contemporary talks, an air-minded observer might wonder about the qualifications shown at the highest levels of government to discuss aviation matters. Indeed, taken out of context, Thurnheer's words that 'British airmen ought to be able to (ascertain their precise position) by sighting Lake Constance' would denote a paucity of cognisance in aeronautical navigation. One ought however take into account that the statement came right on the heels of the deliberate overflying of Switzerland, on 20 June 1943, by the Friedrichshafen RAF raiders on their way to Africa. Thus, what could be interpreted as blatant ignorance of how critical wartime flight can be at night and under adverse weather conditions, was indeed a clever use by the Swiss representative of one of the RAF's calculated blunders. The timely outcome was in any case a British statement on 11 August that '... (referring to rail transits between Germany and Italy through Switzerland), the Swiss government has given (HM's Government) satisfactory replies on their determination to observe their obligations of neutrality most strictly'. It thus appears that at least one case of RAF infringements on Swiss neutral airspace played in favour of Switzerland.

* * * * * * * * *

Mr Pilet-Golaz, the wartime Swiss Head of Foreign Affairs, was known for his lukewarm sympathy towards Britain. Regarding bombs which fell on Zurich on 17/18 May 1943, Pilet knew there was no reasonable doubt that the bombs were British. Nevertheless, three days later Pilet told British Ambassador in Berne Clifford Norton that he had instructed Minister Walter Thurnheer in London, 'to deliver a protest in not very strong terms'. He, Pilet:

> was not letting the Press know of this protest since he very much hoped... an early [British] reply expressing regrets, even if [the UK] did not admit absolute responsibility, and agreed to pay compensation for the damage. In that case, the reply could be published simultaneously and any public excitement would be allayed.

Such words disclosed the Swiss political resolve to avoid giving undue prominence to an operational accident. Only material damage had been provoked and the tone contrasted with earlier reactions such as those after the initial bombing of Switzerland, on Geneva in June 1940. At the time, the blunder had been fully recognised by the British Foreign Office as early as 18 June with apologies followed by complete compensation.

An incessant by-product of RAF night bombings of Switzerland was the question of maintaining or not black-out of the country at night. There is no doubt, as shown in Chapter 5, that this touchy matter stirred much animation in Berne and London. Another topic eventually found its way in diplomacy in 1940. It stemmed from the irritation of the Italian press at a Switzerland unable to prevent RAF raiders to northern Italy from taking it easy with Swiss airspace.

* * * * * * * * *

If diplomatic deals generally evince much pompous prose, they occasionally display doses of unintentional humour. Witness a couple of pearls extracted from the Foreign Office's association with neutral countries. There was that case of compensation paid by His Majesty's Government for the death of two bullocks hit by anti-aircraft shells from a British vessel being attacked by an enemy aircraft near the coast of Portugal. Witness also, the surprising suggestion appearing in the 1943 Foreign Office records. Its proponent, Walther Thurnheer the imaginative Swiss Minister in London, aired the idea of having an RAF aircraft simulating a forced landing in the Alpine republic. The idea was to counter German accusations of Switzerland's inability and unwillingness to defend her neutrality. The 'timely' downing of a pair of *Lancasters* on 12/13 July halted that extravaganza in the offing.

FOOTING THE BILLS

The British government was, generally speaking, quite willing to pay compensation once RAF responsibility had been ascertained through the presence of dud bombs or other clues. The expenses incurred due to RAF aircraft accidents or incidents were also easily acknowledged. However sometimes, and particularly after VE Day, it took British bureaucracy inordinate delays to come to terms with the bills, resulting in the addition of sizeable amounts of interests at 5 per cent. For instance, on 25 July 1945 the outstanding amount peaked at 385,862.70 Sw.Frcs including 43,132.20 frcs of interests.

The ultimate balance sheet presented to Britain for the damage caused by RAF aircraft has not been clearly established but it must have neared 50 million Sw.Frcs. This comprised indemnification resulting from aircraft crashes or landings between August 1942 (the Berne *Mosquito*) and the end of the war. There were also expenses resulting from the care of crewmembers walking away from accidents, and compensation for the bombings (starting in June 1940).

The aircraft-related amount was just 29,667.45 Sw.Frcs, a sum that had grown by 6215.05 frcs of interests at the end of 1946 due to overdue payment. Clearing the wreckage of downed aircraft or the simple hangarage, guard and maintenance of those that made a safe landing also cost money to their owners. The sums involved could be negligible as in the case of the roundel-carrying French '*Lightning*' welcomed in Geneva just after VE Day: 165.40 Sw.Frcs. Often the fee was more tangible. The couple of *Mosquito*es stored in Dübendorf were responsible for a bill of 38,229.40 Sw.Frcs[1] presented to the RAF three years to the day after the second such machine had arrived on 30 September 1944.[2]

At Birmenstorf, the hole in the ground dug by Sgt. Avery's *Wellington* cost 490,- Sw.Frcs, whilst clearing the wreckage of Smith's *Lancaster* on the Sihlsee ice amounted to a mere 72,-francs. Its sister machine at Golaten proved comparatively expensive at 5739.20 Sw.Frcs. Surprisingly neither Bertram Noble's *Lancaster* at Alp Grappelen nor the wreck of the Volketswil *Mosquito* entailed bills for damage. However, a most improbable aspect of the two *Lancaster* crashes in July 1943 in Canton Valais, was the Swiss claim for compensation. It resulted from their real or alleged downing of Badge's crew at Le Bouveret and Mitchell's above Sion. At 7,447,40 Sw.Frcs the Bouveret *Lancaster* proved the most expensive of all the British aircraft arrivals in Switzerland, but its twin in adversity at Sion, drained only 300- frcs from the UK treasury. Even if the Swiss did not claim full compensation since they recognised a responsibility in those two demises, the appearance in London's Foreign Office of a telegram from the Berne embassy relaying the Swiss demand, amounted to a mild seism. It was felt that since liability for the crashes was assumed by the Swiss flab, HM Government should ignore the matter. It took several days for drafting a diplomatic answer making the Swiss understand the awkwardness of a claim presented in relation with the loss of fourteen RAF men. Also, solving the issue would delay the settlement of more straightforward pending matters. Eventually the financial liquidation of the Bouveret and Sion affairs was incorporated in the final post-war bill presented to Britain and covering all damages incurred.

TAXING THE GOVERNMENT

What does not seem to have been deducted from the bills issued to foreign parties, is the salvage of aluminium scrap resulting from crashes. Aircraft wrecks were sent to Chippis in Valais where 'Industrie de l'Aluminum' converted them to semi-manufactured goods. However, Swiss Customs did their act, claiming dues from their own government for 'the import of metal scrap'! Contemporary estimates show that wreckage of RAF and USAAF aircraft brought between 200 and 250 tons of scrap aluminium into the country. At about .25 Sw.Frcs per kilo this caused headaches worth some 62,500 frcs. to Berne accountants.

* * * * * * * * *

The total of roughly 50 million Sw.Frcs of compensation indicated above may appear as a lot of money to be paid for just wasting lives and equipment. Not so however in comparison with the cost of aerial warfare. One source sets at $50,000 dollars, then about 214,000- Sw.Frcs, the cost of a single sortie of an RAF bomber! It is extremely difficult to check such a figure. However, even if one sets the benchmark at just a tenth of that amount, a typical 1944 raid, the one to Augsburg on 25/26 February with its 584 heavies, would have cost 12.5 million Sw.Frcs to the British taxpayer. For the whole war, Bomber Command dispatched 389,809 sorties which would mean an expense of some 8,350 million Sw.Frcs at 1945 value. That would be 167 times what was paid to Switzerland in compensations.

Astronomical as they are, such figures should not conceal the true cost of war: the loss of life and the suffering generated in the air and on the ground. Bomber Command's Second World War operations snuffed the lives of no less than 55,573 aircrew. A further estimated 305,000 persons were killed on the ground in Germany alone in the course of bombing operations.[3] Such are the figures that should bring about much humility in considering the material costs of a war.

BOMB BLASTS

The third subdivision of indemnities was related to bombings and here laid the bulk of the sums involved. Switzerland's Federal Council (Government) decided in the summer of 1942 to help victims of foreign intrusions by paying up to fifty thousand Sw.Frcs per event. This covered much of the material damage incurred due to foreign interference; cases where damage exceeded that figure were to be settled after the war.

The amount of compensation paid for the twenty-odd Royal Air Force bombings of the country has not been clearly established, one of the reasons being the dispute over who ought to pay for certain deterioration. For instance, no agreement was ever reached on who should pay about 2,000.-Sw.Frcs for broken windows and the setting afire of stocks of chemicals in the Ciba facilities in Basle. The damage could just as well have been due to Swiss flab, German flak or RAF gunners approaching the Kembs dam on 7 October 1944.

A close approximation of the bombing compensation can however be derived from a figure of 32,272,034.32 Sw.Frcs[4] appearing at the end of 1946. In any case, a lawyer, Me.Félix Paschoud, headed a Commission Fédérale d'Estimations in charge of appraising damages and a few examples of its findings can be quoted. For instance the body felt entitled to claim 1,136,629- Sw.Frcs plus interests at 5 per cent since from the time of the bombing, for the Geneva incident on 12 June 1940. Another early bombing, on Basle and Binningen on 16/17 December 1940, resulted in a claim for 1.2 million Sw.Frcs. Later on, the attack on Raron airfield, a by-product of the raid on Turin on 11/12 December 1942, cost together with the damage at Sins, 114,914,-Sw.Frcs. Bombs widely scattered over the country in the course of the raid to Italy on 12/13 July 1943 cost 418,771.15 Sw.Frcs to HM's treasury. At the lower end of the scale, repairs to the six houses and power lines damaged by the few missiles dropped on Zurich-Seebach on 17/18 May caused damage worth only 9,634- Sw.Frcs.

UNDER THE WHITE CROSS

The RAF machines destroyed in Switzerland had no other value than that of the scrap metal they yielded. There were, however, two *Mosquitoes* which could be repaired and salvaged after arrival (see Chapters 4 and 15). One was bought by the Swiss who were given the other free of charge as compensation for the cost of their internment.

The senior such machine was DK.310, the reconnaissance *Mosquito* brought in Berne-Belp by Gerald Wooll on 24 August 1942. This was a long-nacelled machine sporting a pointed windshield, two characteristics that should prove important later in this presentation.

From the time it dropped into Belp until April 1953, the stranded *Mosquito* was to live a pampered career. Soon after inadvertently 'acquiring' the hitherto little known *Mossie*, the Swiss military endeavoured to hide it from German curiosity: they kept it hangared and under guard, ironically alongside other interned but swastika-bearing machines.[5] A minimum of maintenance was performed as well, fuel tanks being refilled and the strain taken off the landing gear's oleos.

Simultaneously, the Swiss queried H.M.Government in order to obtain ownership of the machine and be able to test-fly it. On 27 August 1943, one year after DK.310's arrival Air Commodore Ferdinand West, the charismatic British Air Attaché in Berne, was able to give a positive answer: Britain was willing to sell the *Mosquito* for 12,000 pounds. Translated into 208,200 Sw.Frcs the sum was deducted from the growing hoard stemming from bombing compensations. Thus, in a surprising resolve occurring in the middle of the war, Britain allowed a foreign country, albeit neutral, to acquire one of its prominent war machines.

From then on, the aircraft could be test flown by pilots belonging to Switzerland's renowned KTA, the *Kriegstechnische Abteilung*, i.e. the establishment developing, testing and producing weapons. KTA's aircraft branch nested in Emmen, near Lucerne, in central Switzerland. Prior to its ferry flight, DK.310 was provided with 'domestic' radios, given the code 'E-42' with Swiss national markings replacing the RAF cockades. Thus outfitted, the *Mosquito* left Belp at the hands of Capt.Walter Läderach. He was an experienced pilot, chief of *Flieger Kompanie* 7 and one of the few who dared to wrestle with an unfamiliar high performance machine that was not exactly forgiving in take-off and landing configurations.

This initial Swiss flight to Emmen took place the very day, 6 September 1943, of the ill-fated USAAF mission to Stuttgart when five of the raiding *B-17F*s took refuge in Switzerland. One of them, a 306 Bomb Group machine flown by Lt Martin Andrews, went as far south as Magadino-Locarno, almost crossing the path of the Swiss-flown *Mossie* that had made an intermediate stop at Dübendorf-Zürich.

THE MOSQUITO EVALUATED

It seems that no test flight took place during the winter 1943/44. In any case a comprehensive technical description was elaborated under the supervision of Col. Karl Högger, head of technical services, Swiss Air Force. Starting on 17 May 1944, a series of twenty-four sorties lasting 686 minutes occurred, intended for technical evaluation and familiarisation of test pilots such as Ernst (? Karl) Wyss and Lt Mathoz with observer Probst.

Emmen's thorough technical evaluation ended on 13 October 1944 when the *Mosquito* was handed over to Swissair airline and flown back to Dübendorf. At the time, Switzerland was no longer completely isolated in a sea of Axis-dominated territory hence the idea of using the aircraft for night postal runs. As of 20 March 1945, duly provided with a CoA and coded HB-IMO under civilian guise, DK.310 and Capt Läderach started training six commercial pilots.[6] The effort could have been spared since the postal scheme was dropped a year later. Losing its civilian registration on 7 August 1945 and with seventeen hours and fifty-two minutes of Swiss flying time, the aeroplane was returned to KTA, being re-coded 'B-4'[7] in the process.

B-4 did not fly again in 1945. Then, on 27 June 1946, the starboard *Merlin 21* was removed and sent to Rolls-Royce Derby for overhaul and modification into a *Merlin 25*. The engine was replaced on DK.310 by a new one obtained from the factory. On 21 August 1946 the aircraft had accumulated thirty-nine hours and thirty-three minutes of Swiss time when its port engine was in turn taken away. The *Mossie* never flew again. It shed its 'new' right engine[8] on 15 March 1949 for the benefit of the other airworthy 'Swiss' *Mosquito*: NS.993, the fighter-bomber that had become a 'Swiss refugee' on 30 September 1944 and was by now wearing the code 'B-5'.

DK.310 then slowly faded into oblivion. On 1 July 1951, just ten years after being born at Hatfield, the aircraft was reportedly struck off charge. DK.310 thus sadly disappeared in an unrecorded Swiss scrap yard. Its younger stablemate, NS.993, was now free to acquire prominence.

CHESHIRE AND NS.993

NS.993, the second repairable *Mosquito* to arrive in Switzerland, had landed at Dübendorf (see Chapter 15) practically intact but for its failed right engine. A little known aspect of NS.993's life is that it started its operational career within 617 Squadron where famed G/C Leonard Cheshire used its suitability for dive-marking targets. He first flew the machine with his navigator Pat Kelly against the marshalling yards at Paris-Juvisy on 18/19 April 1944. The trio again operated together on 24/25 April over Munich, an occasion when NS.993 almost failed to return due to fuel shortage.[9] In June, soon before being allotted to 515 Squadron, the same aircraft and pilot operated against Le Havre and Watten, the large concrete weapons site near St-Omer in northern France.

Upon reaching Switzerland, and like DK.310 its older 'Swiss' mate, NS.993 was towed out of public view. Air Ministry requested continued maintenance but this was abandoned in December 1947. Even then, guard and hangarage went on to the tune of 130- Sw.Frcs per month. At this time internment costs had reached precisely 11,624.24- frcs. In the summer of 1948 after a long ballet of mail between embassies and headquarters in both countries Britain lost interest in the veteran machine. The UK then gave away the machine and its radios at scrap value i.e. for a symbolic 1,000 Sw.Frcs.Thus administratively cleared to fly, now known as 'B-5' in Swiss parlance, NS.993 was handed over to Capt Wyss for its first flight under the white cross.

The KTA then realised that the exceptional machine sitting aimlessly at Dübendorf could be used to advantage.The idea was to use the fast twin as a test bed for a jet engine.This was a modified Armstrong Siddeley *Mamba SM-01* being developed to propel a new Swiss fighter-bomber: KTA's *N-20 Aiguillon*.[10] It took three months to render the *Mosquito* airworthy again, starting mid–March 1949 with the replacement of the port engine No.151523.That old contemptible,'B-4', thus shed its new *Merlin* (No.105435) which was then grafted upon NS.993, replacing the seemingly time-expired power plant. On 27 June 1949 the aircraft was ferried east to FFA, the *Flug- & Fahrzeugwerke Altenrhein* near the Austrian border.[11]

It took the best part of 1950 to modify the *SM-01* engine and prepare the aircraft by rigging the Swiss *Mamba* in front of the bomb bay. Flight tests took place from November 1950 through 1952 when the *N-20* project was cancelled. One of the mishaps that befell the *Mossie* occurred on 1 December 1950 when the landing gear was damaged: its test pilot had discovered how the *Mosquito* could become a difficult aircraft to handle with its massive gear down.

On 8 April 1953 NS.993 'B-5' flew what was to be its last sortie, at the hands of pilot Mathoz and thus adding the final touch to the forty-one hours, fourteen minutes flown in Swiss livery.The final blow to NS.993 came next day when dismayed Swiss engineers discovered accumulations of a strange yellowish dust which proved to be residues of the glue bonding the various components of the 'wooden wonder'.[12] Callard's machine was finished: it was dismantled on 15 March 1954, the parts mostly heading for the scrap yard.

SURVIVING THE 'SWISS ORDEAL'

Table 3 and Chapter 18 draw a rather comprehensive picture of what happened to RAF aircrew in Switzerland.Three words crudely summarise their fate: internment, departure or burial.

Among those who survived, the early arrivals were confined in the cosy informality of small hotels or *pensions de famille*. Such was the case for Wooll and Fielden in August 1942 (see Chapter 4) who for three days were lodged and treated at the 'alkoholfrei' Restaurant Daheim in Berne for an amount of 43.45 Sw.Frcs to which 3.75 frcs were added for a hairdresser session.

By September 1944, however, when the number of RAF internees had grown, complete hotels were rented, such as the Rothorn'in Arosa and the Grand Hotel in Adelboden. Other men wangled their way into clerical appointments in Berne and Geneva Legation or Consulates. Some even became students in 'university camps', in Geneva for physics courses and Fribourg for architecture and law.

Leaving the country of their unwilling arrival meant either escape or repatriation. Escape from internment was the accomplishment of evaders and escapees intent on pursuing the fight by returning to the United Kingdom; their deeds has been covered in the first volume of this trilogy.[13] Suffice it to say here that those illegal returnees who had the bad luck to be caught by Swiss guards became, for a time, the unhappy inmates of the Wauwilermoos or Hünenberg '*straflagern*', the Swiss versions of better known concentration camps in Spain and Germany.

Repatriation was the exception intended for badly wounded or crippled military personnel. In the case of safe and sound airmen, the measure was only enforced within the framework of a few exchanges of equivalent numbers of RAF and Luftwaffe specialists (see Chapters 5 and 18). The third such exchange does not lack flavour. It involves the nine RAF airmen who, in the early hours of Saturday 13 May 1944, entrained for a long journey to Gibraltar via Germany, occupied France and Spain. They were the six survivors of the Sihlsee *Lancaster*, two others from the Golaten crash, and as a last-minute addition, the pilot from the Lake Constance ditching. Most had been selected by the British Air Attaché in view of their specialist trades that had necessitated long and exacting training.[14] All wore civilian clothes and carried a British passport.

Their German counterparts were the crews of three nightfighters which had arrived on the nights of 15/16 March (ObFw Helmut Treynogga's *Bf.110G*), of 27/28 April (OLt Wilhelm Johnen) and of 1/2 May (Fw Konzack's *Do.217N-2*). The second, a *Bf.110G-4*, had landed in error in Switzerland carrying a state-of-the art radar; it was destined to make much of an impact on Swiss-German relations. Its crew included Paul Mahle who had designed the infamous '*Schräge Musik*' slanted guns that exacted such a high price from Bomber Command.

Epilogue

Altogether, thirteen RAF wartime aircraft ended their careers inside Switzerland, although officialdom catalogues only twelve. Indeed the Steckborn Lancaster was listed by the Swiss as having ditched outside their national boundaries. It remains however that its survivors came ashore in Switzerland and that their machine was later raised and towed into that country. The breakdown by type of aeroplanes was thus eight Lancasters, four Mosquitoes and one Wellington.

NO *WHITLEY*, NO *STIRLING*, NO *HALI*

Why then just those three types? The question may look irrelevant but remains puzzling for those in Switzerland and elsewhere, aware of the RAF's genealogy. What follows is a tentative essay to shed some light on the subject. A preliminary explanation can be that, except for the early *Whitleys* and then the *Stirlings* and *Halifaxes*, the other types did not possess sufficient endurance to reach targets close to Switzerland where they would seek asylum in case of misfortune.

Then, why did no *Whitley* ever show up in Switzerland? Here a combination of luck and small numbers involved is the most obvious answer. During the three years[1] of its Second World War career as long-range bomber, the *Whitleys* took part for certain in just five raids on Italy, skirting Switzerland in the process and losing no more than four of their number. The chances for one of them to end up in Switzerland were thus minimal. The same applies for the *Stirling*, the first and largest of the four-engined RAF bombers to enter service. In all 551 of them raided Italy from February 1941, when the type first went operational, to the summer of 1943 when England-staged raids on Italy were discontinued. On those sixteen occasions, ten *Stirlings* were lost (a loss rate of 1.8 per cent) which – given the right circumstances – could have reached Switzerland but did not. Such was the choice of two F/Sgts, both *Stirling* captains; both were severely wounded over Turin and both were posthumously awarded the Victoria Cross for heroism, Britain's highest decoration. The first was Australian Rawdon

Middleton who on 28/29 November 1942 lost his life after bringing his aircraft back to the English coast. The other was youthful Arthur Aaron: on 12/13 August 1943 and unwilling to risk an hazardous re-crossing of the Alps to reach either Switzerland or England, he and his crew flew their crippled *Stirling* to an Allied airfield in North Africa.

And why no *Halifax* either? The type also took part in the raids against Italy and could indeed have landed or crashed in Switzerland when damaged beyond hope of safe return to England. In the 'Italian period' 693 of them went to the peninsula in the course of sixteen nights, losing fifteen of their number at a 2.16 per cent loss rate.

PROMINENT *LANCASTERS*

To explain why no machine of the type ever visited Switzerland one can again consider the two periods hinging on the 1943 summer which heralded the termination of the England-staged Italian campaign. In the first period haphazard occurrences and luck must have played its role during encounters with adverse weather or with enemy defences, be they Italian or German. In the second period, the numbers involved became the dominant factor: in April 1944 for instance there were almost twice as many *Lancasters* than *Halifaxes* engaged in bombing operations and by the way, more than ten times that of *Stirlings*. A year later the ratio had become three to one against the *Halifax* whilst the *Stirling* had completely disappeared from the bombing offensive.[2]

Another factor was that *Halifax* bombers (as opposed to those on Special Duties) were seldom engaged in long range operations near Switzerland such as against F'hafen and were also less prominent in raids against targets on Southern Germany. There were just two instances when *Halifaxes* and *Lancasters* took part together in a raid that produced RAF arrivals in Switzerland: 25/26 February and 15/16 March 1944. On the later, against Stuttgart (see Chapters 9 and 10) the *Halifax* loss rate was at 4 per cent of the numbers involved, slightly greater than that of the *Lancs* (3.47 per cent). Thus chances were such that Switzerland could just as well have welcomed *Halis*. It just happened that circumstances, for instance geography, sudden crippling damage or crew judgement,[3] precluded the Swiss option for the doomed crews and aircraft. The same can be said of the February Augsburg mission when another *Lancaster* trundled into Swiss skies (see Chapter 8, 'Smith's Sihlsee Spin'). The loss rates had then been equal at 4.3 per cent for both types.[4]

* * * * * * * * * *

The Swiss saga of the Royal Air Force was not just a matter of machines – men were also, and above all, involved. Whatever the aircraft losses, they could be replaced. Human casualties could not. With the forlorn 'Swiss Squadron' came seventy-five aircrew whose fate has been described in 'The men who did (or did not) make it'. Half of them lost their lives and found decent, and always well attended, burial at the splendidly designed British plot in Vevey's St Martin cemetery.[5] To those who rest forever in Swiss ground, that moving epitaph engraved on one of their tombstones does apply:

> *'Let me feel the wind on my temples*
> *when I answer the last great call'*.

Appendix

TABLE 5

MANNED RAF AIRCRAFT DOWN IN SWITZERLAND

No.	DATE	TIME(a)	TYPE	CODE	SERIAL	SQUADR
1	24 August 1942	1403	Mosquito	LY°G	DK.310	1.PRU
2	14/15 April 1943	0043	Wellington	SE°X	HE.374	431
3	12/13 July 1943	0055	Lancaster	EM°Q	ED.412	207
4	same	0108	same	PO°T	ED.531	467
5	25/26 February 1944	0107	same	HW°V	ND.595	100
6	15/16 March 1944	2240	same	DX°F	JB.474	57
7	same	2330	same	LS°A	W.4355	15
8	6/7 April 1944	0012	Mosquito	UP°R	NS.875	605
9	27/28 April 1944	0123	Lancaster	SR°P	LL.750	101
10	same	0141	same	AS°X	ME.720	166
11	same	0215	same	TL°R	ND.759	35
12	30 September 1944	1437	Mosquito	P3°	PZ.440	515
13	same	1523	same	P3°T	NS.993	515

MANNED RAF AIRCRAFT DOWN IN SWITZERLAND

CAPTAIN	TARGET	FATE CREW(b) (+)(int)(PoW)			CRASHED (C)	REMARKS or LANDED (L)
F/Lt Wooll	Venice	2			(L) Berne-Belp	Became Swiss 'B-4'
Sgt Avery	Stuttgart	5			(C) Birmenstorf	--
Sgt Badge	Turin	7			(C) Bouveret	Dubious claim Swiss flab
F/O Mitchell	same	7			(C) Sion-Thyon	Dubious claim Swiss flab
P/O Smith	Augsburg	1	6		(C) Sihlsee	--
P/O Atcheson	Stuttgart	6	1		(C) Saignelégier	--
F/Lt Blott	same	7			(C) Golaten	--
S/Ldr Negus	Intruder	2			(C) Lake Constance off Uttwil	--
W/O Noble	Friedr'fen	6	2		(C) Alp Grappelen	--
P/O Ridley	same	5	2		(C) Hamikon	--
W/O Peter	same	1	5	1	(L) Ditched off Steckborn	
S/Ldr Morley	Intruder	2			(C) Volketswil	Damaged, Swiss flab
F/Lt Callard	same	2			(L) Dübendorf	Became Swiss 'B-5'

Notes: a): times are local Swiss times.

b): (+) means deceased.

c): the tables spreads across pages 218 and 219.

Notes

CHAPTER 1 (LOVE AND HATE)

1 An 'advance notice' of a border violation occurred before the war on 17 April 1936, when a *Ju.52* crashed near Bienne in western Switzerland, one of several which had been shuttling between Germany and Spain to re-supply the 'Legion Condor' operating there to help Franco.

2 At the time the village had yet to be renamed Ferney-Voltaire. The alleged border violation was indeed one in reverse, this being a case of a Swiss aircraft overflying French territory. Other such accidental occurrences were indeed to happen again – for instance, on 23 September 1943 when a student pilot, Cpl. Bongard, took his Bücker *Jungmann* trainer for half an hour over Germany near Friedrichshafen.

3 Flab was and is *Fliegerabwehr* in Switzerland, i.e. 'antiaircraft', the equivalent of the German flak (*Fliegerabwehr Kanonen*) which – for all its efficiency, so unfortunate for too many Allied recipients – has become a generic word.

4 See Chapter 17.

5 Further in the text, the clear RAF notation of, for instance '22/23 September', will be used to denote unequivocally 'the night of the 22nd September' in Anglo-American parlance and 'night of the 23rd' in German.

6 The Swiss government system called for a rotation of its members. Pilet had been President of the Confederation in 1932; he was head of the Département Politique (Foreign Affairs) 1940/1944.

7 A pilot since 1915, Arthur Travers Harris had been an advocate of the heavy bomber. He had commanded No.5 Group, been Deputy Chief of Air Staff and appointed Air Marshal Head of Bomber Command, RAF, in February 1942. In a distinguished career, Harris was always close to his men, air- and ground-crew alike. He died on 5 April 1984, aged ninety-two.

8 AVM Arthur Coningham had commanded No.4 Group of Bomber Command at the time its *Whitleys* bombed Switzerland (Chapter 17). It is, however, doubtful that he took part in operations.

9 Volume III of this trilogy comprises the American bombings of Swiss towns, including hitherto unknown facts about the attack on Schaffhausen on 1 April 1944.

10 Escapees wore civilian clothes in Switzerland and benefited from a larger measure of freedom; this explains why many evaders pretended they had escaped from Prisoner of War compounds. (See Table 4)

11 Figures from different sources are difficult to reconcile, the referenced figures being the best estimates. Altogether there seems to have been 374 deaths among all military internees belonging to all arms and nations.

12 The present volume is the second of a trilogy dealing with the air war over Switzerland. Volume I, *Aviateurs-Piétons vers la Suisse*, was published in 1997 in French and is about evaders i.e. the 'walking aviators'. The third book covers the USAAF involvement with Switzerland.

13 This figure includes two aircrew missing in Lake Constance on 6/7 April 1944, as well as Bradley and thirty-three of his fellow airmen who died in crashes.

14 101 Squadron is the same unit that would 'supply' a *Lancaster* on the Alp Grappelen on 27/28 April 1944 as recounted further on. In 1942 the Squadron's rate of mechanical troubles was notoriously high.

15 Ironically, the spot could have been just south of the village of Gruyères, a name reminiscent of Switzerland where the whole crew hoped to find refuge!

16 See note 12.

CHAPTER 2 (WHY THE RAF?)

1 See on this subject *Aviateurs-Piétons vers la Suisse 1940-1945*, Editions Secavia, Geneva, 1997. An extensive description of how the Swiss battled the Luftwaffe in the hectic summer of 1940 can be found in the French 'Aero-Journal' No.14, August 2000.

2 That episode of Swiss history is to be covered in our third volume, *The USAAF and Switzerland*.

3 Milan and Turin, for instance, involved round-flights of 1,350mi. (2,160km) and twice crossing the formidable Alpine barrier.

4 There were very few departures from this policy until, starting at the end of August 1944, Bomber Command staged both daylight and night raids. Also, the night-only decision marked the implementation of the area bombing policy meant to curtail and destroy war industries as well as the morale of the German population. After the war good-wishers generally too young to have experienced the hardships of the times, questioned the morality of area attacks against large towns. They conveniently ignored the fact that Germany and Japan had started the most dreadful conflicts of all times. There was also the simple reality that for four long years the Allied air arm was the only way to take the war to a ruthless Axis. Those who experienced the early Luftwaffe attacks against cities such as Rotterdam, London and Coventry – to say nothing of this author's village in neutral Belgium – have or had, little compassion for the recipients of the retribution dispensed by Bomber Command.

5 One of the 77 Squadron *Whitleys* (N.1508) was flown by young P/O Thomas 'Hamish' Mahaddie who, endowed with exceptional skills – and luck – was to be one of Bomber Command's stalwarts. From his humble beginnings as a metal rigger, he went on to command 7 (Pathfinders) Squadron, the unit where P/O Joseph Antoine served and died. Mahaddie achieved the rank of Group Captain in charge of a Pathfinders base, and survived the war. Another of the 77 Squadron pilots flying to Turin in that early raid was F/O Jimmy Marks, also slated to become CO of a PFF Squadron. His luck did not hold though: he was killed on 19/20 September 1942, one month after Antoine.

6　By coincidence, the crash site is close to Carrouges, a name reminiscent of the Swiss Carouges, near Geneva, where British bombs were to cause some stir later that same night.

7　Fusilier (Private) Fernand Chollet belonged to *Compagnie Territoriale V/122*, a reservist unit attached to Geneva's military commander, Col Paul Martin; Chollet was the first of the unit's two wartime casualties. Ironically, 'Beau-Séjour' was a medical institution partly taken over by the military.

8　There had been one precedent of RAF bombs striking a neutral country, still earlier in the war, at Esbjerg in Denmark.

9　It has not been possible to ascertain whether or not Bissett is one of four homonyms who later lost their life in Bomber Command.

10　The introduction of the Gee navigational aid in bomber tactics did not begin until November 1941.

11　A contemporary analysis shows, for example, that in November 1940, 65 per cent of the bombers despatched over Europe had failed to find their targets.

12　The figure does not take into account 152 violations by Axis aircraft.

13　Ironically, Genoa was closely connected to wartime Switzerland, being, with Savone and Marseilles, a port of entry through which transited the goods and raw material intended to keep the country going.

14　Altogether, those raids involved around 2,500 sorties from which 'only' two dozen aircraft failed to return, a casualty rate much lighter than that sustained against targets in Germany. More than half of those sorties (1,380) were flown in the course of ten days in mid-August 1943, during which Milan felt the weight of 2,200 tons of bombs, including 500 two-ton 'block-busters'. This hints at what could, and occasionally did, strike Switzerland.

15　The British request was, of course, associated with that of permission to use a Swiss landing place, which could have been Lake Geneva where large flying boats such as *Sunderlands* or *Catalinas* could alight.

CHAPTER 3 (BAFFLING BALLOONS)

1　October 1942 had been fruitful as far as the Swiss balloon crop was concerned: twenty-five had been collected within the two weeks between the 10th and 25th. An incendiary one had landed near Oberkirch, Canton Lucerne, in central Switzerland. It resulted in a comical happening when the farmer who trampled on the firing device accidentally set it alight. Trying to douse the fire, he threw the whole system into a ditch where the water promptly fanned the conflagration… The wretched phosphor-laden contraption finally had to be left to burn itself out on dry ground.

2　It was disclosed after the war that stray British barrage balloons had caused 1,614 of the 2,225 wartime grid faults that occurred in Switzerland!

3　The unit had commenced operations on 1 February 1940, in France, at Buhl, near Sarreguemines, when it launched forty-seven balloons carrying propaganda leaflets intended for Magdeburg.

4　Nigel Smallpage's wartime luck was to be tested once more. Having completed thirty PRU operations, he became staff pilot on *Mustangs* at 41.OTU. There, he survived a bad crash, albeit with a fractured skull and broken pelvis and legs. Grounded, he worked in RAF intelligence and indulged in photography and writing after the war.

5   The Black Forest had been chosen for the experiment because it concealed storage and ammunition dumps. The *Razzle* devices were carried in addition to a normal bomb load. They were made of a piece of phosphorus sandwiched with wet cotton wool (to prevent it from igniting), between two sheets of celluloid about 6in^2. After some time, the wool dried, letting the phosphorus simmer; the celluloid would then burn for around ten seconds and, hopefully, set afire any dry material nearby.

6   This accidental bombing will be clarified with hitherto unpublished facts in our third volume: *The USAAF in Switzerland*.

CHAPTER 4 (PIONEER *MOSQUITO*)

1   By coincidence, the last Allied aircraft to seek refuge in Switzerland – the 244th – arrived exactly three years and one day later: a Soviet *YAK-9* whose pilot had defected from Czechoslovakia... only to be handed back to the USSR! As for the first 'foreign landing' in Switzerland, it had occurred on 3 February 1916 when the Italian Cpl Giacomo Barbatti had landed his Voisin biplane near Agno.

2   In 1942, RAF PRU flew 2,777 sorties, 2,203 of which were successful.

3   Flying an armed machine, pilot F/Lt Victor Ricketts, DFC, and his American observer, F/Sgt Boris Lukhmanoff, DFM, had been downed and killed by flak near Calais, France.

4   Two new Italian cruisers were being built there. Ironically, sixty years later, on 10 May 1992, pictures of the same area would be taken, exempt of any danger for any airman, by just three passes of an *ERS-1* satellite mounting a Synthetic Aperture Radar microwave channel, generating black and white images.

5   The British had acquired twenty *B-17Cs*, called *Fortress I* by the RAF. They were operated by 90 Squadron with rather unhappy results. The one Gerald Wooll brought over was to be coded WP°J (serial AN.522) and seems to have been written off after a crash in Yorkshire as early as 22 June 1941.

6   For comparison, the four *Merlins* of a typical *Lancaster* heavy bomber yielded 0.94 mile per gallon.

7   The Swiss did not use the abbreviation 'Bf.' for their 'Mess'. The *D-3801* was a Swiss-built variant of the French Morane-Saulnier *Mo.406.C1*.

8   *Oberst* (meaning Colonel or Group Captain), Rihner, would, in 1944, become *Oberstdivisionär* and chief of the Swiss Air Forces, then called Flieger- und Fliegerabwehrtruppen.

9   On the early *Mosquito* variants, the control operated an ON/OFF shutter without any intermediate position.

10 Walker's machine, of the same model, was LR.478, and had been taken on charge less than a month earlier. Trying to reach Gibraltar after photographing the Modane railways, it crashed on the southern side of the Pyrenees in Navarre, near Pena-Sanguesa. Richard's aircraft was a *Merlin* 72-engined PR.IX, serial LR.435; it landed at Bultofta-Malmö airport.

11 Since the disaster of June 1940, France was split in two astride a line running from Geneva, west towards the Atlantic and down to the Spanish border. The south-eastern part, run by the Vichy regime, was in principle devoid of German forces. Until November 1942, when Germany overtook the region, the area was less likely to interfere with would-be evaders trying to cross into Spain.

12 Whitaker, a Yorkshire reporter in civilian life, had been on a PRU *Chamberlain* sortie to Trondheim, Norway. His *Spitfire*, AB.314, crashed at Funäsdelen in Sweden. In February 1944, then a F/Lt with a DFC 'gong', Whitaker was on the verge of becoming a distinguished clandestine pilot, flying *Lysanders* in and out of occupied France. He lost his life on the night of 3/4 May 1944, when he was downed again at Guillerval near Paris.

13 It is quite entertaining to notice in this initial report that the pilot is listed as 'Captain G.R. Awooll': the acronym 'awol' meaning 'absent without leave' in Army parlance.

14 An interesting occurrence of such a 'diplomatic' action was to happen in Portugal a year later. The Air Attaché in Lisbon then arranged for P/O Robert Sharpe, the wireless operator of an RAF 53 Squadron *Liberator*, to destroy the IFF and antisubmarine gear inside his crippled aircraft that had landed at Portella on 31 July 1944.

15 The aircraft carried four cameras: one with an f.52 lens with a 36in focal length, and three, including one oblique-mounted (looking to port, on the pilot's side) f.24/14in lenses. The magazines each held film for 500 exposures, none having been made.

16 *Merlin 21* engines allowed the *Mosquito* Mk.IV to reach 285mph IAS (460km/h) at sea level and 329mph TAS at 25,000ft (530km/h at 7,622m); later versions gave, at maximum continuous cruise, 378mph at 30,000ft (605km/h at 9146m).

17 Scharf had at that time a namesake whose face was well-known by many Allied airmen: Hanns-Joachim Scharff who, as master interrogator at Oberursel, did succeed in extracting information from captured airmen.

18 The homeward flight was in a British-registered (G-AGBE) and BOAC-impressed civilian KLM *DC.3* flown by Captain Parmentier. BOAC (British Overseas Airways Corporation) came out of the wartime merging of British Airways and Imperial Airways. Its landplanes had their UK base at Whitchurch, near Bristol, from where they operated to many destinations including neutral countries, with the exception of Switzerland, too dangerously tucked inside enemy territory.

19 'The night Fielden went missing,' remembers Paddy Hope, one of his navigator colleagues, 'we had a heavy drinking session in his memory at the Mess. However, in the papers next day was a report of a *Mosquito* crew landing in Switzerland, so we had another even heavier party to celebrate (his survival).' As seen earlier, Hope was not quite as lucky: he and his pilot, Freddy McKay, were downed and captured in Belgium on 8 December 1942.

CHAPTER 5 (BIRMENSTORF *WELLINGTON*)

1 Coverdale would be killed two months later, on 21/22 June, disappearing without trace with his crew, probably at sea, during the last raid on Krefeld.

2 Before the war ended it would have endured eighteen Main Force attacks, dropping 21,246 short tons of bombs that would destroy 46 per cent of its housings! And this is without taking into account six USAAF raids, with some 1,280 tons of explosives.

3 During his interrogation by the Swiss, Avery stated that his crew had been operational since December 1942. The all-sergeant crew was however classified 'Temporary rank', which would indicate a freshman status.

4 'Pathfinders' (PFF) were selected crews in special Squadrons intended to mark targets ahead of the Main Force bombers. *H2S* was an airborne radar giving air bombers and navigators a rough picture of the ground below.

5   The Vickers *Wellington* structure resembled a metal basket (the so-called geodetic structure) covered by fabric. The corkscrew manoeuvre was initiated by any crewmember who happened to notice the presence of an enemy nightfighter; the pilot then had to react immediately, launching his heavy machine in a series of turns, dives and climbs meant to put off the adversary's aims. It very often succeeded, leaving the exhausted pilot in a sweat, leaving also whatever was not firmly affixed to float crazily around as the floor fell away.

6   'Boost' is fuel pressure feeding the engines; 'rpm' is the number of revolutions per minute for engine shaft and propeller.

7   The figure includes operational (47,268) and non-operational fatalities (8,305).

8   At almost the same spot on 19 June 1988, a *Tobago TB-10* also stalled, killing its pilot.

9   Cleaning up the site generated a bill of 490 Sw.Frcs, presented post-war to Great Britain.

10 What the 'prisoners' did not know was that inter-service bickering was going on between the *Gendarmerie d'Armée* (Army Constabulary) and the Army Group Id (Intelligence and Security) about when and how to interrogate the flyers.

11 The men could, however, receive as many letters as arrived. They all sent a first letter home and to fiancées on 20 April. They all insisted that they were well and decently treated, even if one of them (and surprisingly it was Wilfred Boddy, the only married man in the crew) said '… we do miss the excitement we have become so used to…' The Swiss did censor the letters, going as far as copying them for the records.

12 The hotels were generally in secluded spots in order to ease surveillance: Adelboden, Chaumont, Davos, Evilard, Glion/Caux, Gurten-Kulm (Berne), Klosters, Macolin and Wengen/Wengeralp.

13 Coincidences abound in real life: the day of Avery's last sortie was also the one when Stalin's son, Yakov, a Red Army Lieutenant, died at Sachsenhausen concentration camp. Another famous name was also operative on 'Avery's night': Peter Churchill, no relative but a British underground agent who parachuted into France's Haute-Savoie.

14 Of course those numbers were only the tip of the iceberg: on 1 June 1944, for instance, there were 39,681 military internees in the country, the majority being Italians (19,818) and Poles (10,451). The Americans numbered 689 men, and those from the UK and British Commonwealth were 3,901. Among those were the airmen whose numbers appear in Chapter 1.

15 With them was a case of covert espionage: Allen Dulles, the head of the American OSS intelligence unit in Berne, had Andrews and Titus memorising sensitive information to be delivered in Washington upon repatriation.

16 Another coincidence involving two other Forsters: a British flyer, William, was to arrive as part of the crew of a XV Squadron *Lancaster* on 15/16 March 1944 while the crash at Golaten was to be reported by a local peasant, Robert Forster!

17 The German flyers were Fw. Juchelka, Obgefr. Klünsch, Oblt.Lemke and Obfw.Wörner, lost over the Alps during a ferry flight from Munich to Vicenza.

CHAPTER 6 (BOUVERET)

1   Italian targets were industrial, such as Turin (attacked on twenty-one occasions) and Milan (twelve), or naval bases like Genoa (eleven) and La Spezia (five). Casualties are difficult to assess, but were not negligible; for instance in 1943 alone, Milan reported 1,174 killed. In Turin 300,000 people fled the town after the second attack, and many others were leaving town every night in fear of the RAF bombing.

2   As shall be seen, the total should have been 436 if two waves had not been cancelled with 182 *Halifaxes* and *Lancs II*. Two diversions involved twenty-two mine-laying *Wellingtons* on the Atlantic ports, and nineteen scattering leaflets over the Continent.

3   On 17 April 1942, Nettleton, a South African, had led a small force of twelve *Lancasters* on a daylight low-level raid against the M.A.N. submarine engines factory; only five had returned. The Victoria Cross (VC) is the highest British military award; thirty-two were presented to the RAF in the Second World War, twenty-three of them to Bomber Command personnel.

4   Other markers – or were they the same ones? – fell near Allèves, halfway between Lakes Annecy and Bourget near Chambéry, promptly setting afire an acre (about 4,000m^2) of woods. Both lakes were successively used as turning points to Italy, and accordingly marked by the PFF.

5   This raid, and the twenty-one aerial 'premières' taking place on 17 August 1943, were reconstructed in the book *Forteresses sur l'Europe*, by this writer (Rossel, Brussels, 1980, in French).

6   *Gee*, the RAF transmitter-receiver TR.1335, was a radio device – not radar, contrary to *H2S* allowing a rather precise navigation up to some (depending on altitude) 150 miles (250km) outside the south-eastern shores of England. Its important side-advantage was to give the crews an 'easy' way of finding their bases upon returning.

7   The Swiss air arm did not fly nightfighters until after the war, when *Mustangs* seem to have been used for training, flying from the alpine aerodrome at Munster.

8   By a quirk of fate, the Badge crew came out of HCU the same day as the other crew whose members were to die the same night in Switzerland.

9   The German *Wilde Sau* (*Wild Boar*) saw single-engined fighters – in this case belonging to *JG.300* – take advantage of the illumination provided by a blazing city, searchlights and so on, to perform visual attacks on bombers.

10 RAF Langar is remembered by many as a pleasant and comparatively worry-free station, situated as it was in farming country studded with inviting water holes, such as the Unicorn in the village or Madge's Plough in Stathern. Badge's EM°Q was the fifth letter Q lost by 207 Squadron; there would be two more before the war ended.

11 The 4,000lb *Cookie* blast bomb, combined with a shower of incendiaries, proved effective against industrial targets.

12 It was not until 1943 that the specific wings (brevets) of Navigator (N) or Air Bomber (AB) were awarded.

13 Bain had been Squadron CO for only one day when he died; Parselle escaped in a freak occurrence, being blown out of his exploding aircraft and still strapped to his seat, to become a Prisoner of War.

14 This was the night of the first shuttle raid, mentioned in Chapter 1.

15 Underlining again the frailty of such reports is the fact that among the force of seventy-one aircraft on that raid, there were only twenty-five *Halifaxes*. Then, also, the raid had been dispersed by thunderstorms during penetration.

16 See note 12, Chapter 1.

17 In 1993, fifty years after the crash and soon after *Aeroplane Monthly* published a story by this writer that stirred interest on the accident, a memorial to Badge's crew was unveiled below the crash site. In attendance were the crew members' relatives who could be traced: Jim Wright the

Air Bomber's son, the niece and nephew of Horace Badge, F/Lt. Jepp's widow, and cousins and a niece of rear gunner James Spence.

18 The crash was responsible for the death under stress of a witness, Mr Leupin, a butcher in Vevey, who suffered a stroke and collapsed.

CHAPTER 7 (HIGH ALTITUDE)

1   467 RAAF Squadron was one of the eight Australian bomber Squadrons serving with the RAF in England; it lost 730 aircrew in 104 *Lancasters* in 3,833 sorties. Besides Mitchell's, the Squadron was to loose two more *Lancasters* before the end of the night. There would also be JA.676 captained by F/Lt R.W. Gibbs, most probably lost at sea returning home, and F/Sgt S. Chapman's LM.311, which made it back to base only to break up when turning in to land, the tail appearing to separate from the fuselage. By coincidence, five nights after the loss of Mitchell, one of his namesakes was killed, again raiding northern Italy: flight engineer Sgt Robert Mitchell of Dundee. He belonged to 207 Squadron (the unit which lost Badge's *Lancaster* at Le Bouveret) and crashed at Cislago (Milan).

2   This 'Operation Bellicose' had been mounted to wreck the Zeppelin factories in F'hafen on the northern shore of Lake Constance. Because of the short summer nights offering little opportunity to fly under cover of darkness, the raiders had been instructed to fly on south, to Maison Blanche in North Africa – across Switzerland. This was the first 'shuttle' raid of the war. F'hafen was again to involve Bomber Command and Switzerland ten months later (see Chapters 12, 13 and 14).

3   The general rule was to give new bomber pilots a preliminary operational trip with a seasoned crew in order for them to gain experience while observing their behaviour in dealing with the multiple dangers involving enemy opposition, weather and so on. Dixon was to be shot down and captured during the famed raid on Peenemünde on 17/18 August 1943. He was luckier than his CO, S/Ldr Raphael, lost that night in another aircraft. Raphael had, just two days earlier, replaced his predecessor at the helm of 467 Squadron, W/Cdr Cosme Gomm, killed in action in a raid to Milan.

4   Morgan's relatives were to emigrate to the Southern Hemisphere after the war, in Nelson, New Zealand.

5   RAF Bomber Command losses amounted to 12,330 aircraft of all types. Figures of personnel casualties vary slightly according to reliable sources, but can be reconciled as follows: Aircrew deaths numbered 55,573 including KIA and deceased as PoW, to which must be added 9,838 PoW, 8,203 wounded and 2,951 evaders missing but safe. The numbers above exclude ground staff losses.

6   Returning crews stated that around midnight during penetration, combats with nightfighters took place near Beauvais and that a German *Ju.88* was downed by a *Lancaster* near Dijon. Flak opposition was encountered near Poix, Amiens and Le Creusot.

7   The period coincided with the arrival on the airdrome of the first Swiss Air Force unit, *Detachment 32*.

8   Also spelled Riod.

9   The spot in now easily accessible by road; there is even a ski-lift feeding the controversial 'Piste de l'Ours' that can be seen from the valley, splitting the forest overlooking Sion. Locals have, since the war, developed the habit of forecasting freezing weather whenever snowpatches on the 'Mayen de l'Ours' take the shape of an aircraft.

10 A similar incident did kill two people on 11 April 1980, the crew of a twin-engined German Piper *Navajo*'which crashed in town during its approach to Sion airfield. On two other occasions the same manoeuvre was to end on roofs: on 15 August 1989 for a Robin *DR-400* and on 12 January 1992 for a Piper *Saratoga*.

11 Swiss investigators found two small holes in a fuel tank which they attributed to their flab.

12 A quite similar drama was to be enacted precisely eleven months later to the day, on 12/13 June 1944, when a 408 Squadron *Lancaster* downed near Cambrai, burned its crew with the exception of, again, the tail gunner, Belgian F/O André Dulait.

13 According to François Brunelli, who at the time worked at the girls' chalet, the beads of the broken-up rosary were distributed one to each Girl Guide.

CHAPTER 8 (SIHLSEE)

1 The machine, coded U5+DL, serial 2663, was actually a reconnaissance aircraft from the same unit as a previous example that had landed at Basle-Birsfelden airdrome on 21 April 1940. The wreckage was returned to Germany on 22 November.

2 *H2S* was an inboard radar enabling the operator to see a crude image of the ground through cloud.

3 PFF supporters were carrying coloured flares, dropped in order to 'replenish' the waning target indicators laid earlier by selected precision-flying PFF aircraft. This was besides their bomb load, in the case of ND.595, one 4,000lb (1,816kg), one 500lb (227kg) and five 1,000lb (454kg), all high explosives.

4 In their compendium *Bomber Command War Diaries* (Viking Press, 1985), Middlebrook & Everitt state that at least four of the missing aircraft were lost to collisions.

5 JB.289 (coded HV°T) seems to have been lost on 30 June 1944, at the very ripe age of 452hrs.

6 17,796 RAF pilots were trained in Canada during the Second World War, under the Empire Air Training Scheme, out of 42,110 Britons of all trades. (See also note 7, Chapter 14)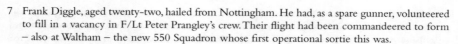

7 Frank Diggle, aged twenty-two, hailed from Nottingham. He had, as a spare gunner, volunteered to fill in a vacancy in F/Lt Peter Prangley's crew. Their flight had been commandeered to form – also at Waltham – the new 550 Squadron whose first operational sortie this was.

8 That Berlin raid cost Bomber Command twenty-five aircraft lost to enemy action and thirty more to bad weather, the total amounting to 9.3 per cent of the force involved! For comparison, 'only' 3.6 per cent of the force raiding Augsburg were lost.

9 There were several other Allied operations over the Continent on this night of 25/26 February 1944. *Mosquito* nuisances and a 'Gardening' (mine-laying) party over and near Holland had drawn German nigthfighters to those parts.

10 The Schräge system of upwards-firing weapons had first been used by the Luftwaffe during the raid against Peenemünde on 17/18 August 1943. The RAF only recognised it in August 1944, after hundreds of aircrews had fallen victim of a technique their own RAF had developed in First World War... and forgotten!

11 In November 1946, Hitz was to achieve fame with a fellow pilot, Viktor Hug, by rescuing, by air, eleven American flyers stranded with their crashed *C-47* on a Swiss glacier, 3,000m (9,840ft) above Meiringen.

12 A typical tour of thirty operations – when achieved! – could mean an average total of 150 dangerous, nerve-straining combat hours.

13 Not infrequently in the Second World War, crippled airmen had to be helped out of their bombers. One such instance occurred on 5/6 August 1944 over Brittany, when F/Sgt Reginald Pool's pilot managed to throw him out of his doomed *Lancaster*. He did not survive, drowning in the Baie de Douarnenez. More fortunate was the American T/Sgt Tyre Weaver, who had an arm severed on 26 July 1943. He was helped out with his parachute near Bremen, and had the good fortune to be captured almost immediately and treated in a German hospital.

14 Sadly, 'Bish' Smith died in 1994 but not before this writer was privileged to meet Hedy, and persuade her into returning the gloves to him, complete with the 'Bishop' cartoon drawn inside for identification of their onetime owner.

15 In Dübendorf, the British crew shared their experience with that of twenty USAAF personnel stranded there following daylight raids on Southern Germany on the 26th. The Swiss Col. Högger was to enjoy rewarding wartime experiences flying interned four-engined American bombers, as will be recounted in the next volume of this series.

16 In Pfäffikon, the parachute disappeared and was not recovered for ten days or so.

17 Benson's belongings were listed on this occasion, describing what a typical aircrew member carried on a winter operation. As per regulation, Benson had left at base whatever could help the enemy in acquiring a better understanding of Britain at war. His pockets revealed only some loose change, six photos (to be used on false identity papers), a printed list of key German sentences, a sketch of Wilhelmshafen(?), a slip of paper with scribbled numbers, some gums and sweets, two keys, a comb and two pencils. Under his life-vest and parachute harness, Benson was warmly clad in his officer's tunic and trousers, a pullover, two shirts and some underwear, a black tie and dark socks. The boots were missing. Not easily noticed, however, were the cellophane emergency ration and the escape packet under the tunic. The brown pouch, numbered 358, contained three silk maps, currency valid in three occupied countries: Holland (25 Gulden), Belgium (350 francs) and France (1,000 francs). By the time this tally had been completed in Switzerland, an orderly had gathered the navigator's possessions at base and forwarded them to the Colnbrook Central Repository, whence they eventually would reach the grieved family.

18 That night, recorded temperature on Sihlsee was minus 26°C (about minus 11°F).

19 BOAC (British Overseas Airways Corporation) came out of the wartime merging of British Airways and Imperial Airways. Its land planes had their UK bases at Whitchurch near Bristol, whence they operated to many destinations, including neutral countries except Switzerland, too dangerously tucked inside enemy territory.

CHAPTER 9 (SAM ATCHESON)

1 Exceptions were when a new pilot was flying with an experienced crew for his first sortie, as for Atcheson in this case. A high ranking officer or, exceptionally, a passenger such as a press reporter, could also be eighth man aboard.

2 'Y training' referred to the use of the *H2S* navigation and target-finding radar. The training had nothing to do with the 'Y' radio interception station at Kingsdown monitoring German radio transmissions, nor of course with the Luftwaffe's Y-beams used for target-finding over Britain.

3 As *H2S*, *Oboe* was one of three aids devised to help navigation and/or bombing. It was an improvement of the German system *Knickebein* (alias 'Y') and relied on two radio beams broadcast from England to guide the aircraft towards a precise spot as far as the Ruhr. *Gee* had been developed earlier and was by now well-known by the enemy, which did its best to jam it.

Like *Oboe* and because of the earth's curvature, *Gee* was not of much use beyond 3° of eastern longitude i.e. outwards from mid-Belgium. Nevertheless, the device remained useful in finding base when returning in bad weather. See also note 6, Chapter 6.

4 The Westland *Lysander* was a single-engined aircraft used by the RAF to deposit or pick-up clandestine agents in enemy-occupied territories.

5 Capt Loderer had, in the morning after Atcheson's crash, flown over the spot as observer with pilot Oberst Schätti, and taken the pictures of a huge black fan-shaped smudge defacing the snowy ground.

6 Not taking into account eight more 'small' nuisance raids by night-flying *Mosquitoes* nor the twelve daylight attacks by the USAAF.

7 More precise figures relating to this Stuttgart raid are typical of the frightful losses of Bomber Command in the European campaign: 267 men missing over the Continent, including 202 killed, 40 PoW, 17 evaders and 8 Swiss internees, plus 24 killed in England upon returning. Among the aircraft lost to nightfighters comparatively near to Atcheson were: 51 Sq. *Halifax* of F/Lt Alwynn Fell, downed in Héricourt village near Belfort: seven killed; 429 Sq. *Lancaster* of F/Lt Harry Heimbecker, crashed at St.Barthélémy, near Lure: three killed, one PoW, three evading to Switzerland; 514 Sq. *Lancaster* of F/O Kaiho Penkuri, down near Vesoul at Villars-le-Pautel: eight killed; 466 Sq. *Halifax* of P/O Wills (six PoW, one evader) probably downed near St Hippolyte, at the foot of Haut Koenigsbourg castle: also of interest since one of the crew (F/O Frederick Cunliffe) walked for days to Switzerland where he became an interned evader. For a full story of the 350-odd 'Swiss' evaders.

8 The string of bombs fell not too far from a secret location – a farm – where Swiss intelligence gathered information about German occupation forces, brought from France by clandestine agents.

9 Almost four years earlier, on 16 May 1940, a German Heinkel *He-111* had crossed into Switzerland over Montfaucon, only to be shot down by Swiss fighters at Kemleten near Winterthur. Montfaucon was also to become the last landing place for a Swiss *Me.109* which crashed there on 22 May 1947.

10 Edi Gyger's crash axe, also entrusted to the author, has since been donated to the Dübendorf Air Museum near Zürich.

11 Also near Saignelegier, close to the crash site, another tremendous explosion occurred on 1 October 1987, when an army depot of explosives blew up following an arson attack.

12 By co-incidence, his name was quite similar to that of the American Air Attaché, Br. Gl Banwell Legge.

13 Although Reece gave the man the initials R.D., the Assistant Air Attaché in Switzerland had been S/Ldr William Jones.

CHAPTER 10 (GOLATEN)

1 Another famous veteran *Lancaster* also served in the Squadron: LL.806, which went on to finish the war with 134 operations. The Squadron, incidentally, was one of the few in the RAF to be numbered with Roman figures: XV. For the sake of continuity in this book, we have chosen to use standard numerals, i.e. 15 Squadron.

2 In 1943, for instance, the flying-life expectancy of operational RAF bombers was a mere forty hours.

3 By 1944, improvements were available to help returning aircrews cope with the difficulties of landing in the often appalling weather prevailing over England. They included homing beacons, ground-fired flares, and – provided enemy intruders were not prowling about – the large lighted circle around aerodromes and the so-called 'Sandra' lights (three searchlights in a cone over the airfield). Also under development then was FIDO, the fog-dispersal technology to be set up on a few aerodromes.

4 At debriefing, some of the returning crews indicated they had not seen those route markers. Anyway, the district proved rich hunting ground for the Luftwaffe that night, as seen in the previous Chapter. Their opponents from the *Nachtjagdgeschwader 6* were also seriously mauled, losing half a dozen *Bf.110* nightfighters, including the one force-landed at Dübendorf, Switzerland by Obfdwbl Helmut Treynogga.

5 The Italian capitulation in September 1943 had seen the hurried transfer of large numbers of Allied Prisoners of War from Italy to Germany. Many had escaped before reaching the German border to seek refuge in Switzerland.

6 This measure proved hardly effective since the number of refugees steadily increased from 16,000 in 1942, to 110,000 in May 1945!

CHAPTER 11 (WATERY CRASH)

1 Apart from the Intruders, there were only forty-nine *Mosquitoes* out that night, spot-bombing Hamburg, the Ruhr and the Rhineland; one was lost.

2 One reliable source credits Hoare with scoring his Squadron's 100th victory on 10/11 January 1944 near Chièvres in Belgium, but another places the event on 15 April. By then, Hoare had been credited with nine aerial victories plus eleven enemy aircraft either damaged or probably downed, and was promoted to Group Captain.

3 Baltringen was a satellite aerodrome for Laupheim, south of Ulm, an area known by Allied intelligence as a seat of much aeronautical development.

4 Both men rest in the Cherbourg cemetery, where the Germans buried them after they were downed in the Cotentin peninsula. The crew of HJ.790 (F/O Kenneth Dacre and Sgt Sidney Didsbury) were killed near Ardorf, one of the airfields defending the approaches to Wilhelmshaven, Bremen and Hamburg in northern Germany. By a strange coincidence, two bomber airmen with the same names also died a few days apart in the summer of 1941!

5 The originality of the name was also observed in the case of Australian P/O Bruce Negus who – like tail gunner Bolger of Chapter 7 – hailed from Auchenflower in Queensland. He, too. was a pilot, and he, too, had been killed in operations (with 207 Squadron, against Hannover on 18/19 October 1943); he, too, has no grave.

6 The Nuremberg disaster cost the Command almost 12 per cent of the force dispatched. They lost sixty-four *Lancasters* and thirty-one *Halifaxes* (with 772 men, including 539 fatalities) out of 795 aircraft participating. Including take-off and landing accidents, the grim total was 108 aircraft. This was the RAF's worst night of the war. *Flower* was the code-name for low-level intruder sorties to enemy airfields.

7 The *Hecht* had just beaten German boats intent at investigating the scene.

8 The *Mosquito VI* stalling speed with flaps up is around 105 knots (200kmh) which, by 1944 standards, fits very well with Swiss observations of 'an aircraft flying at high speed'.

9 Unique underground organisation set up on the Continent for weather-spying, 'Beagle' was the creation of a Belgian, Albert Toussaint. He had reached England in May 1940 and his idea was taken up by the RAF. Toussaint was dropped back by parachute on 22/23 August 1942. The first of his clandestine measurement and broadcast stations was in Rienne, south of Dinant.

10 'Bodan' is the archaic French appellation for 'Bodensee' – 'Lake Constance'.

CHAPTER 12 (ALPINE ADVERSITY)

1 By the end of 1943, the target areas were defined as follows: the 'Baltic' (including Stettin for instance), the 'Berlin Road', the 'Central Complex' (with Schweinfurt, f.i.), the 'East' (Pilsen, etc), the 'South-East', the 'Ruhr' with its heavy industries, the 'Saar' with its steel mills and the 'Upper Rhine' (including Stuttgart f.i.).

2 Also operating this night were sixty-five RAF and USAAF clandestine supply missions to the underground, including that of a 'black *Liberator*' shot down at St Cyr de Valorges, west of Lyons, France.

3 Bernard Noble was destined to have a remarkable RAF flying career; his book, *Noble Endeavours*, is a compendium about the RAF and flying combat aircraft.

4 Much more publicised, thanks to the 8th USAAF public relations units, was the shuttle on 17 August 1943 when the 3rd Division of *B-17*s flew on to Algeria after bombing the large Messerschmitt factories in Regensburg. (Readers mastering French can read *Forteresses sur l'Europe* – Rossel, Brussels, 1980 – by the same author, for a complete reconstruction of the raid.) The most celebrated shuttle raids of the war were, however, the '*Frantic*' missions which took place along the triangle UK–Russia–Italy–UK in the summer of 1944.

5 The Master of Ceremonies was the raid leader; he kept circling the target for the duration of the attack, commenting by radio-telephone on the PFF marking and exhorting main force bombers to aim at such or such coloured marker.

6 The tonnage was that carried by the crews who, at debriefing, actually reported bombing. It does not include bombs in aircraft lost or jettisoning their loads.

7 However, a Frenchman, impressed at the time to work at F'hafen, states the destruction of flying boats was to be credited to a single intruder a fortnight earlier. If that is the case, one would need only a slight stretch of imagination to connect the event with the night of 6/7 April 1944 when S/L Negus was lost in Lake Constance, right opposite F'hafen. (See previous Chapter)

8 During the moon period, the rising half-moon proved a blessing for intruding patrols, but a curse for bombers, even though Bomber Command endeavoured to reduce operations during that period.

9 One of the two evaders that night was Sgt Norman Thom, who reached Switzerland after violent adventures narrated in *Aviateurs-Piétons vers la Suisse* (Editions Secavia, Geneva, 1997). Among the crews killed that night was W/Cdr William (Guy) Lockhart's, the CO of 7 (PFF) Squadron. He died with his crew of high-ranking officers at Reichenbach, near Lahr, Germany. Another CO who lost his life that night was Gp/C Eric Eaton of 156 Squadron.

10 Sgt Hausnik was an American volunteer in the RAF; he had received a commission in the USAAF on 24 March, and was awaiting a transfer to a US Bomb Group. Joseph Kemp was to be killed over Belgium eleven nights later. Both men flew with 35 (PFF) Squadron.

11 At this time of the war, though, voice interference with German controllers was carried on by ground-based male and female 'Corona' operators, at Cheadle in England.

12 The West Kingsdown facilities were on the eastern Kent coast, between Dover and Manston, south of Deal. Another listening station was the main RAF Interception Station at Cheadle, near Birmingham.

13 From October 1940 to November 1943, aircraft such as *P-40*s, *Hurricanes* and light bombers were shipped by cargo or carriers to Takoradi, in the Gold Coast (now Ghana). They were then flown to reinforce British Middle East and North African forces via, for instance, Kano, Fort Lamy and Khartoum. The shortage of pilots on these 'runs' was endemic, and accentuated by malaria, which seems to have struck some 20 per cent of the staff. Many problems plagued the organisation, such as a rivalry between British and Americans, who, with an eye on post-war airlines, were eager to establish a foothold in Africa. A more practical and immediate difficulty arose from the lack of aircraft available to return pilots from Egypt to Tako. On this account, a couple of coincidences are worth noting. At the time, Donald Brinkhurst was a crewmember in antiquated Bristol Bombay transports impressed on such return trips. Don met Bertram Noble on at least one such flight. Later, when shot down as a gunner in their own 101 Squadron, Brinkhurst became an evader in Germany and arrived in Switzerland two months after Noble had found his final resting place there. The second concerns Sgt D. Noble, navigator in, again, 101 Squadron, who died in a raid to Duisburg on 14/15 October 1944, when his *Lancaster* was lost at sea.

14 A 'Mention in Despatches' is denoted by an oak leaf worn on another decoration. The MiD was often awarded instead of a decoration, such as the DFC.

15 The average bomber pilot arrived on operations with some 250 hours of flight experience.

16 The Heavy Conversion (to four-engined bombers) Unit was like the training in various aerial trades, i.e. the Operational Training Units (OTU) and the Lancaster Finishing Schools (LFS), one of the many stages in training. The cost for qualifying a full crew has been estimated at more than £5,000 in British wartime pounds.

17 This was not uncommon practice amongst foreigners in the RAF and Allied forces who did not want their families pestered by the German occupiers should they become Prisoners of War or killed. For instance, Cdt. René Mouchotte, a Frenchman and Commanding Officer of 341 Squadron, flew under the false Canadian identity of René Martin, which made it extremely difficult to identify his body after he was killed over the Channel on 27 August 1943. One first-hand source indicates that 'Special Radio Operators' were not always attached to a particular crew.

18 It was only after VE Day, in May 1945, that the RAF adopted knots for speed instead of miles per hour, and nautical miles instead of statute miles. This was in view of the expected transfer of the RAF's 'Tiger Force' to the Pacific, where the USAAF was using those nautical units.

19 See note 6, Chapter 12. On that night to Nuremberg, 30/31 March 1944, 101 Squadron had lost no less than seven *Lancasters*!

20 The most representative Squadrons among the Bomber Support Units engaged in radio countermeasures were 101 and 214; the later flew *Fortresses B.II* and *III* (the RAF versions of the USAAF *B-17s*).

21 At this time, 101 Squadron was about to begin trials of the Rose tail turret (in May). Had this occurred a month earlier, its twin 0.5in. Brownings and their heavier firepower could perhaps have saved Noble's *Lancaster*.

22 Sgt Walter was to be killed just four nights later on a raid to the German tank depot at Mailly-le-Camp, near Troyes, France. This was on 3/4 May 1944 when he flew in P/O Thomas Drew's crew, one of the four from 101 Squadron downed among the forty-two losses − 11.6 per cent of the force involved!

23 Friedrich had by then been promoted to Major. He was killed with all the crew of his *Ju-88* on 16/17 March 1945 when, in a raid on Nuremberg, he collided with *Lancaster* UL°L2 (PB.785) of 576 Squadron.

24 By one of the numerous coincidences that crop up in war, he had a namesake downed on this very night: Flying Officer D.M. Bridges, pilot of a 166 Squadron aircraft – the unit of the second *Lanc* to arrive on the same night in Switzerland (see Chapter 13).

25 A poignant illustration of the grief suffered by relatives of men lost in the Services, it took a long time for Maurice's mother in Maypole Lane, Birmingham, to accept that her son would not return. Her's and others' dignified letters seeking information about the last minutes of their loved ones from survivors, are monuments of despair setting the tragedies in proper perspectives.

26 Prowse had a brother in a PFF Squadron who could have been Canadian W/O DC Prowse, navigator in an 83 Squadron *Lancaster*. Somewhat less lucky the night before, he was downed and lost a leg at Dahn, near Pirmassens, during the Schweinfurt raid. He was made a PoW but quite surprisingly remained at Dahn until the area was overrun by Allied forces. He later became a QC (lawyer) in Canada.

CHAPTER 13 (SWISS FLAB)

1 On 30 April, W/Cdr Powley relinquished command of the Squadron to take charge of No.1 Lancaster Finishing School. He returned to operations in October, commanding 153 Squadron. He was killed, probably over the Kattegat, on 4/5 April 1945, during a mine-laying raid.

2 In his post-war report, General Guisan, the head of the Swiss military defences, credits his flab with the downing of one German and nine Allied bombers, including one in April 1944.

3 At Kirmington, the X had been painted with great difficulty, owing to the curvature of the fuselage, by one of the aircraft's groundcrew, airframe flight mechanic J.C. Lamming.

4 Records are unclear about this first sortie, which could have been against Augsburg the night after.

5 News of Ridley's death had been ciphered to London by the Air Attaché in Berne as early as 28 April, a few hours after the accident!

6 See note 5, Chapter 12.

7 A mid-upper turret reputedly salvaged from the Hamikon's *Lancaster* ended up in Reinach, later finding its way later into itinerant displays such as those organised by the Utzenstorf-based enthusiast Rolf Zaugg.

8 Nine months later, on 25 February 1945, Hamikon again escaped a similar tragedy when an American *B-17* crashed in trees 2mi.(3km) further up the road, at Müswangen. The saga of this aircraft whose pilot was a Swiss-American, will be recounted in our third volume, *The USAAF in Switzerland*. In a similar vein, one can observe that Hamikon is only 14km (9mi.) away from Dürrenäsch, where a Swissair *Caravelle* crashed after the war.

9 Again, several coincidences. In March 1945 this very 166 Squadron had a F/Sgt Philips flying a *Lancaster* coded AS°X, just like the Hamikon machine. Also, a Clifford Phillips was killed in a 426 Squadron *Halifax* downed in Belgium on 12/13 May 1944; he was (as 'our' Roy) a F/O, a bomb aimer and a Canadian! As for F/Sgt J.A. Phillips, RCAF, a *Lancaster* pilot in 419 Squadron, he was downed, survived and evaded capture on 24/25 July 1944.

10 Achard's interrogation report states that Phillips had jumped near Lausanne when the actual path of his aircraft had ended some 135km (84mi.) to the north-east. He certainly meant Lucerne which is the large town south of Hamikon; that is unless he was deliberately trying to hide from his interrogator that he had been at large for two days; or unless Achard did not want his hierarchy to know of such a breach in the country's security.

11 Ironically, this is only a stone's throw away from the Beromunster broadcasting station which was used by earlier RAF navigators. (See Chapter 4)

12 The small, handy escape boxes contained a host of useful escape items, including money of the countries overflown; they were distributed one to a man after briefing, and handed back upon return in England.

13 The life of evaders in Switzerland is described in *Aviateurs-Piétons vers la Suisse*. (See note 12, Chapter 1 and note 1, Chapter 2)

14 Persons arriving in England from overseas were, until cleared – for instance at Patriotic School in London – considered as possibly dangerous for British and Allied security. MI.9 (Military Intelligence, Department 9), a specialised unit which at this stage of the war operated closely with its American counterpart, MIS-X.

15 ACRU (Aircrew Recovery Unit) started its Annecy operations on 6 September 1944, soon after the area had been liberated. (See *Aviateurs-Piétons vers la Suisse*)

CHAPTER 14 (BORDER DITCHING)

1 It was common that an otherwise all-Australian crew comprised a British flight engineer, reflecting the dearth of men trained in that trade 'down under' .

2 The raid had been twice postponed on the preceding nights due to airfields being snowed in, the crews contributing to their clearing./ Douglas Jackson was killed a few nights later when, again serving as tutor to a new pilot, he was raiding Schweinfurt as did Peter in captaining his first long range mission.

3 AVM Don Bennett, the PFF Commanding Officer, was exceptional not only in being altogether a renowned pilot, navigator and wireless operator, but also – in relevance to this book's subject – because he had, before the war, married a Swiss girl, Ly. His PFF Group had started as a five-Squadron force in 1942 when it began marking targets ahead of the Main Force. In typical British understatement, Peter gives credit to his being accepted for PFF duties to the skill of his crew and particularly to the accuracy of his bomb aimer, Noel Davis. The PFF crews were entitled to wear a special badge and were promoted one rank but had to sign on for an extended 'tour' of initially fifty operations, later reduced to forty-five. Main Force bomber aircrew were compelled to fly a minimum of thirty war operations in their first tour, twenty if they wished to proceed with a second and fifteen for a third. None of those goals was often achieved in view of the high casualty rate.

4 Peter and the rear gunner, Vin Graham, were in their ninth operation; Brereton, the replacement engineer, was in his tenth and all the others in their eighth sortie. The repudiated gunner was to be killed in a freak ground accident early on 27 April when his *Lancaster* was landed upon by a disabled *Mosquito*.

5 The *Lancaster* had six self-sealing fuel tanks containing 2154 Imp.gallons (9792 litres) meaning that the 322 *Lancs* attacking F'hafen had left their bases carrying more than 3.15 million litres (693,600 Imp.gal.) of high-octane fuel, all of which had had to be imported in wartime England!

6   Said a crewmember afterwards: 'We were quite relieved when Davis the perfectionist did not indulge again into a second run into the target!'.

7   Noel Davis was one of the 799 Aussie air bombers trained in Canada during the Second World War. The country trained 9,602 Australian aircrew amongst a total of 131,553 aviators of all trades. (See also note 6, Chapter 8)

8   Over the years suppositions were voiced that this fighter might have been the *Bf.110G-4* which Oblt Wilhelm Johnen landed in error at Dübendorf that same night of 27/28 April 1944. Interesting as this might be, no firm proof supporting this hypothesis has been unearthed. The speculation seems to be based only on Johnen's indication aired in his book *Duel under the Stars* (New English Library, London, 1957), a source which – at least in its English-language version and for all its narrative appeal – does not qualify as a model of accuracy.

9   Being herded to the crash station Vin Graham thought the order crazy as he could not imagine ditching this far from the Channel!

10 Much later the crew pretended they had alighted in German waters and rowed to Switzerland, thus 'escaping' from becoming prisoners. The Swiss were understandably reluctant to accept such a thesis and classified the men as 'Winged internees'.

11 In the RAF 'Pilot Officer' does not indicate the trade of pilot but a rank equivalent to 2nd Lieutenant in the USAAF or Leutnant in the Luftwaffe.

12 This was in accordance with the promotion scheme attached to incoming PFF crews (see endnote 3).

13 Isolated as they were in an Europe overrun by Hitler, the Swiss were greedy for information on Luftwaffe combat tactics and on modern aids.

14 Anzac Day in Australia is the yearly celebration honouring the country's war veterans.

15 Not all of the thousands of Australians who flew with the RAAF or RAF were as lucky: 7024 aircrew failed to return to Australia and in Europe alone, 4,437 of them were killed in operations.

16 The Straflager Wauwillermoos sat on former marshy grounds, west of Sursee and north-west of Lucerne; some 400 internees had the dubious distinction of passing through its rudimentary facilities. Contrary to 'Escapees', 'Winged internees' (airmen who had flown into Switzerland) were punished for attempting to return by themselves to Allied control.

17 According to the Geneva Convention, 'Escapees' (personnel having escaped from enemy prison camps) were allowed to return as soon as passage to their country's control became available across the border. 'Internees', men who had arrived in Switzerland without having ever been caught by their enemy (such as the 'Walking internees' i.e. the 'Evaders', or the 'Winged internees' who had flown into the country) had in principle to wait until the end of the war to be officially allowed to leave. Peter's crew were of a category apart, having paddled into Switzerland; like 'Evaders' who swam across border rivers, they arbitrarily became 'Winged internees'. (See *Aviateurs-Piétons vers la Suisse*)

18 The unit was either Annecy's ACRU-2 (see note 15, Chapter 13) south of Geneva or, north across the Jura mountains, Lt Robert Simpson's PoW & Escapees Detachment at Hôtel 'Les Terrasses' in Malbuisson near Pontarlier. The Annecy outfit is the same that helped Noel Davis after his escape from Switzerland.

19 After the war, 'Bomber Schaffner' raised several aircraft, both military and civilian, from Swiss lakes, including Peter's *Lancaster* and two *B-17*s from the US 384 and 385 Bomb Groups, whose ordeals will appear in the third volume of this series: *The USAAF and Switzerland*. In November 1993, the main spar of another *Lancaster* was also raised from Lake Constance just off F'hafen. The 22m-long (72ft) object did not allow a more precise identification but a possibility is that it could be F/Sgt Robert Stewart's 115 Squadron aircraft whose crew were all killed.

20 Utzenstorf, south of Solothurn (Soleure) and some 50km (32mi.) south of Basle, witnessed the arrival on 17 August 1943 of one of the first two *B-17*s to land in Switzerland during the Second World War, the other having landed at Dübendorf.

CHAPTER 15 (THE LAST)

1 One set of statistics indicates that the RAF could at that time muster about 5,100 aircraft and the Americans 5,060 bombers and 3,730 fighters, against 4,500 Luftwaffe aeroplanes spread over the Continent, including 570 on the Western front.

2 At the time 515 Squadron was operating under the aegis of 100 Group, RAF, a collection of bomber support units protecting the large bombing raids by disrupting German nightfighter efforts.

3 605 Squadron was an 11 Group unit (see Chapter 11); its sorties to Munich had to be abandoned because of weather.

4 Other *Mosquito* Squadrons were also involved in Day Ranger patrols and Morley's and Callard's crews were lucky in comparison with the fate of some 418 Squadron colleagues. For instance on the same day, 30 September, as their Dübendorf affair, *Mosquito* NS.906 (TH°W) crashed at sea off Aalborg, Denmark, killing F/Lt Robin Thomas and F/O Gilbert Allin.

5 'FB' stood for 'Fighter-Bomber', one of the variants of the nimble and versatile de Havilland *Mosquito* whose production reached an overall total of 7781 units. Other variants included fighter, nightfighter, bomber and photo-reconnaissance. One example of the latter type was the first RAF machine to reach Swiss soil (see Chapter 4).

6 According to Fidler, Morley was in the habit of 'discounting a lot of our trips' and their total number of sorties was about twenty when they arrived in Switzerland.

7 St-Dizier had once been a well-appointed French base later taken over by the Luftwaffe and its nightfighters. Mid-September it had become the USAAF's A-64 continental base, housing their 10th PRG and 405 FGp. At the time, St-Diz was also used – as Florennes in Belgium for instance – by B-24 *Liberators* loaded with fuel to sustain the advancing ground forces. The RAF mechanic would be the only man on site capable of caring for a *Mosquito*. In the event, Harper waited two days at St-Dizier before returning to England aboard an American *Liberator*.

8 British and Swiss times were identical at this period in 1944.

9 Navigator Reg. Fidler is adamant that his PZ.440 did NOT stray into Swiss airspace on the way in.

10 Those units were, amongst others, protecting north-eastern Switzerland. Flab assignments were modified several times: in Autumn 1944 orders were to shoot not only at large formations but also at isolated aircraft unless they were clearly in emergency. In 1944, the flab was engaged 180 times on seventy-five days, spending 3,886 7.5cm rounds, 1559 34mm ones and 3,229 20mm and claiming three aircraft destroyed with three more probably falling on foreign soil.

11 Total ammo expended amounted to fifty 20mm shots, just six 34mm and a whopping sixty-three 7.5cm shells for *Flab Detachment 7*, plus forty-four 20mm and just two 7.5cm for *Det. 2*.

12 Single-engine safety speed at maximum weight of 25,500lb (11,577 kg), not PZ.440's situation, reached the unusual figure of 184 knots, ie. 213mph or 340km/hr!

13 Coincidence again, on 27 October 1945, a *B-17* being ferried back to England crashed at practically the same spot.

14 The crew mistakenly reported the area as 'Prien Lake' and their prey as Dornier Do.217, these being twin-engined land planes.

15 Most probably a machine from 7.*Seenotstaffel* recently arrived from the Black Sea via Vienna.

16 One cannot help wondering, as stated in Chapter 4, why so many *Mosquito* starboard engines developed such a tendency to overheating? In this case however the fault may be traced to debris hitting the cooling system.

17 F.F. Lambert later became one of the most useful researcher at PRO, the Public Records Office (now National Archives) in Kew, where RAF records are stored.

18 Both Squadrons were co-residents at Little Snoring.

CHAPTER 16 (MISLEADING COCKADES)

1 French pilots in North Africa were converted there to *Spitfire* and to American aircraft: *P-38*s, *P-39*s and *P-47*s. New pilots were also trained in the USA to fly *P-47*s and *B-26*s at such American fields as Hawthorne near Orangeburg, South Carolina. Returning to Europe they flew aircraft adorning French markings. In England, French 'North African' pilots were converted on *Halifaxes* by the RAF to man two heavy bomber Squadrons within Bomber Command: the 346 'Guyenne' and 347 'Tunisie'; these however sported standard RAF markings.

2 VE-Day is the day of Victory in Europe, 8 May 1945. Around this date several aircraft of other nationalities still made it to Switzerland. Some brought in refugees, some were lost or, in the case of some American liaison aircraft, some were on a sightseeing jaunt. In 1947, two more French fighters ended up in Switzerland: a *Spitfire* in March and a *P-47* in June (Düb Tally).

3 This volume is the second of three books covering the implications of the Allied air forces in Switzerland in the Second World War. The first volume *Aviateurs-Piétons vers la Suisse ('Evaders to Switzerland')* was published in French in 1997; the third *The USAAF and Switzerland* is to appear next year.

4 Henri Koechlin had enlisted in 1935; he was now a veteran of the new French Air Force and had downed a *Bf.109* from JG.53 near Stuttgart on 26 December 1944. That day, 20 April 1945, was Hitler's fifty-sixth birthday but more notably several aerial occurrences happened on Europe's vertical battlegrounds. Way north, near Bremen, two other Frenchmen – Pierre Closterman and Capt. Guérin – were hit by adverse fire; both crash-landed their aircraft at their respective bases. Less fortunate, Jacques Groensteen, a Belgian in the RAF, lost his life aboard a *Spitfire* over Berlin-Oranienburg.

5 French coding indicates 'First Escadrille' of 'Groupe de Chasse 7'. GR.2/33 denotes '2e Escadrille of the 33e (Savoie) Groupe de Reconnaissance'. At the time Colmar was still known as the US Advanced Landing Ground Y-53, Strasbourg-Entzheim being Y-40.

6 The Swiss army salvaged some 50 litres (11 Imp.gal) of high octane petrol.

7 Both aircraft had arrived crated in North Africa from the United States and been assembled in Oran.

8   Up to then, 167 USAAF aircraft and 13 RAF machines had landed or crashed in Switzerland.

9   See note 5.

10 By coincidence, Teufen is the village where Wilfred Boddy hoped to visit after his *Wellington* crashed at Birmenstorf (see Chapter 5).

11 The unit to which the pilots belonged was GC.2/9 'Auvergne'. With GC.1/9 'Limousin' and GC.2/6 'Travail', it was one of the three French Groupes de Chasse still flying the *P.39*. Between June and August 1945, the units were re-equipped with an improved version, the Bell *P-63 Kingcobra*.

12 Sgt Laurens had been flying the *P-39* serialed 43914, S/Lt Delvové's being 43044.

13 A second French Zone covered the region west of the Rhine between Karlsruhe and Bacharach; the limit then ran overland to roughly Limburg, Siegen and Prüm. A sector of Berlin was also assigned to the French occupation forces.

14 A new *P-39* could clock up to 380mph (600km/h) but it can be surmised that the tired machines showed lessened performances and speed would have been reduced in view of the prevailing visibility.

CHAPTER 17 (BOMBING)

1   Those figures reflect the number of locations known to have received belligerent bombs. What follows lists British-induced incidents by dates only.

2   There were seventy-seven instances of Allied and German bombs dropped on Switzerland and thirteen strafing sessions. German aircraft were mostly involved in 1940 and USAAF's in 1945.

3   RAF photo reconnaissance had been – quite 'illegally' – started with one civilian machine: a Lockheed *12A* operated early in 1939, some six months before the war started. The first good high altitude photographs by a PRU *Spitfire* were taken on 18 November 1939 over Belgium, at the time a neutral country like Switzerland.

4   Duds, i.e. bombs that failed to go off, were more common than expected. For instance, to pick out the oil refineries where the tally was easy to make, they amounted to 16.4 per cent of the total dropped.

5   Among the many books about this period, one certainly makes compulsory reading: Goulding's excellent *Uncommon Valour* (Air Data Ltd, Wilmslow, 1985).

6   See note 5.

7   Düsseldorf had received the same treatment on 4/5 and 7/8 December 1940, albeit with weaker forces. The Mannheim raid was repeated on a smaller scale on the next night and again on 20/21 December.

8   Some sources quote 'Operation Rachel' instead of 'Abigail'.

9   The twin-engined Bristol *Blenheim* was a light bomber soon to be phased out of operations by the RAF.

10 Hess' voyage finally took place on 10/11 May 1941. Although this was a political fiasco, the flight itself was a masterpiece of long-range night navigation in view of the scarcity of radio aids then

available: lifting off a Stuttgart airfield, Hess reached his target, a lonely castle in Scotland, some 765mi.(1,225km) away!

11 The Novobax missiles were 20in. (about 54cm) in length and were 4-pounders weighed by the Swiss at 1.7kg. The octagonal objects struck the imagination of contemporary Swiss advertisers: in Reinach, the 'Indiana' cigar manufacturers packed their products in boxes of such a shape.

12 The failure cost the RAF twelve aircraft, including a *Whitley* (Z.6801 of 77 Squadron, pilot nineteen-year-old P/O Roger Lloyd) that crashed at Daussois, Belgium, where it became the first RAF machine this author had to investigate within the framework of underground assignments.

13 That maximum-effort operation proved to be a disaster with the loss of thirty-seven bombers due to weather: almost a staggering 10 per cent of the force despatched, with 119 killed and 75 PoW, all for a raid that was a failure. The event was to be instrumental in the replacement in February 1942 of the then commander of Bomber Command, Sir Richard Peirse, by the forceful Arthur Harris.

14 Swiss reports estimate correctly at twenty to thirty the number of aircraft infringing upon their neutrality that night. A 'near miss' as far as bombing Switzerland goes, brought bombs on Annecy in nearby France where five people were killed.

15 Revetment of the runway was started in 1943 on this small fighter base squeezed in the deep Rhône valley in the Swiss Alps.

16 Targets were labelled 'primary', 'secondary' or 'of opportunity' according to their importance in the bombers assigned tasks. 'Expediency' is a quite unofficial attribute given here to accidental bombings of Switzerland.

17 Back in November 1941, 105 Squadron had been the first unit to be fully equipped with the ubiquitous new de Havilland *Mosquito* day bomber.

18 Allied and German weather synopses have been collected for most of the wartime years by specialist meteorologist Frederic Haldiman in Geneva.

19 Weather forecasts at the time were much less reliable than nowadays. A notorious example of wrong expected winds happened on the 'night of the jet stream', on 24/25 March 1944 during a raid on Berlin. Wind speeds forecast at 70 knots were discovered to be at 135 knots. It was only years later that such high values were attributed to the jet streams phenomenon usually occurring at much higher altitudes.

20 Under the management of former German officer Emil Bührle, Oerlikon had developed 20mm guns for airborne and anti-aircraft purposes; spare parts were exported to Germany where the weapon was also built at or for the Semag company. The gun had also been tested or used by France, Britain and even the USA.

21 The Swiss population was, particularly in the western part of the country, sensitive to any sign of commercial collaboration with Germany. For instance, at the end of September 1941, pamphlets appeared on the walls at Le Locle suggesting that the Federal government was provoking the RAF by allowing German goods trains to transit to Italy. Likewise, thousands of RAF insignias were made and sold in Geneva, the proceedings going in part to help British internees in Switzerland.

22 Had such a raid been considered, it would probably have been a *Mosquito* daylight precision attack; such a sortie had been mounted against the Liège FN armament works in Belgium on 12 February 1943 and the Schott glass works in Iena on 27 May.

23 The *Würzburg* tracking radar developed by Telefunken as their *Funkmessgerat 62D* was but one element in a panoply of sophisticated radio-electric measures used in the defence of the Reich. Others included the *Freya, Würzburg-Riese, Wassermann* and *Jagdschloss* radio-detection devices.

24 Doubts remain about the victim's identity: either the *Maloja* or the *Albula*. The wartime Swiss merchant marine comprised up to sixteen ships, half of which were chartered from Greece. It lost four of its own merchantmen and a chartered one.

25 The raid was the fourth in the 'Battle of Berlin' which was fought between 18/19 November 1943 and mid-February 1944; the offensive cost the RAF 384 bombers in the course of 7,403 sorties.

26 Such a move was later to stall the US 1st Army's progress across the Urft River, south of Aachen when breaching of the dam there failed.

27 The 11,885lb *Tallboy* (4,860kg) comprised three 4,000lb (1620kg) *Cookie* bombs plus tail fins; the object was 21ft (6.4m) long with a body diameter of about one metre (3.28ft). Leaflets of dubious origin had been found near Basle in 1943, warning of RAF intentions to bomb the Kembs dam.

28 Swiss observers reported what was probably the high fighter cover 'flying higher than the bombers'. They did not notice the flak-suppressing action.

29 No.627 *Mosquito* bomber Squadron shared Woodhall Spa, south-east of Lincoln, with 617 Sq. whose *Lancasters* specialised in pin-point targets.

30 Swiss civil defences were quick to repeat that air attacks were not just a show for all and sundry to watch but were a real danger for onlookers, neutral or not, even at a distance. On this occasion no casualties were recorded, apart from a woman in town who had to be hospitalised in a state of nervous shock.

31 As for Bomber Command, it had resumed daylight operations on 27 August 1944 (to Homberg), three years after the last one on 12 August 1941. It was by now apparent that the Luftwaffe's day fighters did not continue to pose a serious threat to the RAF heavies.

32 The 801st Provisional Bomb Group had been activated at the end of 1943 in order to supply the European underground by night. It 'acquired' the remnants of the 492nd BGp in mid-1944. After the liberation of Western Europe, some of its aircraft flew at least twenty-one night bombing missions such as the one on 28 February 1945 against Freiburg-im-Breisgau.

33 Valbert is right under the path followed by the Saignelégier *Lancaster* in the last seconds of its final flight two months earlier (see Chapter 9). One purpose of Floege's 'Operation Sacristan' was to continue hindering German-controlled production at the nearby Peugeot-Montbéliard plants.

34 That same night many other clandestine drops occurred, including twenty-one by US Carpetbagger's *Liberators*. One of them released sixteen containers of arms and ammunition just outside Lomont near Lure, 50km to the north-west. It has not been ascertained who the crew was over Ocourt, nor if it was an RAF or USAAF operation.

35 There were 695 *Lancasters* dispatched on this last area attack on the Bavarian town. Another coincidence occurred this night when a 166 Squadron machine (see Chapter 13) was shot down at Münsingen a German village near Stuttgart with the same name as its counterpart in Switzerland, which became the resting place of many Allied aircrew in the Second World War.

CHAPTER 18 (THE MEN)

1 The actual crew member complement was 76 but one had parachuted to become a Prisoner of War in Germany. Another who drowned whilst entering Switzerland is not included in this tally since he was an evader; his saga appears in the preceding volume of this trilogy. The figures include, however, the six French pilots listed in Chapter 16. (See also Table 3)

2 In his *Histoire de la Neutralité Suisse* (La Baconnière, Nauchâtel, 1970), Edgar Bonjour mentions 43,000 troops which seems to contradict his figure of 29,503 Frenchmen (Vol.6 p.80,82).

3 Bonjour also refers to 29,503 French, 12,295 Poles, 539 Belgians and 94 British, i.e. a total of 42,531 military internees but he fails to make reference to the 1600-odd US flyers who landed in Switzerland.

4 Not counting the four FAF airmen in Tally/Table 3.

5 No foundation has been discovered for the fable that Allied aircrew had ever been exchanged against fuel shipments, certainly not for Switzerland, nor for that supposedly 'neutral' country: Spain.

6 The four French Air Force pilots who survived landing in Switzerland just before or after V-E Day, were allowed to return across the border after a brief spell in hospital, or within about twenty-four hours.

7 Other radio facilities initially included the Uttligen 1.5kw short-wave military transmitter, improved to 10kw and moved to the Kleine Scheidegg mountain in 1943. Towards the end of the war, two radio aids were also operating on or near Dübendorf airfield, the main Swiss military base: HEZ was on, in daylight only, on 340kHz and HBZA, a bad weather beacon, broadcasting on a nearby frequency.

8 Re. *Aviateurs-Piétons vers la Suisse* p.214. It remains unclear whether or not the stations were actually jammed or if Lamus' assertion was a ploy to mislead his opponents. Another recurrent bone of contention between Switzerland and Germany (and even Britain for opposite reasons) was the question of black-out which, if enforced, hindered night navigation of RAF bombers (see Chapter 5). In 1943 the Swiss gave way to Germany: they elected to keep their black-out effective; their radio stations schedules remained however unchanged.

9 IBM spent 102,810.40 Sw.Frcs on this scheme, to which its president Mr Watson added 8,000.- Sw.Frcs of his own money.

10 Three more aircraft crashed in England upon returning. Out of the nine aircraft shot down, three came down in Belgium, two of which ended in the author's 'jurisdiction' where his underground assignment was to try and salvage sensitive equipment and possibly help evaders. They were *Halifax* LK.749 EY°J of 78 Sq. down at Pry (crew F/Sgt Frank Lovatt) and *Lancaster* LL.839, UM°X2 of 626 Sq. down Thirimont, on the French–Belgian border (crew F/O Douglas Laidlaw).

11 This was a Canadian 419 Squadron *Wellington* from which there was only one survivor, Sgt W. Ledford, who evaded capture through the Belgian 'Comète' line only to be killed one year later. In a rare twist to the rule barring evaders from returning to operations lest they risk giving away their helpers if captured, Ledford flew again operationally, this time with Sgt R.S. Harrison of 434 Squadron. Their *Halifax* was shot down, again in Belgium, on 22/23 August 1943 during a raid on Leverkusen. This time Ledford's luck ran out: he died with his seven comrades. In a freak coincidence a Canadian friend from his 419 Squadron, Sgt H. D' Aperng, survived a crash in October 1942 and was killed in Germany one week after Ledford.

12 Another *Halifax*, from 158 Squadron, crashed here on 14/15 February 1945 after developing engine trouble on its way to Chemnitz; the crew survived.

13 There has been considerable speculation as to the function of 'Paul' Bell who indeed was a crewmember and not an SAS as indicated in several sources.

14 One spectacular 'coup' of *Stockbroker* had been twice sabotaging production equipment in the Peugeot tank turret factory at Sochaux.

CHAPTER 19 (AFTERMATH)

1   Slightly different sums are quoted in available sources, depending upon the inclusions of ancillary internment and/or damage costs. For comparison purposes, the bill to Germany for her twenty-three aircraft that ended in Switzerland between 25 July 1942 and 8 May 1945, amounted to 45,593.80 Sw.Frcs. The United States had 167 aircraft in the country between roughly the same dates. They paid a whopping 1,928,603.80 Sw.Frcs for them. Again as a comparison, Swiss banks agreed in 1997 to contribute 100 million Sw.Frcs to fund compensations to victims of the Jewish holocaust.

2   There were actually three *Mosquito*es which landed in Switzerland: one at Berne and two at Dübendorf but one of the latter had been reduced to scrap on arrival (see Chapter 15).

3   This estimate of 305,000 German casualties quoted from the 1947 US Strategic Bombing Survey is at odd with other sources reckoning from about 220,000 to 600,000. The number can however be compared with those attributed to Luftwaffe bombings of seven Allied towns: 104,000 and on Britain alone: 66,400.

4   In 1945 1 Sw.Frc was worth 0.23364 US dollar and it took 17.35 Sw.Frcs to acquire one British pound.

5   *Mosquito* operations had started on 30/31 May 1942 in the Millenium raid to Köln with the first loss occurring on the same night; also, by then the Press had been able to report on the machine. Air Ministry could thus surmise that Germany had collected data on the new aircraft, rendering secrecy less stringent.

6   The six civilian pilots were Hans Ernst, Robert Fretz, Otto Heitmanek, Ernst Nyffenegger, Anton Von Tscharner and Franz Zimmermann. They flew a puny total of two hours and forty-seven minutes of familiarisation time.

7   Opinions did differ as to which of the two *Mosquito*es by then available to Switzerland bore the codes 'B-4' and 'B-5'. To this writer, the chronological order seems self-evident with 'B-4' going to the 'Berne' (PR) *Mossie* and 'B-5' to the 'Dübendorf' one. Concurrently, pictures show the flat-windshielded (i.e. the fighter-bomber variant such as *Mosquito* NS.993) as 'B-5'. The PR machine with its triangular windshield (the bomber/PR variant) must thus have been 'B-4', ex-'E-42', ex-DK.310. At least one photograph correctly shows DK.310 as 'B-4'. Even so, many authors perpetuate the erroneous coding 'B-5' attached to the 'Berne' machine.

8   This power plant, Rolls-Royce No.105435, can now be seen in the Dübendorf Air Museum east of Zurich.

9   Cheshire's – and NS.993's – deeds on this raid were instrumental in the pilot being awarded the Victoria Cross, the highest British wartime decoration.

10 The N-20 *Aiguillon* was to be propelled by four Swiss-made turbofans sunk in its wings. Technical hitches caused them to be replaced by the modified *Mamba* which originally was an axial-flow turbo-prop engine.

11 Prior to the lifting of the ban on aircraft construction in Germany, the Altenrhein factory had conveniently been set up by the Dornier company of Germany, across the lake from its parent unit at Friedrichshafen.

12 This was formaldehyde cement, a synthetic resin that had replaced casein for surface joining. Time and some ambient conditions caused it to powderise.

13 See note 12, Chapter 1.

14 They were F/Lt Walter Blott, F/O Basil Medcalf, P/O George Alistair Smith, W/O Robert Peter, F/Sgt Ronald Carr, Sgts George Beever, Gordon Gill, Eric Hiley and Arthur Truscott.

EPILOGUE

1 The Whitley served as a bomber from the first day of the war, 3 September 1939, until 5 May 1942.

2 According to the official 'Strategic Air Offensive against Germany', the daily averages of RAF heavy bombers and *Mosquitoes* available with their crews for operations was 1,097 in April 1944 and 1,607 a year later; they were as follows:

	April 1944	April 1945
Lancasters	614	1,088
Halifaxes	353	349
Stirlings	58	0
Mosquitoes	72	170

3 The chance factor intervened in captains' decisions to press on to return to England or to proceed to North Africa rather than seek asylum in Switzerland. Also damage due to enemy defences close to neutral territory determined arrivals there whilst, if sustained further afield, they entailed losses over occupied Europe. For instance, in the course of the raid on Stuttgart on 15/16 March 1944 which saw two *Lancaster* arrivals in Switzerland, two *Halis* (out of ten lost) came down within 16-40km (10-25mi.) of her border. A mild stretch of imagination visualises a scenario where the stricken bombers would have turned on a south-easterly heading, thus reaching Switzerland in their predicament. Actually out of one of them (LW.690 of the Canadian 429 'Bison' Squadron flown by F/Lt Harry Heimbecker) three of the survivors evaded capture and walked into Switzerland.

4 From the calculated figures above, comparative loss rates in the course of raids on Italy between June 1940 and August 1943 were: *Whitleys* 10 per cent, *Stirlings* 1.8 per cent, *Halifaxes* 2.16 per cent. During the two 1944 raids on Southern Germany in which bombers arrived in Switzerland, the loss rates for *Halifaxes* and *Lancasters* were respectively 4.17 per cent and 3.9 per cent; although these two figures rely on a very low statistical base, they can be indicative of the general reliability of both types.

5 The bodies of the two French pilots killed just after the war (see Chapter 16) were repatriated by air within days of their demise. The procedure entailed the reimbursement of 1,332- Sw.Frcs covering the expenditure of 900 litres of aviation gasoline at 1.48 Sw.frc/litre. This amounted to about 4.44 frcs at present value i.e. 2.85 times the cost of untaxed 100LL aviation spirit in June 2002.

Index

P = picture
M = map

If you are interested in purchasing
other books published by Tempus, or in case you have
difficulty finding any Tempus books in your local bookshop, you can also
place orders directly through our website

www.tempus-publishing.com